3 0050 05427 9467

j 523.8022 Asi

DATE DUE

1-17-08

DISCARD

DEMCO, INC. 38-2971

D1207990

MAR 3 0 2005

DAVENPORT PUBLIC LIBRARY
321 MAIN STREET
DAVENPORT, IOWA 52801

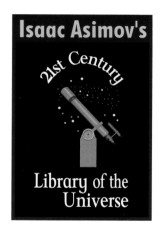

Isaac Asimov's

21st Century

Library of the
Universe

Fact and Fantasy

A Stargazer's Guide

BY ISAAC ASIMOV

WITH REVISIONS AND UPDATING BY RICHARD HANTULA

Gareth Stevens Publishing
A WORLD ALMANAC EDUCATION GROUP COMPANY

Please visit our web site at: **www.garethstevens.com**
For a free color catalog describing Gareth Stevens Publishing's list of high-quality books
and multimedia programs, call 1-800-542-2595 (USA) or 1-800-387-3178 (Canada).
Gareth Stevens Publishing's fax: (414) 332-3567.

The reproduction rights to all photographs and illustrations in this book are controlled by the individuals
or institutions credited on page 32 and may not be reproduced without their permission.

Library of Congress Cataloging-in-Publication Data

Asimov, Isaac.
    A stargazer's guide / by Isaac Asimov; with revisions and updating by Richard Hantula.
      p. cm. — (Isaac Asimov's 21st century library of the universe. Fact and fantasy)
    Includes bibliographical references and index.
    ISBN 0-8368-3953-6 (lib. bdg.)
    1. Astronomy—Observers' manuals—Juvenile literature. 2. Stars—Observers' manuals—Juvenile
literature. I. Hantula, Richard. II. Title.
    QB64.A754 2004
    523.8'022'3—dc22
                                                   2004048168

This edition first published in 2005 by
Gareth Stevens Publishing
A World Almanac Education Group Company
330 West Olive Street, Suite 100
Milwaukee, WI 53212 USA

Revised and updated edition © 2005 by Gareth Stevens, Inc. Original edition published in 1988
by Gareth Stevens, Inc. under the title *The Space Spotter's Guide.* Second edition published in
1995 by Gareth Stevens, Inc. under the title *A Stargazer's Guide.* Text © 2005 by Nightfall, Inc.
End matter and revisions © 2005 by Gareth Stevens, Inc.

Series editor: Betsy Rasmussen
Cover design and layout adaptation: Melissa Valuch
Picture research: Kathy Keller
Additional picture research: Diane Laska-Swanke
Artwork commissioning: Kathy Keller and Laurie Shock
Production director: Jessica Morris
Production assistant: Nicole Esko

The editors at Gareth Stevens Publishing have selected science author Richard Hantula to bring
this classic series of young people's information books up to date. Richard Hantula has written
and edited books and articles on science and technology for more than two decades. He was
the senior U.S. editor for the *Macmillan Encyclopedia of Science.*

In addition to Hantula's contribution to this most recent edition, the editors would like to
acknowledge the participation of two noted science authors, Greg Walz-Chojnacki and
Francis Reddy, as contributors to earlier editions of this work.

All rights to this edition reserved to Gareth Stevens, Inc. No part of this book may be reproduced,
stored in a retrieval system, or transmitted in any form or by any means, electronic, mechanical,
photocopying, recording, or otherwise, without the prior written permission of the publisher except
for the inclusion of brief quotations in an acknowledged review.

Printed in the United States of America

1 2 3 4 5 6 7 8 9 09 08 07 06 05 04

Contents

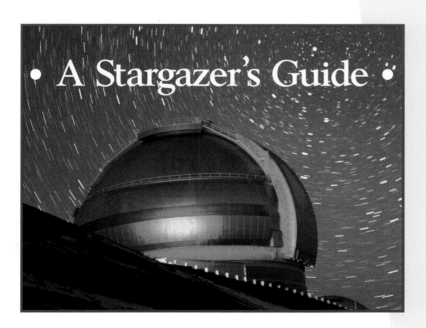

• A Stargazer's Guide •

We live in an enormously large place — the Universe. It's only natural that we would want to understand this place, so scientists and engineers have developed instruments and spacecraft that have told us far more about the Universe than we could possibly imagine.

We have seen planets up close, and spacecraft have even landed on some. We have learned about quasars and pulsars, supernovas and colliding galaxies, and black holes and dark matter. We have gathered amazing data about how the Universe may have come into being and how it may end. Nothing could be more astonishing.

People who live in big cities may find it difficult or even impossible to see the stars and other features of the sky. But in places away from the bright lights and dust of big cities, the sky can be observed with the naked eye and through binoculars and telescopes. In this book, you will discover how to spot some of the wonders of our Solar System, our Galaxy, and beyond!

A Sky of Surprises

If we could stay awake through the night, we would see the stars rise and set. Stars are huge balls of hot gases. The gases light the stars from within. This is unlike planets, which shine because of reflected light. The Milky Way, our Galaxy, is home to upwards of four hundred billion stars. And that is just one galaxy. Scientists think more than one hundred billion galaxies exist in the incredibly vast sky.

From night to night, the sky shifts. A pattern of stars seen at midnight on one night won't appear again exactly as it is until an entire year later. The patterns change with the seasons. That's because Earth revolves around the Sun.

Left: In this time-lapse photograph, the Sun, Moon, and stars appear as streaks wheeling across the sky, an illusion caused by the spinning planet on which we live.

The Moon's Monthly Travels

As you might guess, the brightest object in the night sky is the Moon. The Moon shines by reflecting light from the Sun. It travels around Earth in a little less than one month. In that time, we see its various phases, or shapes.

When the Moon and Sun are on the same side of Earth, we face the Moon's unlighted side. This is the "new Moon," which cannot be seen. The next evening we see a bit of the Moon's sunlit side as a crescent just after sunset. From night to night, the crescent gets thicker until there is a full Moon, and then the Moon becomes thinner and thinner until there is a new Moon again.

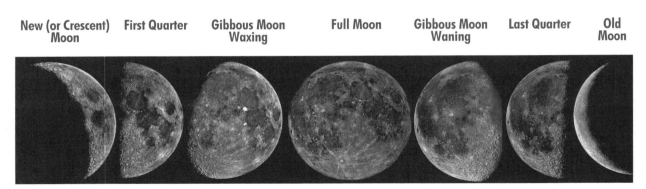

New (or Crescent) Moon First Quarter Gibbous Moon Waxing Full Moon Gibbous Moon Waning Last Quarter Old Moon

Above: The phases of the Moon. The Moon's appearance changes as it orbits Earth each month.

Stonehenge — a prehistoric observatory?

Before modern astronomical instruments were invented, people had their own ways of watching the stars. In England, there is a circle of large upright stones with other stones in the center. It is called Stonehenge. Some astronomers think it might be what is left of a prehistoric observatory. Did ancient people look across the stones to see where the Sun would rise at the summer solstice — or to predict lunar eclipses? No one knows for sure.

A dramatic shot of our nearest neighbor in space.

The Spring Sky

The next eight pages of this book show a portion of the sky as seen by a person in the Northern Hemisphere looking south. For someone in the Southern Hemisphere, the stars would appear higher in the sky, and some of the highest stars shown in the pictures would not be visible at all.

As you face south, imagine that the top of the picture is folded toward you and passes over your head. The bottom of the picture would then be south, and the top would be north.

Above: The Zodiac of Dendera – a star map of ancient Egypt.

As you face south in the spring and look way up over your head, the Big Dipper – part of the constellation, or pattern of stars, known as Ursa Major (the Great Bear) – will stretch across the sky above you. If you follow the curve of the handle of the Big Dipper back toward the southern part of the sky, you will come upon the constellation Boötes (the Herdsman). The star Arcturus in Boötes is one of the brightest stars in the spring sky.

Continue to follow the imaginary curve south, and you will come to the constellation Virgo (the Maiden), and its bright star Spica. To the west (right, as you face south) of Virgo is Leo (the Lion), with its bright star Regulus. Virgo and Leo are two of the twelve constellations of what is known as the zodiac. The Sun, Moon, and most of the planets travel through the zodiac as they move across the sky.

8

Polaris

URSA MAJOR

BOÖTES

Arcturus

LEO

Regulus

VIRGO

EAST

SOUTH

WEST

Spica

Right: Spring in the Northern Hemisphere is autumn in the Southern Hemisphere.

The Summer Sky

One of the easiest constellations to spot in the summer sky is Sagittarius (the Archer). Its outline looks like a teapot in the southern sky.

The Milky Way is visible as a band of foggy light crossing the sky. It passes through Sagittarius and is brightest there. With the use of even a small telescope, you can see many stars in the Milky Way.

To the west, to the right of Sagittarius as you face south, is a curve of stars. This constellation is Scorpius (the Scorpion), with its bright red star Antares. Antares is a red supergiant and is hundreds of times wider than our Sun.

Over your head as you face south, and halfway between Sagittarius and Polaris (the "North Star"), is Lyra (the Lyre), with its bright star Vega. To the east of Lyra is Cygnus (the Swan), with its bright star Deneb. Halfway between Deneb and Sagittarius is the bright star Altair, in Aquila (the Eagle). The three stars Vega, Deneb, and Altair form a star pattern known as the Summer Triangle.

Left: The constellation Sagittarius (the Archer).

Deneb

CYGNUS

Vega

LYRA

Altair

AQUILA

Antares

SAGITTARIUS

SCORPIUS

EAST

SOUTH

WEST

Right: Summer in the Northern Hemisphere is winter in the Southern Hemisphere.

11

The Autumn Sky

The constellation Pegasus (the Flying Horse) is high in the autumn sky (nearly overhead as you face south). Its four bright stars form the Square of Pegasus. Immediately to its northeast (above and to the left of Pegasus), is Andromeda (the Chained Maiden). Within Andromeda, you can spot a small, foggy patch of light. When observed through a telescope, this patch turns out to be a huge collection of stars called the Andromeda Galaxy. It is bigger than our own galaxy.

To the southeast of Pegasus (lower left as you face south) is Cetus (the Whale), which has a rather dim star that is variable. A variable star grows brighter, then dimmer. When astronomers first saw this star, the changing brightness seemed so unique that they named the star Mira, which means "wonderful."

Left: The Andromeda Galaxy, also known as M31, in the constellation Andromeda. A space telescope called *Galaxy Evolution Explorer* made this picture in 2003 using ultraviolet light.

How far in the sky can we see?

The most distant object you can see clearly without binoculars or a telescope is the Andromeda Galaxy, or M31. It looks like a dim, fuzzy star, but it is actually a galaxy larger than our own Milky Way. It is more than two million light-years away. Scientists can see much farther with powerful telescopes. For instance, the nearest quasar is several hundred million light-years away, and other quasars might be as many as 13 billion light-years away. Astronomers do not expect to see many things much farther away than that!

ANDROMEDA
Galaxy M31

PEGASUS

Mira

CETUS

EAST   SOUTH   WEST

Right: Autumn in the Northern Hemisphere is spring in the Southern Hemisphere.

13

The Winter Sky

In the winter sky, you can see Orion (the Hunter). This beautiful constellation can help identify other star groups in the winter sky, as well. On Orion's northeastern edge (the upper left, as you face south) is the huge red supergiant star called Betelgeuse. Orion's southwestern edge (lower right) is marked by an even brighter star known as Rigel, which is actually about 50,000 times brighter than our Sun. (Our Sun seems much brighter to us because it is much closer.)

Between Betelgeuse and Rigel is a row of three stars called Orion's belt. Below the belt is another row of stars, Orion's sword. The middle "star" of the sword is in reality a huge cloud of gas and dust called the Orion Nebula.

Orion's belt points down and to the left (southeast) at the bright star Sirius, in the constellation Canis Major (the Great Dog). Sirius is the brightest star in the sky as seen from Earth — not counting our Sun, of course!

Orion's belt also points up and to the right (northwest) toward Aldebaran, the brightest star in Taurus (the Bull).

Above: The Orion Nebula is a giant gas cloud in which stars are born.

Did Sirius change color?

Certain ancient writers described Sirius as being red in color. In reality, Sirius is a brilliant white star. Could it have been red in ancient times and later turned white? Astronomers don't see how. The ancient Egyptians knew that Sirius rose with the Sun in the time of year when the Nile River was going to flood. So they watched it closely. When Sirius rose, it may have looked reddish, just as the Sun does. That may have been why ancient people thought of Sirius as being red.

TAURUS

PLEIADES

Aldebaran

Betelgeuse

Procyon

ORION

Rigel

Sirius

CANIS MAJOR

EAST　　　　　　**SOUTH**　　　　　　　　　　**WEST**

Right: Winter in the Northern Hemisphere is summer in the Southern Hemisphere.

The zodiac constellations are *(counterclockwise from the top)* Leo (the lion), Virgo (the Maiden), Libra (the Balance), Scorpio (the Scorpion), Sagittarius (the Archer), Capricorn (the Goat), Aquarius (the Water Bearer), Pisces (the Fishes), Aries (the Ram), Taurus (the Bull), Gemini (the Twins), and Cancer (the Crab).

Heavenly Journeys

Not all the objects in the sky turn in one group or follow the same path.

The Moon moves across the sky through the twelve constellations of the zodiac, making a complete circle in a little less than one month. The Sun moves along the same path. But it travels much slower, staying in each constellation of the zodiac for one month and making a complete circle in one year.

Five bright, starlike objects — the planets Mercury, Venus, Mars, Jupiter, and Saturn — also move along the zodiac. They take different lengths of time to move across the sky. For example, Jupiter takes about twelve years to circle the sky, while Saturn takes more than twenty-nine.

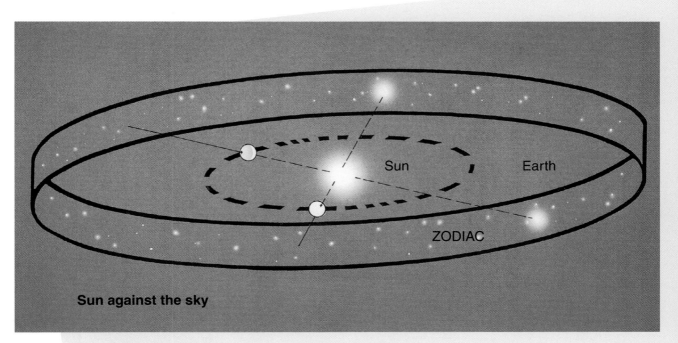

Sun against the sky

Above: As Earth moves in its yearly orbit around the Sun, the Sun appears to move against the background of stars in the sky. The constellations it passes through make up the zodiac.

A naked-eye view of Mercury, Venus, and a crescent Moon. Mercury and Venus, as seen from Earth, go through a cycle of phases, just as the Moon does.

The Sun's Nearest Neighbors

The planets Venus and Mercury are closer to the Sun than Earth is. For that reason, we always see them near the Sun. They only become visible to us shortly after sunset or shortly before sunrise.

Venus is the third brightest object that we can see in the sky, after the Sun and the Moon. When it appears in the western sky, it's often the first "star" we notice as evening falls. At these times, Venus is called the Evening Star. When it is on the other side of the Sun, Venus shines in the eastern sky in the hours before dawn and is called the Morning Star.

Mercury is much harder to see than Venus. Because Mercury never moves far from the Sun, we cannot see it in a dark sky.

Above: Venus is covered by a thick atmosphere that hides its surface from human eyes but not from human technology. This photo of Venus was taken by the spacecraft *Magellan*. The planet's face was revealed using radar.

The Farthest Planets

Mars, Jupiter, and Saturn are all farther from the Sun than Earth is. They shine in the midnight sky. Since we see only their sunlit portions, they always appear "full" when observed from Earth.

Jupiter and Saturn are giant planets. Through a telescope, Jupiter appears as a small globe, and its four largest natural satellites, or moons, can be easily seen. Saturn also has a big moon that can be seen with almost any telescope, as can the planet's many bright rings. These magnificent rings are made of countless pieces of rock and ice. They make Saturn one of the sky's most beautiful sights.

There are still farther planets — Uranus, Neptune, and Pluto. You can spot Uranus and Neptune easily with a small telescope, but you need a more powerful one to see Pluto.

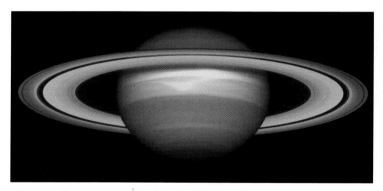

Above: Saturn, as seen by the Hubble Space Telescope.

Above: Jupiter, photographed by the space probe *Cassini*.

How far is "far" in space?

The farthest known planet in the Solar System is Pluto. Traveling at 186,000 miles (300,000 kilometers) per second, light takes about four hours to reach Earth from Pluto when the two planets are closest to each other and seven hours when they are farthest apart. The nearest star (not counting our Sun) is Proxima Centauri. It is so far away from Earth that its light takes 4.2 years to reach us. We say it is 4.2 light-years away. Our Milky Way Galaxy, a huge collection of stars shaped like a pinwheel, measures about 100,000 light-years from end to end!

Inset: Mars, the "Red Planet," in a Hubble Space Telescope view.

Jupiter *(upper right)* and Venus, together with a young Moon.

Types of Telescopes

At first, a good pair of binoculars will be fine for viewing the heavens. You will be able to see great views of the Milky Way and stars as much as ten times too faint for your eyes alone. But you can do all this and more with a telescope!

Telescopes collect light from an object in space, bring the light into focus, and magnify the image that is produced. There are three main types of telescopes – refracting, reflecting, and catadioptric. Refractors use lenses to collect and focus light; reflectors use mirrors; and catadioptric (or "compound") telescopes use both lenses and mirrors.

Whatever type of telescope you choose, you will be astonished by the sights overhead. You will be able to observe artificial satellites, study the surface of the Moon, and see comets in glorious detail.

Right: A catadioptric telescope, such as this "Schmidt-Cassegrain" type made for amateur astronomers, uses a combination of lenses and mirrors to collect and focus light.

The tiniest stars pack a powerful punch!

The matter in some stars is squeezed together extremely tight – so tight that the stars are smaller in size than Earth even though they may contain as much matter as our Sun. One such type of star is called a white dwarf. An even smaller, more tightly packed type exists, in which all the particles are pushed together until they touch. This type, called a neutron star, may have somewhat more matter than our Sun. But while the Sun is about 865,000 miles (1.39 million km) wide, scientists think a typical neutron star may be only 10 miles (16 km) across.

Left: A refracting telescope uses a large lens to collect and focus light. The telescope shown here is at the Griffith Observatory in Los Angeles.

Right: A reflecting telescope uses a large mirror to collect and focus light. Shown here is a "Cassegrain" type of reflector at the Sperry Observatory in Cranford, New Jersey.

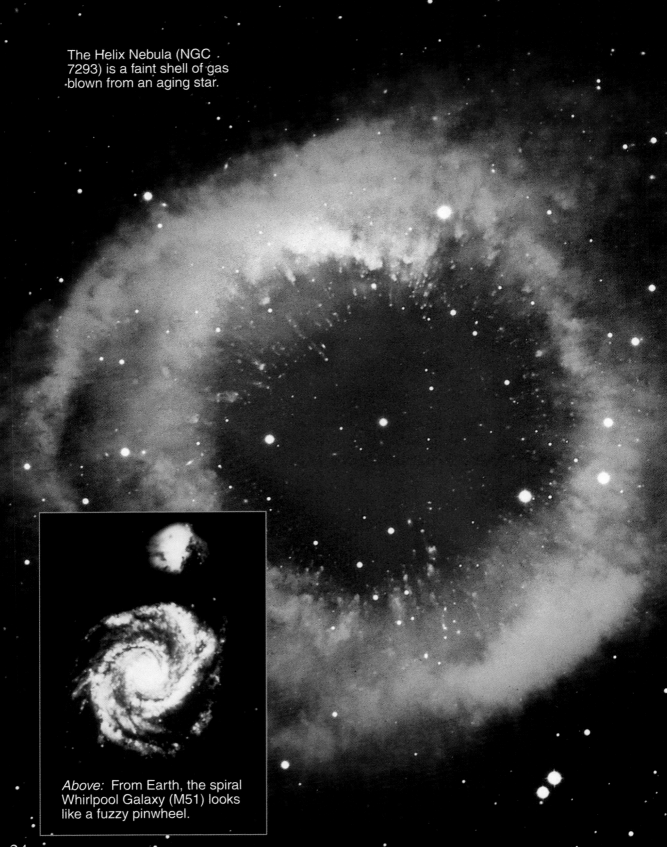

The Helix Nebula (NGC 7293) is a faint shell of gas blown from an aging star.

Above: From Earth, the spiral Whirlpool Galaxy (M51) looks like a fuzzy pinwheel.

Our Vast Universe

The objects you can see in the sky with your eyes alone are only the nearest and brightest ones. With a small telescope, you can see many more objects, some of them very distant from Earth.

Astronomers peer even deeper into the Universe by using huge telescopes on Earth as well as instruments aboard probes and satellites in space, such as the Hubble Space Telescope. Pictures made with these instruments — many of them can be seen on the Internet — reveal marvels that we once could only have imagined.

With the help of powerful instruments like these, we can see star clusters containing up to thousands of stars, and we can see groupings of galaxies, some of them billions of light-years away. In these groupings, we can spot dwarf galaxies, along with much larger galaxies of various shapes — such as elliptical galaxies, which look like oval pieces of fog, and spiral galaxies, which look like pinwheels.

Above: A 2004 image from the Hubble Space Telescope showing galaxies billions of light-years away.

Even astronomers can't always believe their eyes!

About one hundred years ago, an astronomer saw a small moon of Saturn that was never seen again. Perhaps it was an error or maybe there was a flaw in the telescope. In 1937, an asteroid was spotted flying just 500,000 miles (800,000 km) from Earth. It has never been seen again. Sometimes, astronomers see small changes on the Moon, which is supposedly a dead world. Are these mistakes, or is the Moon not quite dead? The sky is full of mysteries — even today!

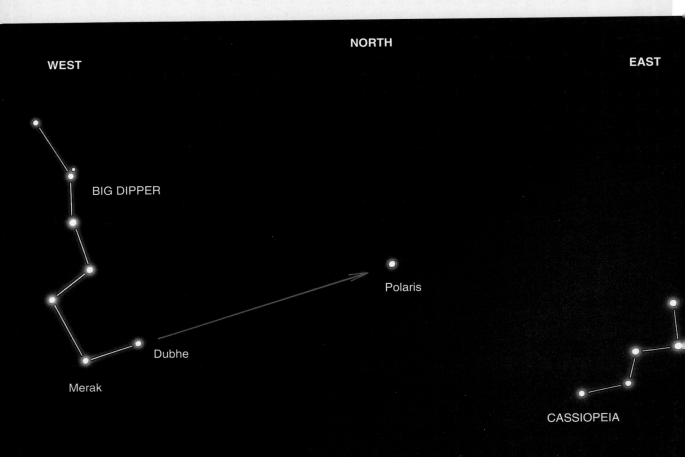

The Big Dipper and Cassiopeia are visible throughout the year in the Northern Hemisphere.

Fact File: Constellations of the Northern Hemisphere

In the Northern Hemisphere, stars turn in large circles around a star called Polaris. Polaris is also known as the North Star or Pole Star because it constantly stays in the North, almost directly above Earth's North Pole.

From the Northern Hemisphere, certain constellations can be seen circling Polaris. They never set and are always visible in the night sky. One of them is Ursa Major (the Great Bear). Seven of its stars form the famous star pattern, or asterism, known as the Big Dipper. The two stars at the bowl end of the dipper — Merak and Dubhe — are called the "pointers." Follow an imaginary line through them to find Polaris. On the other side of Polaris from the Big Dipper are five stars in a W shape. This constellation is Cassiopeia (the Queen), which also is always visible.

Right: If you look in the northern sky at the same time each night for a year, you will see the Big Dipper and Cassiopeia slowly chase each other around Polaris, the North Star.

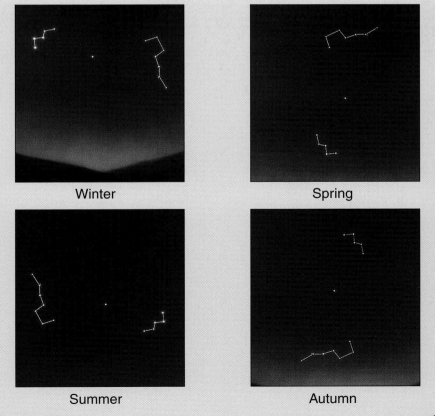

Winter

Spring

Summer

Autumn

Fact File: Constellations of the Southern Hemisphere

Many of the constellations of the Northern Hemisphere were mapped a very long time ago. They were often named after the gods and heroes of ancient Greek mythology or after objects commonly used in ancient times.

However, the sky in the Southern Hemisphere was not mapped until much later. It was mapped because explorers needed information about the southern sky in order to navigate their ships at night. So when astronomers gave names to the constellations of the Southern Hemisphere, they did not use names from ancient myths. Instead, they often named the constellations after the animals found in explorers' travels and the instruments the explorers used to find their way amid the sea and stars.

When humans travel to distant planets, stars, and galaxies in the future, the star patterns seen from their point of view will be different from the constellations we know from Earth. What will they name their constellations after?

Some Southern Constellations

Name of Constellation	Description	Named by	Year
Apus Dorado Tucana	Bird of Paradise Goldfish Toucan	Johann Bayer (Germany)	1603
Antlia Circinus Horologium Telescopium	Air Pump Compasses Clock Telescope	Nicholas Louis Lacaille (France)	1750s

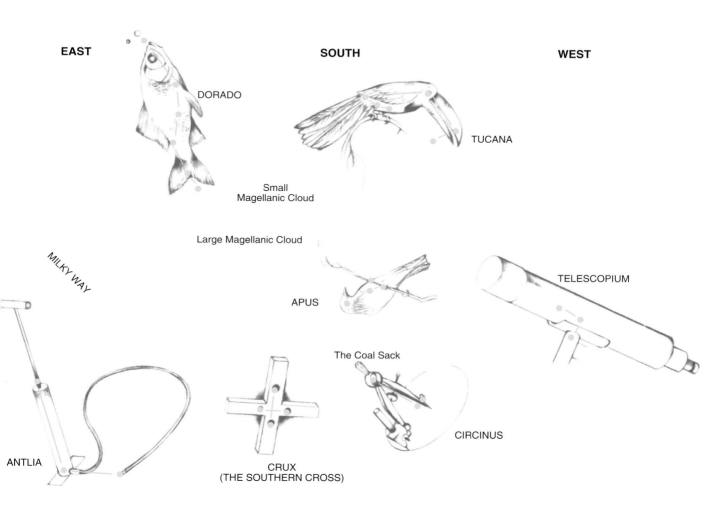

EAST

SOUTH

WEST

DORADO

TUCANA

Small
Magellanic Cloud

Large Magellanic Cloud

MILKY WAY

APUS

TELESCOPIUM

The Coal Sack

ANTLIA

CIRCINUS

CRUX
(THE SOUTHERN CROSS)

Above: A view of the sky in the Southern Hemisphere showing some of the constellations featured in the chart *(opposite).* The constellation Crux (the Southern Cross) points to the spot the southern stars circle around. This spot is opposite Polaris. The Southern Cross is a key constellation for navigating south of the Equator. The Large and Small Magellanic Clouds are small "satellite" galaxies of our Milky Way Galaxy. The Coal Sack is a dark dust cloud, or nebula.

More Books about Astronomy

The Book of Constellations: Discover the Secrets in the Stars. Robin Kerrod (Barrons)

Find the Constellations. H. A. Rey (Houghton Mifflin)

Hubble: The Mirror on the Universe. Robin Kerrod (Firefly)

The Sky Observer's Guide: A Golden Guide. R. Newton Mayall, Margaret Mayall, Jerome Wyckoff (St. Martin's)

Telescope Power: Fantastic Activities & Easy Projects for Young Astronomers. Gregory L. Matloff (Wiley)

A Walk Through the Heavens: A Guide to Stars and Constellations and Their Legends. Milton D. Heifetz and Wil Tirion (Cambridge University Press)

DVDs

Atlas of the Sky. (Space Holdings)

The Standard Deviants: Astronomy Adventure. (Cerebellum)

Web Sites

The Internet sites listed here can help you learn more about the objects in the sky and the telescopes and other instruments used to observe them.

AbsoluteAstronomy.com. www.absoluteastronomy.com/
Astronomy.com. astronomy.com/
The Constellations. www.dibonsmith.com/
Sky & Telescope. skyandtelescope.com/
Windows to the Universe.
www.windows.ucar.edu/tour/link=/the_universe/the_universe.html

Places to Visit

Here are some museums and centers where you can find exhibits about the stars and constellations, along with other aspects of astronomy.

Adler Planetarium and Astronomy Museum
1300 S. Lake Shore Drive
Chicago, Illinois 60605

American Museum of Natural History
Rose Center for Earth and Space
Central Park West at 79th Street
New York, NY 10024

National Air and Space Museum
Smithsonian Institution
6th and Independence Avenue SW
Washington, DC 20560

Odyssium
11211 142nd Street
Edmonton, Alberta T5M4A1
Canada

Scienceworks Museum
2 Booker Street
Spotswood, Victoria 3015
Australia

StarDome Observatory
One Tree Hill Domain, off Manukau Road
Royal Oak, Auckland
New Zealand

Glossary

asterism: a pattern of stars that has a name but is not an official constellation.

billion: the number represented by 1 followed by nine zeroes - 1,000,000,000.

catadioptric: a telescope that uses both mirrors and lenses to collect and focus light.

constellation: a grouping of stars in the sky that seems to trace out a familiar pattern, figure, or symbol. There are 88 officially recognized constellations.

galaxy: a large star system containing up to hundreds of billions of stars, along with gas and dust. Our own galaxy is called the Milky Way.

light year: the distance that light travels in one year - nearly six trillion miles (9.6 trillion km).

moon: a natural satellite that revolves around a planet.

nebula: a cloud of gas and dust in space.

new Moon: the phase of the Moon where the side not lit by the Sun faces Earth. Since we see none of the sunlight reflected by the Moon, we cannot see the Moon at this time. It's the opposite of a full Moon, where the side facing us is fully lit by the Sun.

Northern Hemisphere: the half of Earth north of the Equator.

observatory: a structure designed for watching and recording celestial objects and events.

orbit: the path one celestial object follows as it circles, or revolves, around another.

phases: the different ways in which the face of Venus, Mercury, or our Moon is partly lit by the Sun. It takes about one month for Earth's Moon to go from full Moon back to full Moon.

pointers: the two stars at the "bowl" end of the Big Dipper that point toward Polaris, the North Star.

prehistoric: the period in history before writing was used.

quasar: an extremely distant object that seems to resemble a star and gives off huge amounts of energy. Scientists think quasars may be galaxies that have an enormous black hole at their center.

red supergiant: a huge star that develops when the hydrogen in the core of an aging big star runs low and the star expands. The surface of such a star is relatively cool and red.

reflector: a type of telescope that uses mirrors to collect and focus light.

refractor: a type of telescope that uses lenses to collect and focus light.

revolve: to go around completely, or circle, just as Earth revolves around the Sun.

Solar System: the Sun with the planets and all the other bodies, such as asteroids, that orbit it.

Southern Hemisphere: the half of Earth south of the Equator.

Stonehenge: a place in southwestern England that may have been an ancient observatory.

summer solstice: the time of year when the Sun reaches its highest point in the sky.

Universe: all existing things, including Earth, the Sun, the Solar System, galaxies, and all that which is or may be beyond.

zodiac: the band of twelve constellations across the sky that represents the paths of the Sun, the Moon, and most of the planets.

Index

Born in 1920, Isaac Asimov came to the United States as a young boy from his native Russia. As a young man, he was a student of biochemistry. In time, he became one of the most productive writers the world has ever known. His books cover a spectrum of topics, including science, history, language theory, fantasy, and science fiction. His brilliant imagination gained him the respect and admiration of adults and children alike. Sadly, Isaac Asimov died shortly after the publication of the first edition of *Isaac Asimov's Library of the Universe.*

The publishers wish to thank the following for permission to reproduce copyright material: front cover, 3, Gemini Observatory/NOAO/AURA/NSF; 4-5, © Anglo-Australian Telescope Board, David Malin, 1980; 6, Lick Observatory Photographs; 7, 18, 21 (large), © Frank Zullo; 8, Courtesy of Julian Baum; 9 (upper), 11 (upper), 13 (upper), 15 (upper), 26, 27 (all), © Julian Baum 1988; 9 (lower), 11 (lower), 13 (lower), 15 (lower), © Diane Laska-Swanke; 10, Science Photo Library; 12, NASA/JPL/California Institute of Technology; 14, 24 (inset), NASA; 16, © Brad Greenwood, Courtesy of Hansen Planetarium; 17, © Matthew Groshek; 19, NASA/JPL; 20 (left), 21 (inset), NASA and The Hubble Heritage Team (STScI/AURA); 20 (right), NASA/JPL/University of Arizona; 22, 23 (both), © John Sanford/Astrostock; 24 (large), © Anglo-Australian Telescope Board, David Malin, 1979; 25, NASA, ESA, S. Beckwith (STScI), and the HUDF Team; 29 (all), © Julian Baum and Matthew Groshek, 1988.

Seed sowing and saving :
REF 635.0421 TUR   744611

Turner, Carole B.,
WEST GEORGIA REGIONAL LIBRARY

D1207915

WEST GA REG LIB SYS
Neva Lomason
Memorial Library

DISCARD

Storey's Gardening Skills
ILLUSTRATED

Seed Sowing and Saving

Step-by-Step Techniques for Collecting and Growing More Than 100 Vegetables, Flowers, and Herbs

CAROLE B. TURNER

A Storey Publishing Book

Storey Communications, Inc.

The mission of Storey Communications is to serve our customers
by publishing practical information that encourages personal independence
in harmony with the environment.

Edited by Deborah Burns, Gwen W. Steege, and Laura Whalen
Cover design by Mark Tomasi
Cover photographs courtesy of Collins & Brown
Cover photographs by Geoff Dann
Text design and production by Mark Tomasi
Production assistance by Susan Bernier, Erin Lincourt, and Cindy McFarland
Illustrations by Nancy Hull, with the exception of those credited on page 212
Indexed by Susan Olason, Indexes & Knowledge Maps
Copyright © 1998 by Storey Communications, Inc.

All rights reserved. No part of this book may be reproduced without written permission from the publisher, except by a reviewer who may quote brief passages or reproduce illustrations in a review with appropriate credits; nor may any part of this book be reproduced, stored in a retrieval system, or transmitted in any form or by any means — electronic, mechanical, photocopying, recording, or other — without written permission from the publisher.

The information in this book is true and complete to the best of our knowledge. All recommendations are made without guarantee on the part of the author or Storey Communications, Inc. The author and publisher disclaim any liability in connection with the use of this information. For additional information please contact Storey Communications, Inc., Schoolhouse Road, Pownal, Vermont 05261.

Storey Publishing books are available for special premium and promotional uses and for customized editions. For further information, please call the Custom Publishing Department at 1-800-793-9396

Printed in Canada by Transcontinental Printing
10 9 8 7 6 5 4 3 2 1

Library of Congress Cataloging-in-Publication Data

Turner, Carole B., 1964–
       Seed sowing and saving / Carole B. Turner.
          p.   cm. — (Storey's gardening skills illustrated)
       "A Storey Publishing book."
       ISBN 1-58017-002-1 (hc : alk. paper). — ISBN 1-58017-001-3 (pbk. : alk. paper)
       1. Vegetables—Seeds. 2. Flowers—Seeds. 3. Vegetables—Sowing. 4. Flowers—Sowing. 5. Vegetable gardening.
6. Flower gardening. I. Title. II. Series.
SB324.75.T87   1997
635'.0421—dc21
                                                                              97-30671
                                                                                           CIP

❖ D E D I C A T I O N ❖

In memory of my father,
Charles E. Beeson

Contents

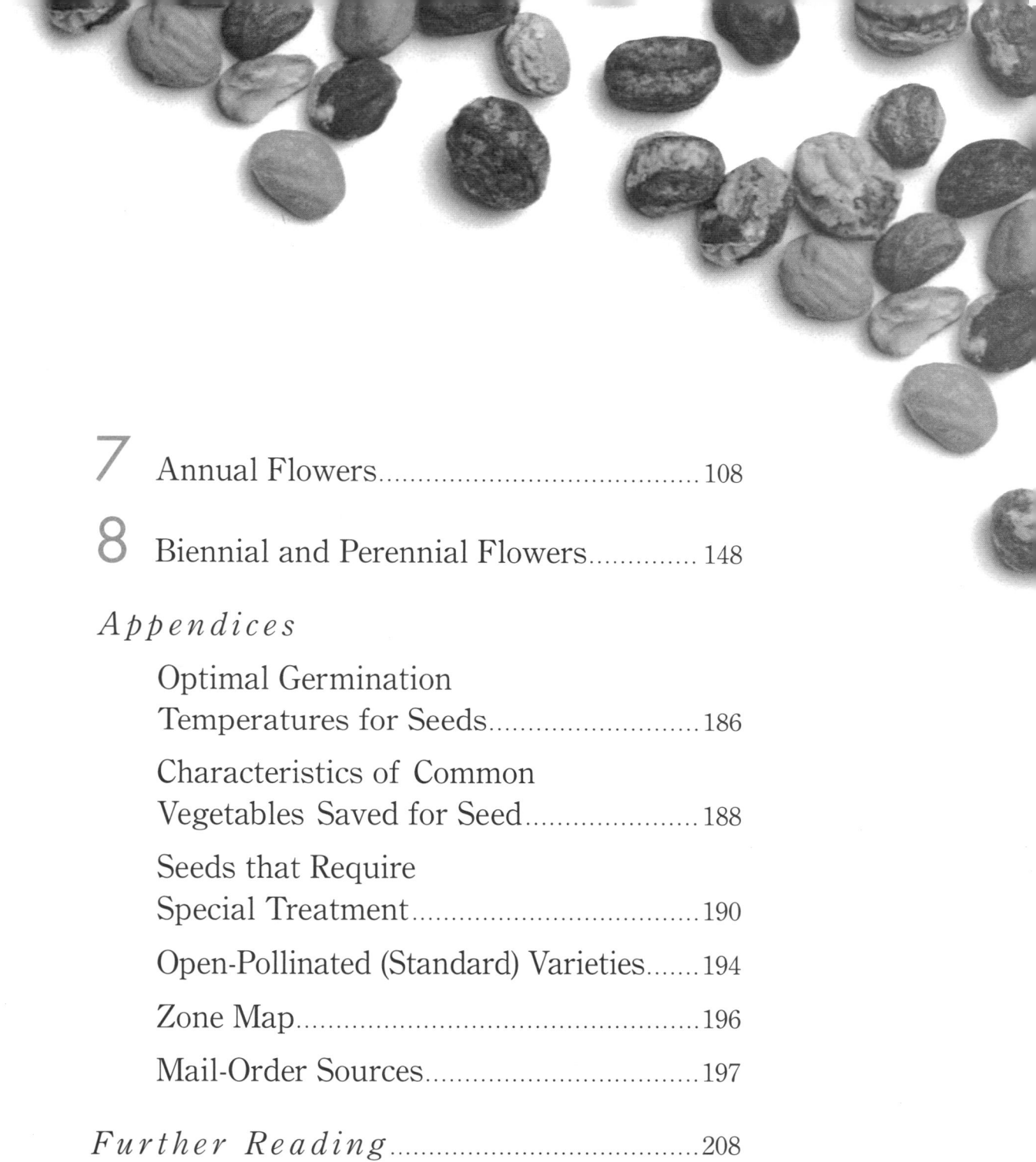

Tomato plant and mature seeds

Introduction

There's nothing quite as miraculous as growing an entire plant from one tiny seed. As I plucked ripe tomatoes from my garden last summer, I wondered at the fact that these 4-foot plants, now nearly toppling with the weight of their bounty, had begun life as tiny seedlings in pots on my windowsill. And the sunflower towering high over my head, with a stem almost 2 inches thick —could it really have grown from one dark, satin-coated seed?

Nature is generous with her miracles. As summer turns to fall, my garden plants begin spilling out their seeds in great abundance, so that future generations will be guaranteed. Columbine seeds, shiny and black in their unfurling papery flutes. Poppy seeds sprinkled from fat little kettles like brown and black grains of pepper. Gaillardias and coneflowers tempting the birds with their bristling gray seed heads. And my lone sunflower, the only one that escaped marauding deer, generously offering up a broad platter of perfect plump seeds, enough to sow a whole garden full of sunflowers.

I've been fascinated with seed-starting ever since I scratched away at my first morning-glory seeds with my mother's emery board, and then hovered over the little pot on the windowsill every day until — wonder of wonders — a tiny green sprout appeared. I was hooked! Fortunately for me, my parents owned a garden center, so I was able to experiment with all kinds of seeds. Being a typical child, I always went for the most unusual things I could find on the seed rack: spaghetti squash, giant pumpkins, scarlet runner beans, and, of course, "the amazing loofa-sponge plant." I wasn't always successful with these novelties, but I sure had fun trying. Today, as I hover over my many flats of seedlings and newly sown seeds, it's clear that things haven't changed much.

Sunflower

1

Why Seeds?

Why bother with collecting and growing seeds if you can buy plants at a nursery? After all, seeds take time and patience, not to mention planning. You must sow them at the right time, often crowded on a windowsill in late winter, so that they have enough time to produce flowers or fruit during the growing season. You must carefully tend the fragile seedlings until they are strong enough to take root in the garden, and then transplant them once or even twice. And then you must diligently guard the tender young transplants against nibbling rabbits, late frosts, and scorching sun.

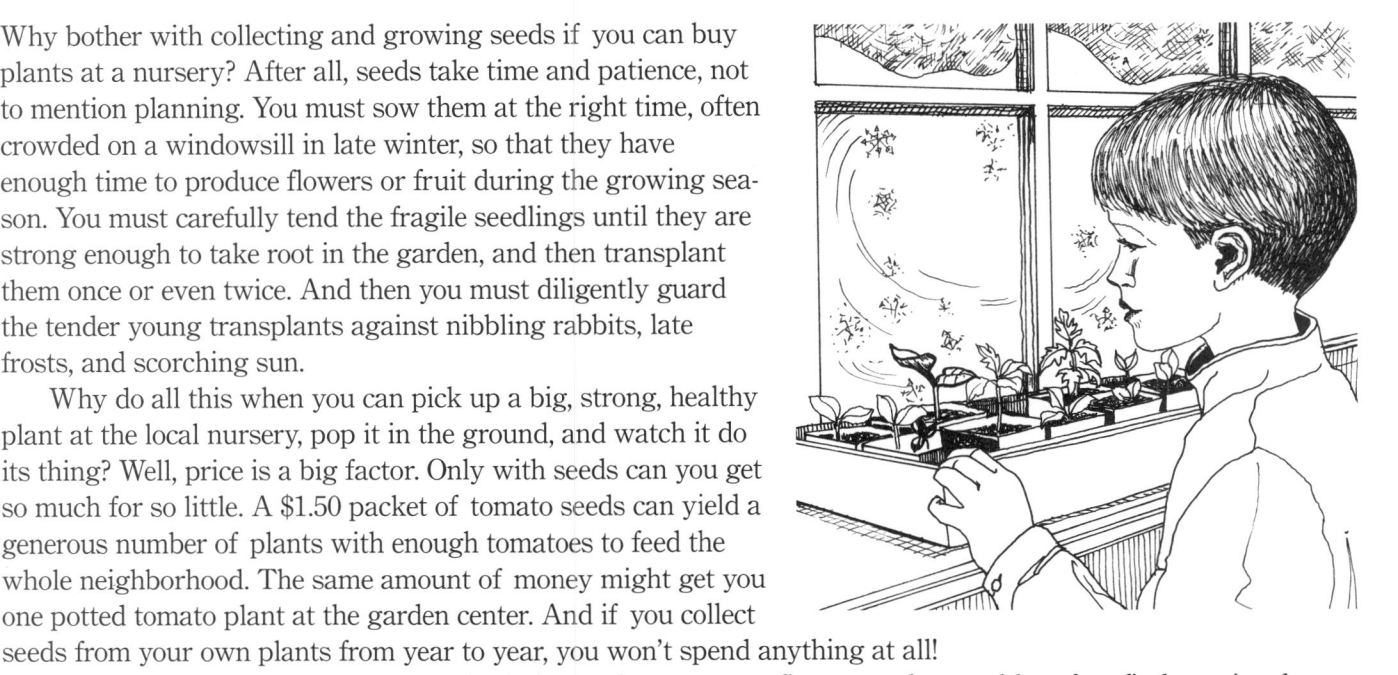

Why do all this when you can pick up a big, strong, healthy plant at the local nursery, pop it in the ground, and watch it do its thing? Well, price is a big factor. Only with seeds can you get so much for so little. A $1.50 packet of tomato seeds can yield a generous number of plants with enough tomatoes to feed the whole neighborhood. The same amount of money might get you one potted tomato plant at the garden center. And if you collect seeds from your own plants from year to year, you won't spend anything at all!

Gardeners who want to expand their choices to less common flowers and vegetables often find starting from seed essential. Most nurseries carry only the most popular varieties of plants in containers, but seed catalogs often list unusual, exotic, or rare varieties that can be impossible to obtain in flats, already started. Some wildflowers, for instance, are difficult to find at garden centers, but there are plenty of seed suppliers that sell them by mail order.

Growing plants from seed is also simply a lot of fun. Children especially enjoy checking the pots or flats each day to spot the first tiny green shoots emerging from the soil.

Another reason to grow plants from seed is to avoid introducing some diseases to your garden. Some potted plants may carry soil-borne diseases such as anthracnose and rhizoctonia, and these can spread to the rest of your garden.

Buy Seed or Harvest Your Own?

When you're just starting out, you'll naturally have to buy most of your seed from the garden center or from seed catalogs. And when those catalogs begin filling up your mailbox every winter, it's hard to resist the temptation to try a few new varieties. If you're a plant collector, you might just want to try them all.

Once you have an established garden, however, you can harvest enough seed from it to plant several more gardens. By selecting the best plants to collect seed from, or by hand-pollinating selected specimens, you can carry on outstanding traits, improve on a plant's best qualities, or perhaps even stumble upon a new variety.

Collecting seeds from your own garden plants is a way to preserve heirloom varieties and pass them along to family and friends. And you'll find that trading seeds with other gardeners is a fun way to share your own plants and try out someone else's favorites. Several seed exchanges have been organized to help seed collectors find each other and find particular plants (see box).

Of course, certain plants — hybrids and other cultivated varieties — often can't be grown from collected seed. If they do produce viable seed, the resulting plants are usually inferior to the parent plant. If you're trying to propagate such plants in your garden, a vegetative method (such as cuttings, division, or layering) is recommended in order to get an exact replica of the parent plant. On the other hand, if you're just interested in experimenting to see what new characteristics might emerge, feel free to sow as many seeds as you wish.

MASTER GARDENING TIPS

Heirloom Plants and Seed Exchanges

The term "heirloom" gets tossed around a lot these days in reference to plants, but what does it really mean? Heirlooms are generally open-pollinated varieties that were introduced over 50 years ago but are no longer commercially available (although some seed catalogs have now begun to offer them, due to popular demand). These plant varieties were kept from extinction by some individual (or individuals) who faithfully saved the seeds and grew the plants year after year (protecting them from cross-pollination to make sure the strain remained pure).

Why bother preserving old varieties when so many "new and improved" hybrids have been created? The main reason, beyond historical preservation, is to protect genetic diversity. Without it, plants may become inbred and susceptible to disease, pests, and drought. The most notorious example of this was the U.S. corn crop of 1970. More than 80 percent of that crop consisted of hybrid corn, and 15 percent of the crop failed that year because of a gene that made the hybrids susceptible to blight. All the nonhybrid corn survived. In 1988, drought wiped out 40 percent of the U.S. corn crop, or $7 billion worth of corn. Hybrids have made a huge contribution to horticulture, and especially to our food supply, but there would be no new hybrids without the genetic material supplied by the old varieties. Saving seeds of nonhybrid varieties is just one way to plan for the future and keep the gene pool from drying up.

Often the only way to obtain seeds of heirloom varieties is through a seed exchange. Since the issue of seed saving has been a low priority for most of our elected officials, seed exchanges were set up as a grass-roots effort to preserve the plants that have played an important part in our heritage and may even end up feeding us in the future. Members of these exchanges grow heirloom varieties and trade the seeds with one another, thus keeping old strains going by sharing them with gardeners all over the country. Some seed exchanges have grown quite large; the nonprofit Seed Savers Exchange, for instance, has 8,000 members and has even set up its own 170-acre farm near Decorah, Iowa, for growing heirloom plants. Many plant societies also operate exchanges among their members. For a list of seed exchanges, see page 205.

Creating soilless mixes for starting seeds, page 12

Stratifying seeds, page 9

Avoid damping-off disease, page 13

CHAPTER·1

Sowing Seeds

Seed-sowing instructions are frequently so complicated that many beginning gardeners simply give up and either buy plants or just toss the seeds out on the ground, hoping for the best. After reading about "gourmet" soil-mix recipes, space-consuming fluorescent light setups, heating pads and cables, cold frames, and computer programs for keeping track of the whole operation, I begin to wonder if I'm planting seeds or preparing for an expedition to Mount Everest. What seems like such a simple process in nature — a seed falls to the ground, is watered by rain and warmed by the sun — becomes a complex undertaking in human hands.

Yet many seeds require only a pot of soil, consistent moisture, and a sunny windowsill to germinate. Start out with things that are easy to grow from seed, be encouraged by each success, and gradually work your way up to the trickier plants.

Indoors or Out?

Annuals, which grow, bloom, and die in the course of one year, are usually sown directly outdoors in spring. Plants with deep taproots, such as carrots and parsley, should generally be sown directly outdoors or in individual peat pots indoors, since they resent transplanting.

On the other hand, warm-weather vegetables like tomatoes need a head start in cold regions, and must be started indoors under lights. You may also want to start annual flowers indoors in late winter to give them a head start for a longer season of bloom.

Perennials and woody plants should almost always be started indoors in late winter, unless the seeds are sown outdoors in seedbeds right after fall harvest. Most perennials that are started indoors early will bloom in the first year, but if the seeds are sown outdoors in spring, the plants may not have time to develop a good root system before the next winter arrives.

In This Chapter

- Testing Seed Viability
- Containers
- Special Seed Treatments
- Timing Indoor Seed Sowing
- Average Last Frost Dates
- Soils and Soilless Mixes
- Light and Heat
- Sowing Seed Indoors
- Successful Seed Sowing
- Labeling
- Watering Methods
- Nurturing Seedlings
- Pricking Out
- Hardening Off
- Transplanting Step-by-Step
- Protecting Young Plants
- Caring for Seedlings
- When and Where to Sow Seeds
- Sowing Seeds Outdoors

Testing Seed Viability

Seeds that are kept in storage rather than sown fresh may, for a number of reasons, lose their viability and become unable to germinate. You will find some guidelines in the chart on page 188, but whether you have collected and stored seed from your garden plants, or you have packaged seed left over from previous years, you may want to test its viability before spending a lot of time trying to grow it.

Some seeds naturally have longer viability than others. Most seeds will stay viable (capable of germinating) for several years after harvest if kept in cool, dry storage. With some seeds, you can tell by their weight and by the way they look if they have lost viability. For instance, a viable sunflower seed will be plump and smooth, not thin and puckered. If a few seeds feel lighter than all the others, chances are they've deteriorated and lost their viability. But if you really want to make sure, try the test shown here.

MASTER GARDENING TIPS

Covering Seeds

When testing seeds that need light to germinate, cover the tray loosely with clear plastic wrap to retain humidity. If seeds do not require light, cover them with another layer of damp paper towels. Place the tray in a warm (70° to 80°F) location, and keep the paper towels consistently damp but not dripping wet.

Judging Viability

Calculate the percentage of viable seeds by dividing the number of seeds that germinated by the total number of seeds tested. If germination is 50 percent or higher, the seeds are viable and worth planting. A rate between 25 and 50 percent indicates that the seeds are viable but should be sown thickly for best results. If the germination rate is below 25 percent, you should probably discard the seed batch, or sow the seeds very thickly and hope for a few plants out of it.

The more seeds you can test, the more accurate your results will be; test no fewer than 20 seeds, or as many as 100 seeds if you can spare them. To avoid mix-ups, be sure to test only one variety per tray.

1 Place several layers of paper towels in a shallow tray. Draw a grid on the top sheet of the stack, dampen, and place a seed in each square. Be sure to label..

2 In two or three days, check the seeds. If you see anything breaking through the seed coat, it means the seed has germinated. Keep checking them for up to three weeks.

Containers

Seeds can be started in almost any kind of container, as long as there is good drainage and water-holding capacity. The best containers are relatively shallow, about 2 or 3 inches deep. I've grown seeds in all sorts of homemade containers and ordinary household containers, in old wooden flats (very heavy ones!) and rectangular plastic flats, and I finally broke down and bought seed-starting kits from a garden catalog. They were somewhat expensive, but well worth it.

Clay pots are acceptable, but they have several drawbacks: They tend to absorb water and need frequent watering to keep the soil moist. They are also heavy, expensive, and space-consuming.

Ordinary household containers, such as cardboard milk cartons, yogurt containers, Styrofoam cups, and plastic margarine tubs, can be used for small numbers of seedlings. Aluminum loaf pans also work well, but pie pans are too shallow and won't hold enough soil or moisture.

MASTER GARDENING TIP

Seed-Starting Kits

The seed-starting kit I use includes a bottomless Styrofoam flat with individual seedling cells, a plastic-lined tray for holding water, a capillary mat to conduct water from the tray to the seedling cells, and a clear plastic humidity cover. I've grown seeds in these setups under my heat lamps, and germination was 100 percent. Most of the seeds germinated in less than a week, and the seedlings were strong and healthy. I highly recommend these types of kits if your seed-starting setup is not too extensive.

HINTS FOR SUCCESS

▶ Make sure all containers have drainage holes in the bottom.

▶ Thoroughly clean and then sterilize containers in a bleach/water mixture before using.

For larger seed batches, and more convenience, use plastic pots, peat pellets or peat pots, plastic flats, or cell trays.

For plants that are difficult to transplant, sow the seeds in individual peat pellets or pots; you can then plant the entire thing in the ground without disturbing the roots and causing transplant shock. (Cucumbers, squash, eggplant, and melons are some good candidates for peat pots.)

Special Treatments for Seeds

Built-in mechanisms prevent some seeds from germinating until all conditions are ideal. These are usually the seeds of perennials and woody plants native to cooler regions, and they will not germinate until the winter has passed. If they did not have this germination-delaying mechanism, the seeds would sprout after being dispersed in fall, and the tiny seedlings would freeze and die in the cold winter weather. If you have collected seeds from such plants, you must treat them to "break dormancy" before they will germinate. Two methods of doing this are *scarification* (penetrating the seed) and *stratification* (chilling the seed).

Scarification and Soaking

Some seeds have a very hard seed coat that keeps moisture out and prevents germination until it is gradually worn away by the elements, eaten away by microorganisms in the soil, or broken down by passing through the digestive tract of a bird or animal. In nature, this weathering process takes several months, delaying germination until spring arrives and the conditions are right for the plant to grow and survive.

If you are trying to grow these kinds of seeds, you must nick, scratch, or otherwise penetrate the seed coat before the seed will germinate. This is called scarification.

Sometimes the seed coat must be softened rather than nicked; this can be done by soaking the seeds in warm water for at least 24 hours. Really tough seeds should be nicked and then soaked, for best results. Occasionally, the seed coat is not particularly hard but contains a germination-inhibiting compound that must be dissolved before the seed will sprout; a good example of this is parsley. These seeds should also be soaked for a day or two before planting.

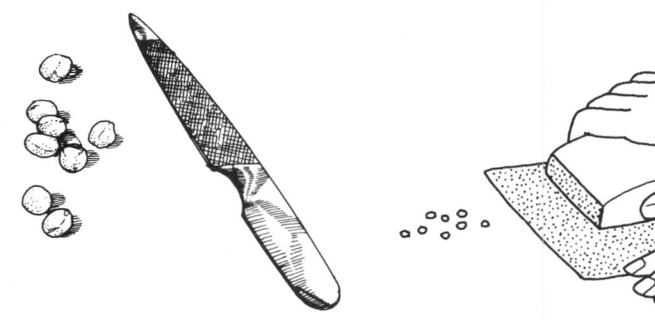

Larger seeds can be nicked with a file, knife, or razor blade. Cut a shallow notch to one side of the hilum (the scar where the seed was attached to the pod), being very careful not to cut into the embryo inside.

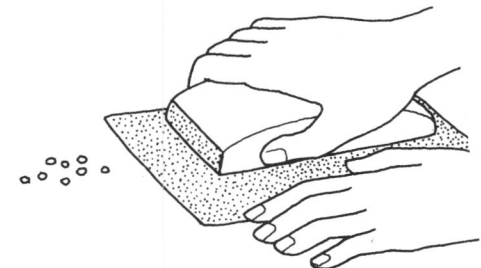

To scarify smaller seeds, rub them between two pieces of medium-grade sandpaper.

Common Plants That Require Scarification

Asparagus (soak)
Beans (soak)
Beet (soak)
Carrot (soak)
Corn (soak)
Lupine (nick and soak)
Morning glory (nick and soak)
Parsley (soak)
Peas (soak)
Primrose (soak)
Spinach (soak)
Sweet pea (nick and soak)

Common Plants That Require Stratification

Aster
Bachelor's button
Bee balm
Bellflower
Black-eyed Susan
Blazing star
Clematis (stratify in freezer)
Columbine
Coneflower
Coreopsis
Delphinium
Lupine (stratify in freezer before soaking)
Pansy
Primrose (not all varieties)
Snapdragon
Spider flower

Stratifying Seeds

Seeds of many perennials and woody plants will not germinate if planted immediately after being harvested. These seeds must go through a cold, dark, moist period before they can sprout. In the wild, this happens naturally and is called "winter," but if you've collected the seeds and plan to sow them indoors, you must provide an artificial cold period before they will break dormancy. The chilling time will vary depending on the plant; some require only a few weeks, while others must be chilled for several months. A few finicky plants have even more complex requirements, and must have alternating periods of cold and warmth before germination is triggered.

Stratification used to be done — and sometimes still is — by digging a hole or trench outdoors and placing in it layers ("strata") of seed and moist sand. You can also create a simulated winter indoors by placing the seeds in a refrigerator. Here is the method I use:·

MASTER GARDENING TIPS

Timing Pointers

▶ Seeds of most trees and shrubs must be stratified longer than seeds of annuals and perennials.

▶ Seeds should be stratified just before planting. Don't chill them and then put them into storage. However, most seeds can be stored, if thoroughly dry, in the refrigerator in envelopes or paper bags.

1 Sow the seeds in pots or flats filled with moistened seed-starting mix and cover the containers with plastic wrap.

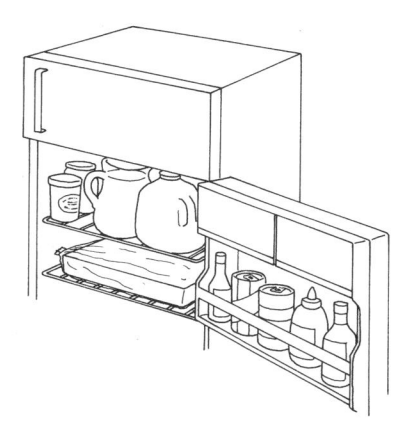

2 Place the containers or bags in the refrigerator (not the freezer). Check them occasionally to make sure the soil stays moist. They can stay in the refrigerator for anywhere between 24 hours and several months, depending on the plant.

3 After the chilling period, remove the containers from the refrigerator or the ground, uncover them, and put them in a warm, sunny place indoors. Water them frequently until the seedlings appear.

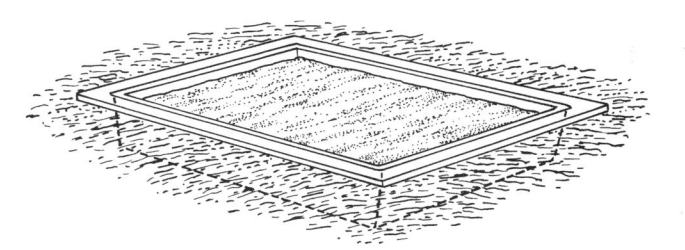

Or, if you don't have space in your refrigerator, you can cover the containers with a piece of glass, bury them to the rim in a protected spot outdoors, and leave them there for the winter.

Timing Indoor Seed Sowing

When to sow seeds indoors generally depends on the last spring frost date for your area, and also on how fast the plant grows. Slow-growing plants like perennials and woody plants can be started indoors as early as 12 weeks before the last expected spring frost. Refer to the map and tables opposite to predict safe planting times for your region. Most annuals and vegetables should be started six to eight weeks before the last frost. You will enjoy indoor seed starting much more if you don't get carried away and plant more seeds than you can handle. When you are working with healthy, fresh seed, you can count on a good germination rate, so you won't need to overplant.

Assemble the materials needed for sowing seeds indoors. These include seed-starting mix, flats and/or pots, labels, a watering can, and a heating pad (optional).

MASTER GARDENING TIPS

▶ Better to sow seed a little too late than too early; seedlings that stay indoors too long can become spindly and weak.

▶ The same holds true for transplanting the seedlings outdoors. In cold regions, it's hard to predict the actual date of the last spring frost. The average date given in most books is just that, an average.

▶ Start small at first, and gradually work up to a larger seed-starting operation.

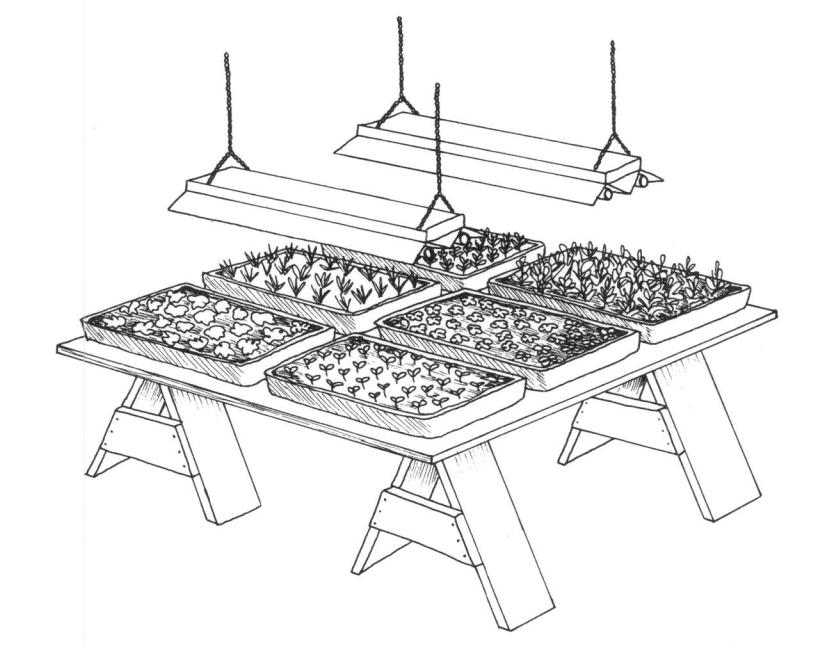

Create a light table by supporting a 4 x 4 piece of plywood on two saw horses. Suspend fluorescent shop lights overhead by chains that can be raised as the plants grow.

Average Last Frost Dates

Average Last Frost Dates in the United States

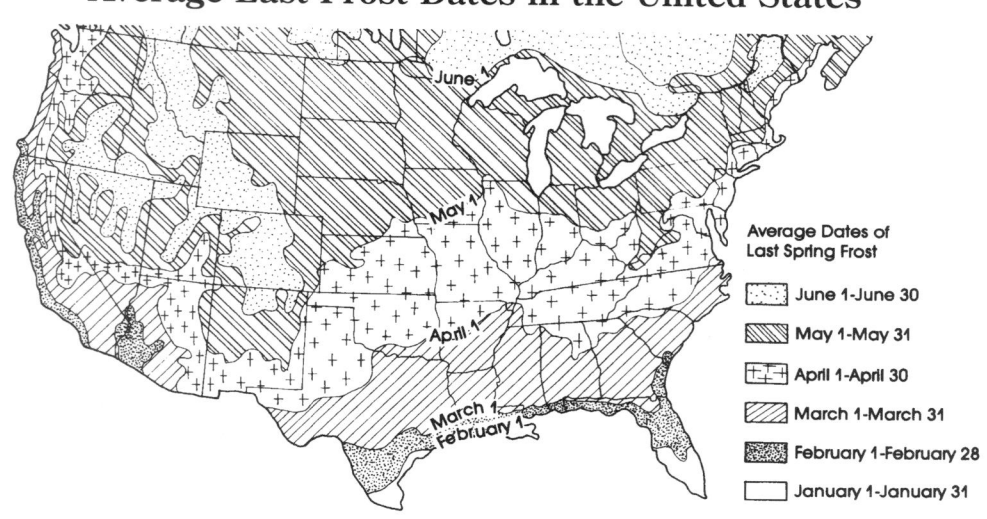

Average Dates of Last Spring Frost

June 1-June 30	
May 1-May 31	
April 1-April 30	
March 1-March 31	
February 1-February 28	
January 1-January 31	

Average Last Frost Dates in Canada

Station	Last Frost	Station	Last Frost	Station	Last Frost
British Columbia		Regina	May 21	Montreal	May 3
Chilliwack	April 6	Saskatoon	May 21	Quebec	May 13
Dawson Creek	June 5	Weyburn	May 22	Rimouski	May 13
Kamloops	May 1			Sherbrooke	June 1
Kelowna	May 19	**Manitoba**		Trois-Rivieres	May 19
Nanaimo	April 28	Brandon	May 27	Thetford Mines	May 28
Port Alberni	May 8	The Pas	May 27		
Prince George	June 4	Thompson	June 15	**New Brunswick**	
Terrace	May 5	Winnipeg	May 25	Bathurst	May 19
Vancouver	March 28			Edmundston	May 28
Vernon	April 29	**Ontario**		Fredericton	May 20
Victoria	April 19	Barrie	May 26	Grand Falls	May 24
		Hamilton	April 29	Moncton	May 24
Northwest Territory		Kingston	May 2	Saint John	May 18
and Yukon		London	May 9		
Whitehorse	June 11	Ottawa	May 6	**Prince Edward Island**	
Yellowknife	May 27	Owen Sound	May 12	Charlottetown	May 17
		Parry Sound	May 17	Summerside	May 9
Alberta		Peterborough	May 18	Tignish	May 23
Athabaska	June 1	St. Catharines	May 2		
Calgary	May 23	Sudbury	May 17	**Nova Scotia**	
Edmonton	May 7	Thunder Bay	June 1	Halifax	May 6
Grande Prairie	May 18	Timmins	June 8	Kentville	May 16
Lethbridge	May 17	Toronto	May 9	Shelburne	May 14
Medicine Hat	May 16	Windsor	April 25	Sydney	May 24
Red Deer	May 25			Yarmouth	May 1
		Quebec			
Saskatchewan		Baie Comeau	May 28	**Newfoundland**	
Moose Jaw	May 20	Chicoutimi	May 17	Corner Brook	May 22
Prince Albert	June 2			Grand Falls	June 2
				St. John's	June 2

Data from Environmental Canada as published in Canadian Gardening magazine.

Soils and Soilless Mixes

There are two ways to obtain an excellent propagation medium for starting your own seeds. The simplest way is to buy a bag of premixed sterile artificial medium. You'll find it sold under several different brand names (like Jiffy Mix, Pro Mix and Metro Mix), but most consist of the same basic ingredients: peat moss, vermiculite, perlite, and possibly some fertilizer (see below). These so-called soilless mixes are available at most garden centers and hardware stores. (Soilless mix is *not* the same as "potting soil.") I have always used them for seed starting, and because they are sterile, I have never had problems with damping-off or other fungal diseases.

If you prefer to mix your own propagation medium, I recommend using equal amounts of peat moss, perlite, and vermiculite. Some gardeners also include garden soil in their mix, but I don't recommend adding it. Most soils are too heavy for seeds and do not provide the air space seeds require. Also, it must be sterilized before seed sowing, to avoid damping-off and other diseases.

HINTS FOR SUCCESS

A good seed-starting mix should have several characteristics:

▶ It should be lightweight, to provide needed air spaces for the seeds.

▶ It should absorb water; moisture is absolutely essential for seed growth.

▶ It should be sterile, so that the seedlings will not be susceptible to fungi, weeds, and diseases.

▶ Finally, it should not be high in nutritive value, since seeds draw only moisture, air, and warmth from the soil, getting their nutrients from the endosperm or cotyledons.

MASTER GARDENING TIPS

Ingredients of a Basic Propagation Mix

Peat moss. Milled sphagnum moss is essentially sterile, light in weight, and can hold over 10 times its weight in moisture. Peat moss also contains a natural substance that inhibits damping-off fungus.

Perlite. Volcanic rock that has been ground up and heated, perlite looks and feels like small, crunchy white pebbles. It usually comes in different grades. You'll want a fine grade for seed mixes, while coarser grades are good for growing cuttings. Perlite is added to soil mixes to lighten and separate. It is not highly absorbent.

Vermiculite. Mica (a shiny, scaly mineral) that has been heated, causing the particles to expand, vermiculite is added to seed-starting mixes to hold moisture and nutrients and to lighten the mix.

Sterilizing Soil

If you want to add garden soil to your planting mixture, you should consider sterilizing it first or you may invite disease problems, including damping-off. Unfortunately, sterilization is a messy, smelly procedure. You can sterilize small amounts of soil in an oven or a microwave.

To sterilize soil in the oven, spread out the soil in pans, wet it thoroughly, and bake it at 275°F. Larger quantities of soil may have to bake for an hour and a half; smaller quantities (up to a gallon) need about half an hour. This method uses steam to kill unwanted nematodes, fungi, viruses, insects, and weeds, so be sure the soil is completely wet before baking it. Plan to do this just before leaving the house for a long weekend, or you may be driven out of the house by the smell.

To sterilize soil in a microwave, put some in an open plastic bag and microwave for 7 or 8 minutes. Many authorities advise against this procedure, since it can change the makeup of the soil (pH, mineral content, etc.).

To sterilize soil outdoors, you can solarize it, a slower method without the annoying smell. Drape a sheet of clear plastic over a garden bed in full sun for a couple of weeks, or put the soil into black plastic pots, place each pot in a clear plastic bag, and tie shut. Put the pots-in-bags in the sunniest spot you can find, and leave them there for two weeks. Pouring boiling water over soil is another muchtouted method of sterilization that actually does not sterilize the soil completely, although it will destroy many microorganisms.

Solarizing is an easy but slow way to sterilize soil.

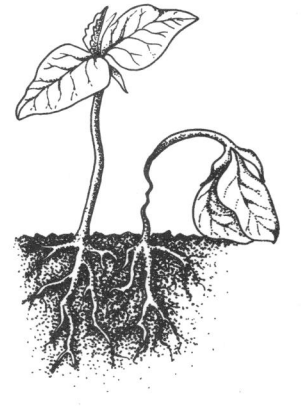

Damping-off is a fungal disease that rots seeds as they germinate or seedlings once they emerge from the soil. It is most often caused by *Pythium* or *Rhizoctonia*, which thrive in stagnant air and high humidity. Once plants contract the disease, they cannot be saved. In this case, prevention is the best care (see box at right.)

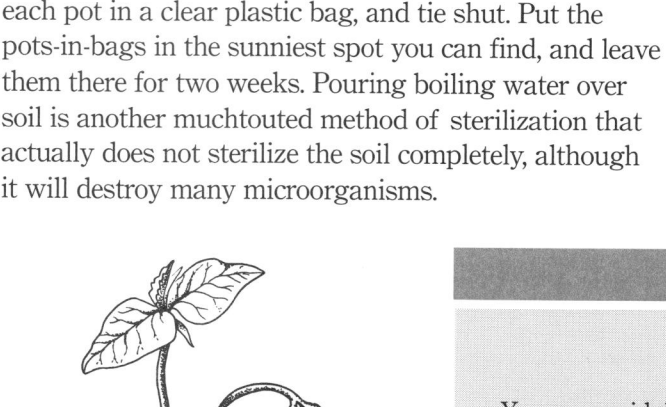

MASTER GARDENING TIPS

Preventing Damping-Off

You can avoid damping-off disease by maintaining a healthy environment for your seedlings.

▶ Sterilize your containers in a solution of 4 parts water to 1 part bleach.

▶ Be sure to use a sterile propagation medium.

▶ Wash your hands and tools thoroughly and often.

▶ Plant only fresh, healthy seed.

▶ Put the containers in a place where they will get good air circulation, heat, and plenty of light.

▶ Don't sow the seeds too thickly.

▶ Thin out any crowded seedlings as soon as they can be handled.

▶ Don't overwater the seedlings.

▶ Give minimal amounts of fertilizer (if any) to avoid burning the roots.

Light Requirements for Germination

Some seeds require light to germinate, but most will germinate in complete darkness. After they have sprouted, however, immediately move the seedlings to a place with plenty of light. A sunny windowsill may do for some plants, but most will get weak and leggy unless they are placed under artificial lights.

Fluorescent light fixtures can be hung almost anywhere. I have a metal shelving unit in my basement, and I hang a light fixture above each shelf. It makes a convenient, if somewhat chilly, place for my seedlings.

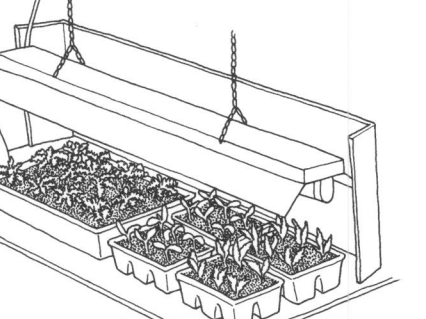

Fluorescent lights come closest to reproducing the natural color spectrum of sunlight. The pink-tinted fluorescent bulbs are best; these are meant specifically for growing plants, since they provide the optimal light spectrum for photosynthesis.

HINTS FOR SUCCESS

► Keep seeds out of direct sunlight, from the time they are collected until just before they germinate.

► Athough ordinary incandescent light has some effect, fluorescent is preferred for seedlings.

► Seedlings should be placed about 6 inches from the light source for best growth.

► Most seedlings will grow well with equal lengths of light and dark. Set timer to keep lights on for 12 hours at a time.

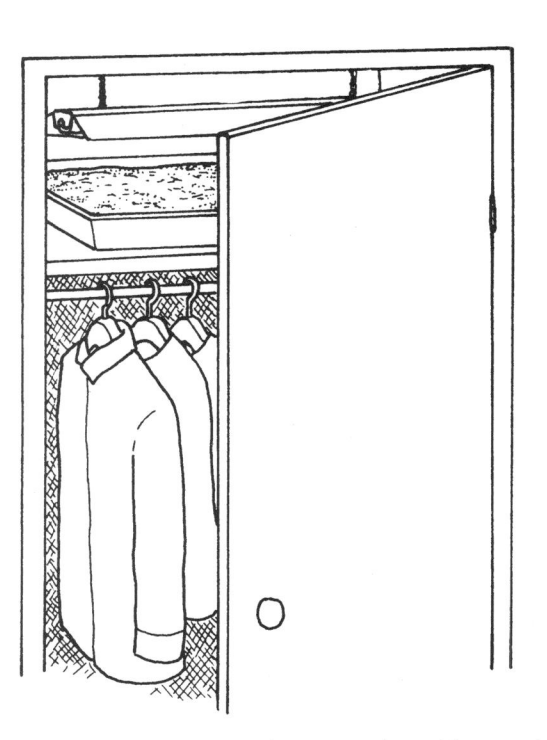

Light fixtures can also be hung in closets, under tables, and inside unused cabinets. The surrounding area can be dark since the fluorescents provide all the light the plants need.

Heat Requirements for Germination

At a temperature of about 60° to 75°F, most seeds will germinate in a few weeks. For most annuals and vegetables, a temperature of 72°F is just about perfect for germination; many perennials can tolerate a slightly lower temperature. You'll probably read a lot about providing "bottom heat" to help seeds germinate. Many gardeners place their seed flats on top of a refrigerator, furnace, radiator, hot-water heater, or heating pad to provide bottom heat, but sometimes these sources produce inconsistent heat, too much heat, or too little heat. I've had success providing general warmth, instead of bottom heat, with a common clip-on lamp.

Attach an aluminum clip-on utility lamp to a shelf near your seed flats (I use a 75-watt Gro 'N' Show bulb, but any incandescent light will do). One lamp provides all the heat necessary for two flats, and my seeds always germinate quickly. If the seeds need darkness to germinate, I simply cover the flat with something opaque, like newspaper, until the seedlings emerge. The lamps can stay on 24 hours a day until the seeds germinate.

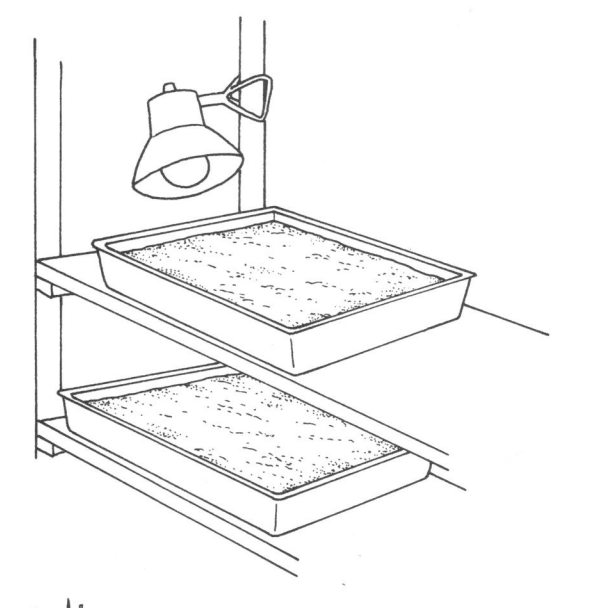

You can buy heating pads from many garden-supply catalogs. These are more useful for cuttings and seedlings than for seeds, as they tend to be too small for seed flats and rather expensive.

....
HINT FOR SUCCESS

Heating cables are also available; these are buried beneath the soil in a cold frame (turning it into a "hotbed") or greenhouse, and usually come with a thermostat to prevent overheating.

Sowing Seed Indoors Step-by-Step

Seed-starting mixes are usually light and fluffy, and the slightest breeze (or sneeze) can scatter the particles. Because of this, it's difficult to make trenches or holes for seed planting, and it's also hard to water the containers without washing away most of the medium. For these reasons, it's usually best to moisten the mix before sowing, but don't overdo it. You should not be able to squeeze any water out of a handful of soil.

MASTER GARDENING TIPS

Providing a Good Environment

▶ To provide extra warmth to the seeds and aid in germination, use warm water (about 80°F).

▶ Once the mix is moist, don't let it dry out.

▶ It's critical for seedlings to have good air circulation, to avoid damping-off and other fungal diseases.

1 Put mix in a bucket, add warm water, and mix with your hands or a long-handled trowel until soil is evenly moist but not dripping.

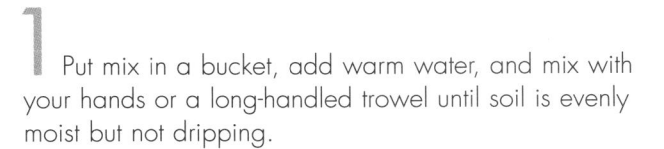

½"

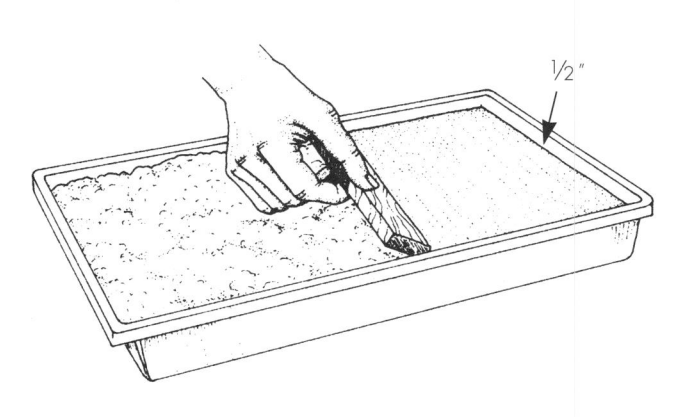

2 Fill the container three-quarters full, tamp down the mix gently but firmly, and then add more seed-starting mix. Tamp the mix once again, and repeat the process until the surface of the mix is about ½ inch from the top of the container. Use a piece of scrap wood to even surface.

3 When the surface of the mix is level, make holes for large seeds or furrows for small seeds, using a dibble, a pencil, or even your finger. Small seeds may be scattered over the surface and covered as recommended with sowing medium (see specific plants.)

4 Soil mix will still be damp, but sprinkle with a bit more water to be sure the surface doesn't dry out, then cover the flat or container with plastic wrap or some other clear material to keep in humidity. To provide air circulation, don't seal the flat completely. If the seeds need darkness to germinate, cover the container with an opaque material like damp newspaper or burlap. If they need light to germinate, leave the lights on for 24 hours a day until they sprout.

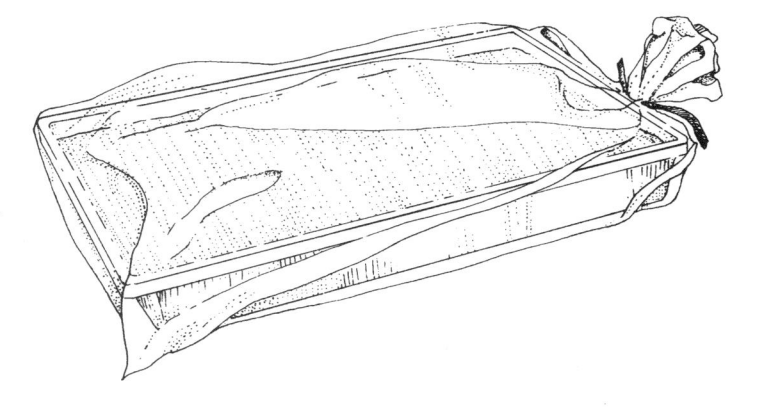

5 Never let seeds dry out. Keep the soil consistently, evenly moist or you may have erratic germination. Use water that is tepid or room temperature (65° to 70°F); the extra warmth aids in germination. To avoid disturbing seeds, bottom water by placing the flat in a large container of water until soil mixture is moist throughout, or use a fine overhead spray.

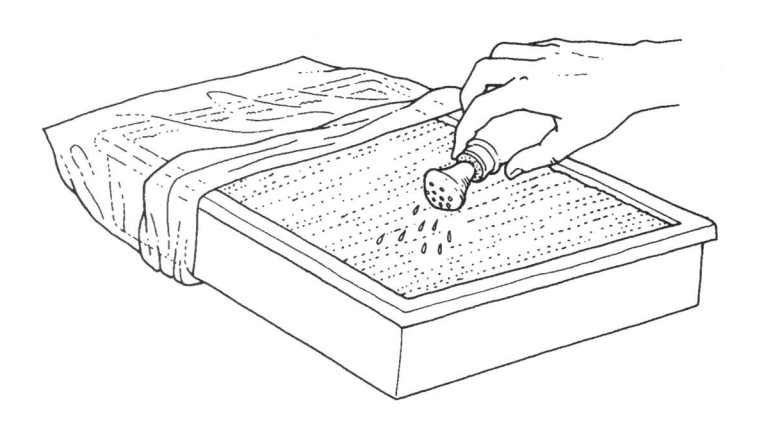

Hints for Successful Seed Sowing

Be careful not to plant seeds too deeply. Follow the instructions on the seed packet to get the right depth, or make a hole about a half-inch deeper than the diameter of the seed. You might want to lay out rows with a straightedge first, to keep your holes from wandering. Furrows are a better way to plant small or fine seeds. To make a furrow, lay a pencil or ruler on its side, and mark out a light row in the propagation mix. Try to keep the rows at least 1½ inches apart, to give the seedlings enough room to grow.

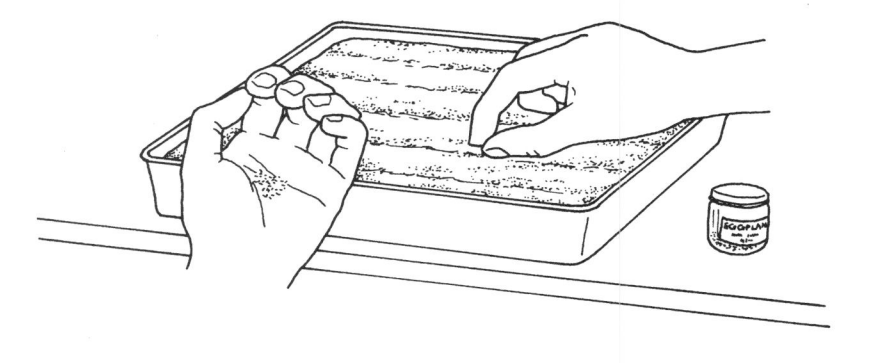

With fine or small seeds, make a furrow in the soil and drop seeds in about ⅛ inch apart.

HINTS FOR SUCCESS

Small seeds can be more challenging to sow, especially if, like me, you have unsteady hands. Here are some suggestions:

▶ Hold the seed packet on its side just above the furrow, and carefully tap the top edge with your forefinger.

▶ Take a pinch of seeds between your thumb and forefinger and rotate them gently over the furrow.

▶ With the finest seeds (some are as fine as dust), use a salt shaker for even distribution; be sure the shaker is clean, dry, and completely free of salt before putting seeds in it.

▶ Mix tiny seeds with a small amount of sand or soil, and then sprinkle this mixture along the furrow.

▶ You can sow all but the largest seeds by teasing them out of their containers with a tweezers.

MASTER GARDENING TIPS

Rules of Thumb

Unless you have a special reason for doing so — for instance, if you know the seeds have a poor germination rate — you should try not to sow thickly. Heavy sowings turn into crowded seedlings, and you'll end up having to thin out a large number of them. It's also important to plant seeds at the correct depth. Follow the spacing instructions on the packet, or use these rules of thumb:

Spacing:

▶ Sow small seeds ⅛ inch apart.

▶ Sow medium seeds ½ inch apart.

▶ Sow large seeds 1 inch apart.

Depth:

▶ Sow very fine seeds on the surface or ⅛ inch deep.

▶ Sow medium-sized seeds ¼ to ½ inch deep.

▶ Sow large seeds 1 to 2 inches deep.

Labeling

When you're sowing seeds, you may think you'll remember what you put where, but inevitably, several weeks later when everything has sprouted, that's harder and less obvious than expected. The bigger your seed-starting operation gets, the more important it becomes to label things properly, especially if you're growing several varieties of a certain plant and need to be able to tell them apart.

As far as I'm concerned, plastic or wooden stakes labeled in permanent marker are best. When I planted seed outdoors, I used to put the seed packet over a wooden stick and cover the whole thing with a baggie to protect it from rain, but it became a sad, crumpled mess in no time, and was very hard to read. Now I keep my seed packets indoors, safe and dry and readable, and use white plastic stakes to label plantings both indoors and outside. After harvesting the vegetables, I pull up the stakes, bring them indoors, and reuse them the following year.

You can use a number of things for labeling: Popsicle sticks, old cut-up aluminum or vinyl blinds, plastic containers of any kind (for example, yogurt cups) cut into strips. One year I even used drinking straws. Although it was a little hard to write on them, they were all I had on hand.

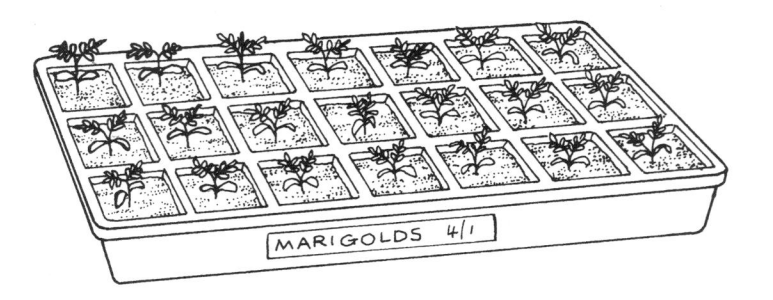

Garden centers sell plastic labels, or you can use adhesive paper labels stuck to the side of the flat or container (these don't tend to last long outdoors). Be sure to use a pen or marker that will not easily wash off or fade outdoors.

MASTER GARDENING TIPS

Labels

Labels are a gardener's memory. They remind us what is in the garden, where it is, and how long it has been there.

► Combine labeling with pest monitoring. Paint a wooden label yellow. Use one side as a plant label and smear the other side with Vaseline. When the pests crawl or fly to the greasy surface, they become stuck to it, producing an exact record of which pests bother which plants.

► When labeling plants, use the front of the label to record the plant name and variety. Use the back of the label to record important dates, such as planting, flowering, and harvest. At the end of the season, collect the labels and write the information in a garden diary.

► Artistic labels for indoor plants can be made from shards of old clay pots. Gently sand any sharp edges and write the plant name on the smooth side of the shard with a fine-tipped marker.

► Small white plastic labels can be used for more than marking flats of seeds started indoors. They are also excellent tools for pricking out the seedlings when transplanting them into pots.

► Before reusing labels, be sure to clean and disinfect them in a solution of 4 parts water to 1 part bleach. Rinse before re-using.

Watering Methods

Your seeds need to stay moist and warm in order to germinate — but the soil mix should not be waterlogged. Water gently to avoid washing away fine seeds.

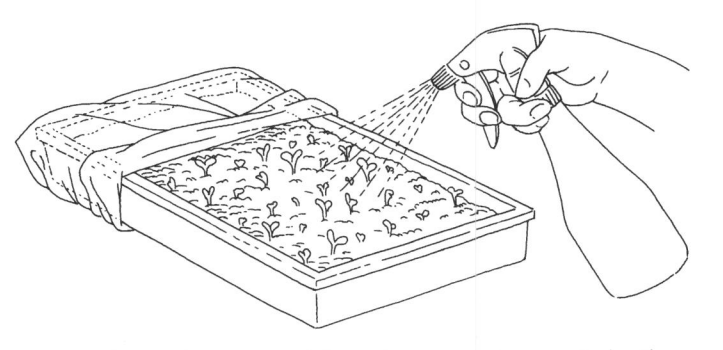

Newly sown seeds can be watered from the top with a squirt bottle or spray bottle, or even by dripping water with an eye dropper. A watering can with a good rose (a nozzle that disperses water gently) can also be useful for top-watering without dislodging the seeds.

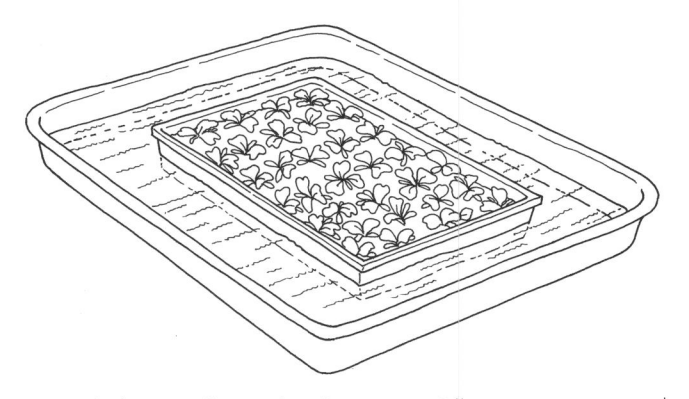

Bottom-watering helps seedlings develop roots. Fill outer container about half full with water and soak your seed flat for an hour. Then pour out excess water and let the flat drain. Do this a couple of times per week, or as needed.

MASTER GARDENING TIPS

How Much Watering and When

Water is essential for nearly all plant functions, and plants do best when just the right amount of water is available. The trick is to know just how much water to apply, and when to apply it.

▶ To get the highest percentage of seeds to germinate indoors or outdoors, keep soil evenly moist from sowing until emergence. Even a short dry period at this time can cut germination rates in half.

▶ Rapidly growing plants need more frequent waterings than slow-growing ones. In general plants need more water in the spring and less in late summer and fall.

▶ Plants grown indoors should be hardened before being moved outdoors. This can be done by letting the plants dry out a bit more between waterings for about two weeks before they are moved.

▶ Water plants in the morning. This is especially true for indoor plants during winter. Plants watered in the morning are less prone to disease and grow better.

▶ Water thoroughly. Plant roots grow only in moist soil. Deep watering encourages larger root systems that are more tolerant of dry periods.

Nurturing Seedlings

Check your flats carefully every day, because as soon as the seedlings emerge, they will need bright light, water, air circulation, and cooler temperatures (60° to 70°F during the day, 55° to 60°F at night). If you let them sit too long in the same conditions they needed to germinate, they will become leggy and weak. If the plants are growing too quickly and you're not yet ready to put them outside, you can slow them down by reducing the temperature while keeping the light levels high.

MASTER GARDENING TIPS

Lighting

The most common way to provide light to seedlings is to set the flats beneath fluorescent light fixtures. The lights should be hung very close to the seedlings at first, and the distance should be increased as the plants grow. Most fluorescent light fixtures (also known as shop lights) come with adjustable chains so that you can raise or lower them. If you can't do this, just place your seedling flats on stacks of cardboard and remove the layers one by one to lower the flats as the seedlings grow.

Thinning

If seeds were sown too thickly, they will have to be thinned out. "Thinning" simply means removing excess plants that are too close together, and leaving one or two in place to grow larger. If you don't thin crowded seedlings, they will compete with each other for water and nutrients. Thinning also provides better air circulation for the remaining plants.

When thinning, try to keep the healthiest-looking, most vigorous seedlings. It's best to thin when the seedlings are small, before they have developed their first true leaves. To avoid damaging the roots of the plants you keep, use small scissors to snip off the extra plants at soil level.

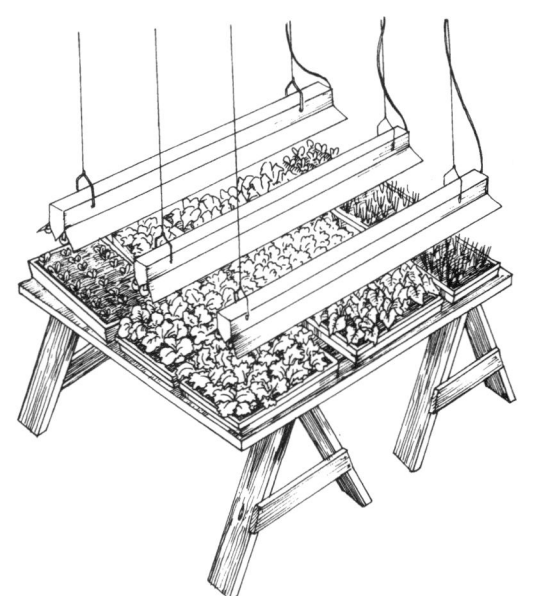

Keep the lights on for 12 consecutive hours a day, allowing the seedlings eight hours of darkness. During the period of light, the plants produce food through photosynthesis, and they use the period of darkness to digest that food and grow.

Thin when seedlings are small, before the first true leaves appear. Snip the plants with scissors rather than pulling them out with your fingers.

Pricking Out

When the seedlings have two or more sets of true leaves, it's time to transplant them to larger individual containers (unless they are already in peat pots and are to be transplanted directly outdoors). Transplanting groups of seedlings from flats to individual pots is called pricking out. This gives each seedling better air circulation and more room for the roots and leaves to grow.

MASTER GARDENING TIPS

Potting Mix for Seedlings

Before you transplant, prepare the receiving containers. Seeds should not have a nutrient-rich potting mix to grow, but seedlings should. Don't use the same soilless propagation mix that you sowed the seeds in.

For transplanting, use a commercial potting mix, or prepare your own. The mix should be composed of equal parts builder's sand, sphagnum peat moss, and clean garden loam or compost. If you wish, add in a little perlite and vermiculite to keep the mix light and absorbent.

Fill your containers almost to the rim, then firm and even off the mix by tamping gently, adding some more, and tamping again. Don't firm the soil too much, or the tiny roots will not be able to push through and expand. Make a hole in the mix with your finger or a pencil.

HINTS FOR SUCCESS

▶ Plant the seedlings into their new containers as quickly as possible; do not let the roots remain exposed, or they may dry out.

▶ Be sure the planting hole will be big enough to contain the roots with room to spare; you don't want to have to stuff the roots into the hole.

1 To prick out the seedlings, lift a clump of them from the flat, using an old fork or spoon. Carefully separate the roots by teasing them apart with your fingers or with toothpicks. The roots are very fragile at this stage, so try not to damage them.

2 Handle the seedlings by their leaves — **never** by the stem. Place the roots carefully into the prepared hole and push the soil in around it, firming gently as you do so. Set the plant a little deeper than it was in the germination flat. You can plant it all the way up to the seed leaves if you wish, but no deeper.

3 Water the new transplants immediately, and put them back under fluorescent lights. Never let them dry out, but don't allow them to become waterlogged, either. Keep the humidity high around the plants, and provide good air circulation. For faster growth, you can fertilize the transplants with a half-strength solution of general fertilizer each time they are watered.

Hardening Off

In all but the warmest regions, seedlings should always be hardened off before being transplanted from their comfy, warm, indoor environs to the cold, harsh, unforgiving outdoors.

"Hardening off" is just what it sounds like: The plant is gradually toughened up for its transition to the garden. If you do not harden off your seedlings before transplanting them, the tender leaves are likely to be damaged by wind, sun, and cold temperatures. Start the hardening-off process a week or so after transplanting the seedlings from flats to individual containers, when you are sure they have fully recovered from transplanting. Here is how to proceed:

1 Take measures to slow down the metabolism of seedlings and toughen their cell walls. This includes cutting back on water and fertilizer, and gradually reducing the temperature.

2 When the outdoor temperatures reach 50°F or higher in the daytime, you can set the plants outside in a cold frame or other protected area. Leave them there for half a day at first, and gradually increase that time over the course of a week. Make sure the soil in the pots stays moist.

3 Eventually you can move them to a less sheltered spot that gets more sun and wind. The whole process should take no more than a week or so, depending on your weather conditions.

HINT FOR SUCCESS

To harden off seedlings in a cold frame, place the flats or pots inside the frame a few weeks before the last expected spring frost. Keep the frame closed at first (make sure it does not get hot enough inside to wilt the plants), and then prop it open for a little longer each day until the danger of frost is passed and the seedlings can be transplanted to the garden.

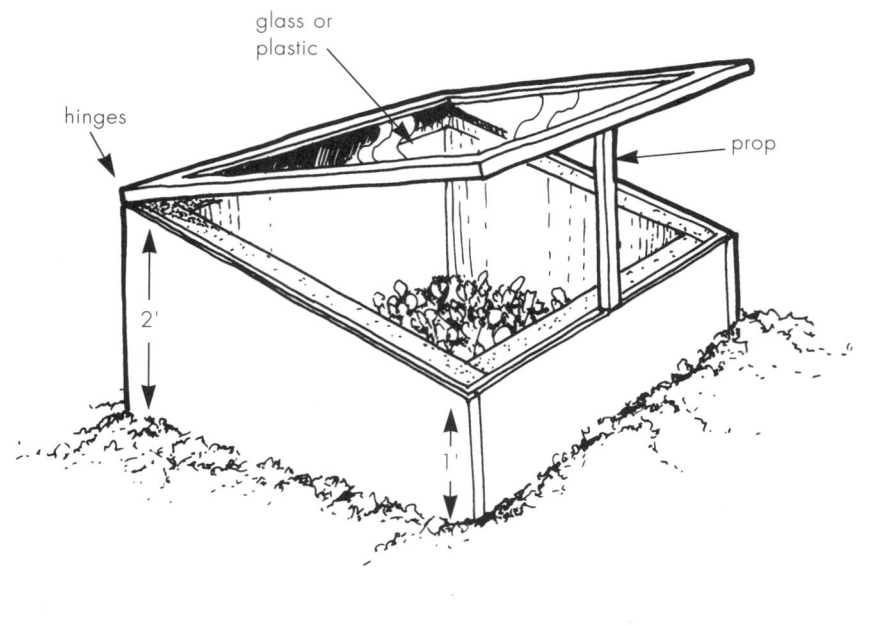

glass or plastic

hinges

prop

2'

1'

A cold frame can serve a multitude of purposes, and one of them is hardening off seedlings. You can buy a cold-frame kit or make your own from weatherproof lumber.

A cold frame is no more than a square or rectangular box, about 2 feet deep in the back, angling down to about 1 foot deep in the front. It must have some kind of sturdy lid made of a transparent material (glass or plastic) to admit sunlight, and this lid should be propped open when the sun is strong and direct. A cold frame is usually partially buried in the ground. It should be located with the front facing south, and should be protected from cold winds.

Transplanting Step-by-Step

Never set out transplants on a hot, sunny day. The shock of transplanting, combined with the sun beating down, may just kill them. Instead, wait for a cloudy day, or plant in the evening when it is cool. Make sure the soil is moist before you start planting.

HINT FOR SUCCESS

If you are setting out seedlings in peat pots, you don't have to remove the pot; just put the entire thing in the hole with the rim of the pot below the soil surface. (Some plants, like tomatoes, can be planted much deeper than they were in the pot.)

1 Prepare the hole first; it should be a little bigger than the plant's root ball. After excavating a hole, mix in some compost or transplanting fertilizer.

2 Remove the seedling from its container by holding the pot upside down and tapping on the bottom. Cradle your hand around the base of the plant to keep it from falling out suddenly and getting damaged.

3 Place the plant in the hole at about the level it was in the pot, or a little deeper. Fill in around the plant with soil, tamping very gently to firm the soil. Water by letting a hose trickle around the plant, or use a watering can with a nozzle that provides a gentle shower.

MASTER GARDENING TIPS

Using Water Efficiently

▶ If you are putting in more than a few seedlings, it's best to water each plant as it goes in rather than waiting until the whole group has been planted. Be sure the water doesn't just run off; it needs to soak in around the roots.

▶ If the plants are on a slope, make a little saucer or trough of soil around each one to hold the water and keep it from running down the hill.

Protecting Young Plants

It's important to choose the right time for planting out. As eager as you may be to get those little plants out into the garden, it's not worth the heartbreak if a late frost hits and mows them all down. Believe me, I know from experience. Fortunately, when it happened to me, I had reserved half the seedlings to plant out a week or two later, so when the first batch was brought down prematurely, I had more to fall back on.

Be familiar with your area's frost dates (see map on page 11) and with the microclimates in your own garden. Don't go strictly by the calendar; every year is different. Wait to plant until you see signs of spring: migrating birds returning, trees budding, flowers blooming. Be on the lookout for signs of frost, such as calm, dry air; clear skies; and a drop in temperature to 40°F or lower in the evening.

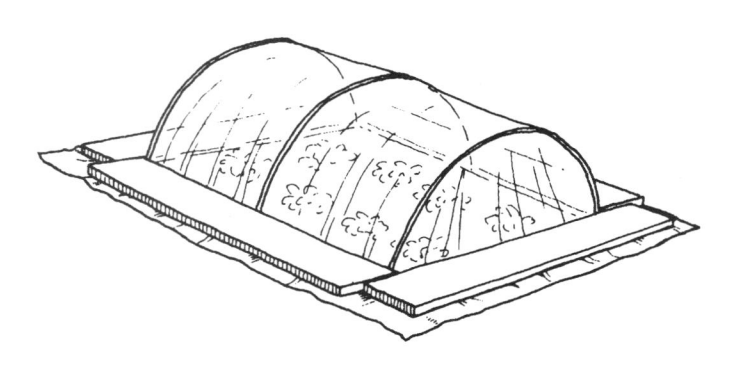

Use plastic row covers (left) or purchased cloches (such as Wall-O-Water, right) to protect your plants. Don't leave any covering on during the day, or your plants may overheat and possibly be damaged.

MASTER GARDENING TIPS

What to Do When Frost Threatens

If you've already put your plants in the ground and frost threatens, cover them with whatever you can find.

▶ Bushel baskets, flower pots, plastic cartons, cups, and glass jars will work.

▶ Containers with holes may be risky if the frost is severe, especially if the hole is at the top where the cold air can descend right through it.

▶ Remember that metal conducts cold, so if you use metal cans as frost coverings, be sure the plant leaves are not touching the inside of the can.

Caring for Seedlings

Once the seedlings are up and thriving, general care includes thinning, weeding, watering, and fertilizing. Here are some tips for each:

Thinning

When your seedlings begin to crowd each other, it's time to thin out some of them. I admit this is sometimes hard to do. Most gardeners feel every plant is valuable, and it isn't easy to yank up those beautiful little sprouts and toss them aside. But when you're growing vegetables, or even flowers, for that matter, it's important to thin the seedlings if you want strong, sturdy, healthy plants eventually. With some vegetables — especially leafy crops like lettuce — you can use the thinnings in salads, so you don't have to feel bad about pulling them. In fact, the young, tender leaves are a tasty and special treat.

Weeding

Don't forget to keep the area weed-free. Weeds will overtake a bed in no time, and your young plants will be robbed of water, nutrients, and even sunlight. Pull weeds by hand before they get too big, and try to do it when the soil is moist so that they come up more easily.

Watering

When the seedlings are well established, you should be able to cut back watering to once a week, or less often if you have some rainy days. Check the individual requirements of the plant so you don't end up drowning it with loving care or letting it die of thirst.

Fertilizing

You can fertilize every so often if the plants need a boost, but fertilizing can sometimes work against you if you choose the wrong formula for the plant. For instance, nitrogen is good for leaf growth, so a high-nitrogen fertilizer is a good choice for lettuce, spinach, and other leaf crops. If you're trying to produce good-looking flowers or fruit, you'll want a fertilizer that is higher in phosphorus, and root crops should have a good dose of potassium (potash). When looking at the three numbers on the fertilizer package, remember that the first one is the percentage of nitrogen, the second one stands for phosphorus, and the third one indicates potassium. Many general garden fertilizers have a balanced formula that can be beneficial for almost any plant.

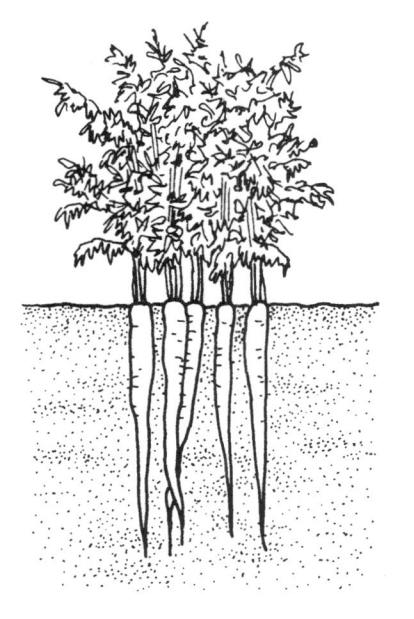

The first time I grew carrots, I was so pleased with the thick, fluffy foliage they were putting out that I didn't thin them until it was too late and they were choking each other out. Of course, the foliage wasn't even important. What I wanted were big, long carrots, and what I got were little stunted carrots that were tangled and grown together, like these pictured above.

When and Where to Sow Seeds

The decision about whether to start seeds indoors or to plant them where they will grow outdoors is dependent, first, on whether you are dealing with plants that tolerate transplanting and, second, on your own needs. For instance, an annual flower may very well germinate and grow outdoors quite easily, but if you wait to start it outdoors, it may not bloom until late summer, while your neighbors' plants that were started indoors have been blooming colorfully for a month or two earlier. A general rule is that seeds of annuals — flowers and vegetables — are generally sown directly outdoors in spring after all danger of frost has passed. Since annuals grow, bloom, and die in the course of one year, the seeds sprout quickly and are soon on their way. Likewise, although many slower-growing perennials and biennials should be sown indoors in order to develop a well-established root system by the time fall rolls around, some can be sown directly outdoors in early spring, and will grow big enough to withstand the winter and return the following year. For gardeners in cold regions, the following charts provide suggestions for the best way to manage your plantings.

Seeds best sown indoors in late winter or early spring

Asparagus	Marigold	Pot marigold
Broccoli	Onions	Scarlet sage
Cabbage (early and mid-season varieties)	Pansy	Snapdragon
	Parsley	Tobacco, flowering
Eggplant	Peppers	Tomato
Leeks	Petunia	

Seeds best sown directly outdoors in spring or summer

Bachelor's button	Hollyhock	Primrose (sow in late summer)
Balloon flower	Lettuce	Radish
Beans	Lupine	Spider flower
Beets	Melons	Spinach
Cabbage (late varieties)	Morning glory	Squash
Carrots	Moss rose	Sunflower
Corn	Nasturtium	Sweet pea
Cosmos	Peas	Zinnia
Cucumber	Poppy	
Four-o'clocks	Poppy, California	

Seeds that can be sown either indoors or directly outdoors

Aster	Canterbury bells	Coreopsis
Astilbe	Cauliflower	Delphinium
Bee balm	Chives	Foxglove
Bellflower	Clematis	Pinks
Black-eyed Susan	Columbine	
Blazing star	Coneflower	

Sowing Seed Outdoors Step-by-Step

Seeds grown outdoors have the same needs as those grown indoors: warm soil, light or darkness (as the case may be), and consistent moisture. Even those seeds that require stratification germinate best in warm soil once they have been chilled. However, extreme summer heat is not good for most seeds. If planting in summer, give the seedbed some light shade, and water frequently to keep the seeds from drying out.

MASTER GARDENING TIPS

Awakening Your Soil

▶ **If you're starting a large bed from scratch,** use a tiller to loosen and aerate the soil, and to work in amendments.

▶ **If the area is relatively small,** and the soil is loose to begin with, you can simply turn it by hand with a spade.

▶ **Use compost, manure, leaf mold, peat moss,** or some other form of organic matter to amend soil. Perlite and vermiculite are not generally incorporated into outdoor soil, since water retention is not as much of a problem as it is in containers.

▶ **The soil need not be sterilized,** although you'll want to remove as many weeds as you possibly can before sowing. Weeds can be hoed out or pulled out by hand. Never use chemical weed killers in a seedbed, as they can damage or kill seedlings.

▶ **If you are sowing seed in an already-established bed** — for instance, sprinkling seeds of annuals in a perennial border — loosen the soil carefully with a hand cultivator or trowel. Avoid digging around the roots of established plants, or you may damage them. The soil should be cultivated just enough for the germinating seeds to take hold and get enough air.

▶ **Do not work fertilizer into a seedbed.** Once the seedlings are established, however, you can give them a liquid feeding or a topdressing of fertilizer.

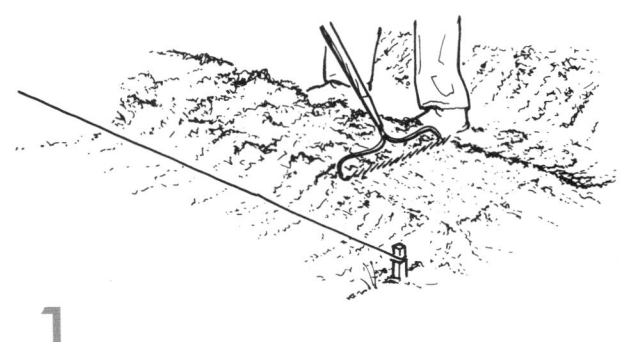

1 Thoroughly till the soil, working in compost or other organic matter and removing all weeds and grasses, and then smooth out the soil with a rake so that it is level.

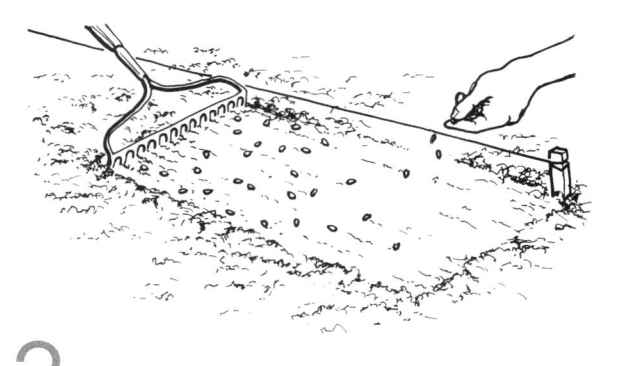

2 Sow small seeds as thickly as you can and plan to thin out plants later. The drawing shows a method known as broadcasting, in which seeds are scattered over the entire surface. Larger seeds should be dropped at intervals along a furrow, spacing them as directed (see individual plant descriptions for suggested spacing).

3 Cover seeds with about the same amount of soil as the diameter of the seed. Leave extra-fine seeds uncovered or sow them ⅛ inch deep if they need darkness to germinate. Gently firm them with the back of a hoe to ensure close contact between the seeds and the soil.

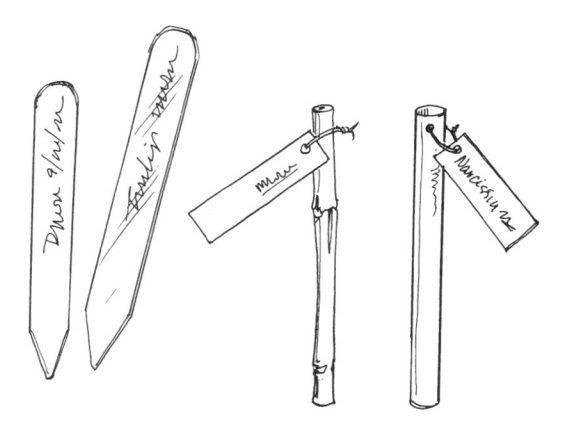

4 Be sure to label your rows so you know what you have planted where. On the label, you'll want to indicate the type of plant and variety, date of sowing, number of days until harvest, and other pertinent information.

5 Use a gentle spray of water to settle seeds into their new location. Continue to keep the seeds moist until you see signs of germination. Then you can gradually cut back on watering as the plants grow and become established.

HINTS FOR SUCCESS

Cold frames are useful for sowing seeds of tender plants early in the spring, when frost still threatens, or for sowing a late vegetable crop in summer or fall. A frame can be used for propagating cuttings, as well. You can put layers of sand or soil inside it, and plant directly into the layers; or merely set flats or pots inside the cold frame. The soil inside the frame should be well-drained, even if you are just setting containers inside the cold frame.

For some seeds, you may need a hotbed, which is simply a cold frame with bottom heat, provided by heating cables or a layer of heat-producing raw manure.

MASTER GARDENING TIPS

Easy Ways to Sow Seeds

▶ If you're planting a vegetable garden or a cutting garden, mark off straight rows by pounding stakes into the ground at either end of the bed and running a string from one stake to the other. Then make a shallow furrow (or "drill") along the row with the corner of a hoe.

▶ Another way to sow vegetable seeds is in "hills." A hill is not literally a mound of soil; the term refers to a number of seeds planted in a cluster rather than a row. Squash and other vining crops are often planted in hills, as is corn. You'll get more plants in a small space by sowing in hills.

▶ Fine flower seeds can simply be broadcast over the ground (after the soil has been prepared). If the flower seeds are larger, make a small indentation with your finger or other instrument, and drop in one or two seeds.

Wind-pollination, page 34

Plants with imperfect flowers, page 33

Soil for seed starting, page 37

Seed anatomy, page 35

From Seed to Bloom

Most plants, like humans and other animals, reproduce sexually. Flowers contain the sexual parts of a plant and produce offspring in the form of seeds.

The seed is like a womb; it holds the embryo of a new plant and the food needed to support that embryo. Unlike a baby in a womb, however, the embryo plant remains dormant within the seed coat until certain outside influences — water, heat, light — stimulate it to begin its growth process.

Seed propagation is called sexual propagation because the genes of the parent plants are combined in a new individual. Just as a human baby is a distinct individual with some characteristics of each of its parents, a seedling takes on qualities of one or both of its parents, but it is not a clone of either one. Some plants are termed self-fertilizing because they contribute both the pollen and the egg cell that develops into the new plant. The self-pollinated seedling offspring come close to being clones of the parent plant, but to produce an *exact* replica of a particular plant the plant must be propagated asexually. Methods of asexual propagation include taking cuttings, grafting, dividing plants, layering, and cloning through tissue culture. In all these cases, a new plant is produced directly from a part of the parent plant.

In this book we are concerned with sexual propagation as we discuss how to identify, harvest, store, and then sow the seeds of a variety of flowers and vegetables. In order to do this successfully, it's helpful to understand how flowers produce pollen, which fertilizes egg cells that eventually develop viable seed. The process is a fascinating, but quiet one, constantly recurring wherever plants flourish. The excitement for the gardener comes when you can capture some of those seeds and nurture them in your garden the following year.

In This Chapter

- Flowers and Pollination
- Imperfect Flowers
- Attracting Pollinators
- The Anatomy of a Seed
- The Miracle of Germination

Flowers and Pollination

The making of a seed begins within the flower. Some flowers, referred to as "perfect" or "complete," have both male and female reproductive parts. Imperfect or incomplete flowers are either male or female, and do not have both parts on the same flower.

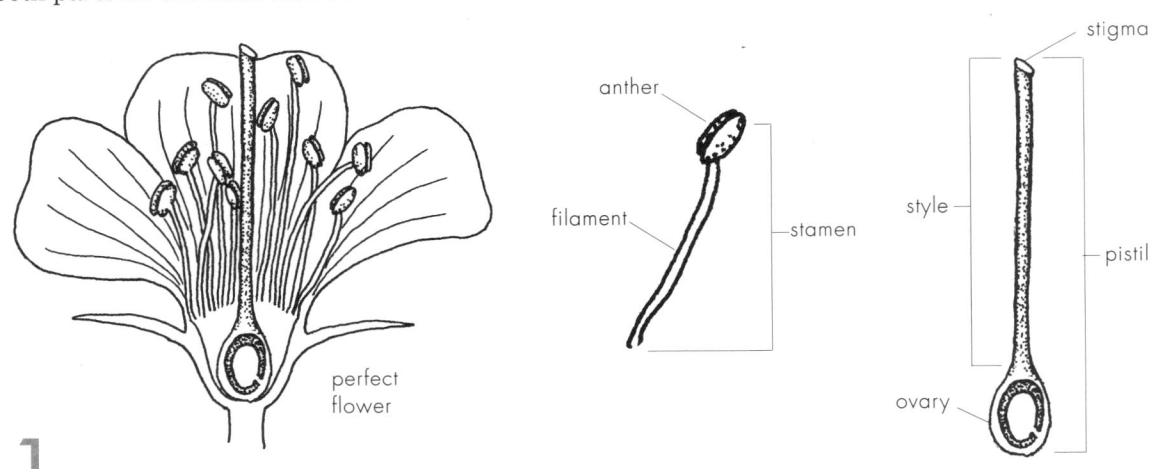

perfect flower

anther
filament
stamen

stigma
style
pistil
ovary

1 The male reproductive parts of a flower, known as **stamens,** consist of thin stalks **(filaments)** topped by the pollen-producing **anthers.** In a perfect flower, these stamens surround the female part **(pistil),** which is situated at the center of the flower. At the top of the pistil is a sticky area called the **stigma,** which captures pollen.

Pollen can be deposited on the stigma from the same flower or from other flowers. It is carried by the wind or by pollinators like bees, butterflies, birds, and even bats. Once the pollen has adhered to the stigma, it germinates and extends a **pollen tube,** which grows down through the **style** to the **ovary.**

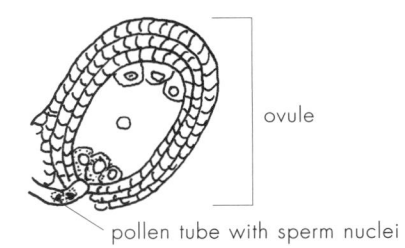

ovule

pollen tube with sperm nuclei

2 As the pollen tube grows, it carries a generative cell at its tip. This cell then divides into two sperm nuclei.

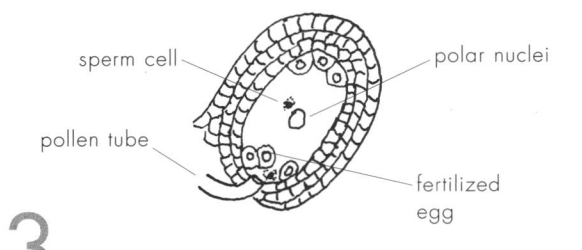

sperm cell
polar nuclei
pollen tube
fertilized egg

3 Fertilization occurs in individual **ovules** of the ovary when one of these cells unites with the egg cell to form a single cell, or **zygote.** This zygote begins to divide and form the plant embryo.

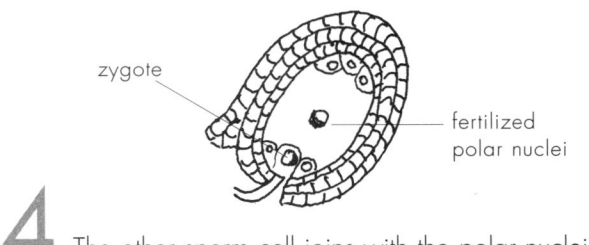

zygote
fertilized polar nuclei

4 The other sperm cell joins with the polar nuclei in the embryo sac to form the **endosperm** — the part of the seed that nourishes the embryo.

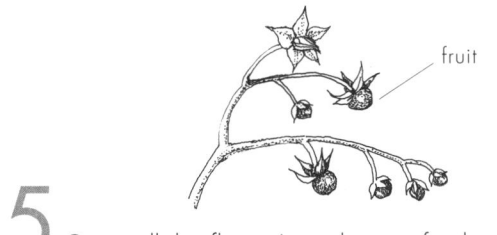

fruit

5 Once all the flower's ovules are fertilized, the ovary matures and swells to form a protective **fruit** or **husk** around the seeds. In vegetables, this fruit is often the edible part of the plant.

Imperfect Flowers: Monoecious or Dioecious?

Some plants with imperfect flowers have both male and female flowers on the same plant. These plants are called monoecious (meaning "one-household"). Sweet corn is monoecious, as is the cucurbit group of vegetables — such as squashes, melons, and cucumbers. In this group, the male flowers bloom first, followed by the female flowers a few days later.

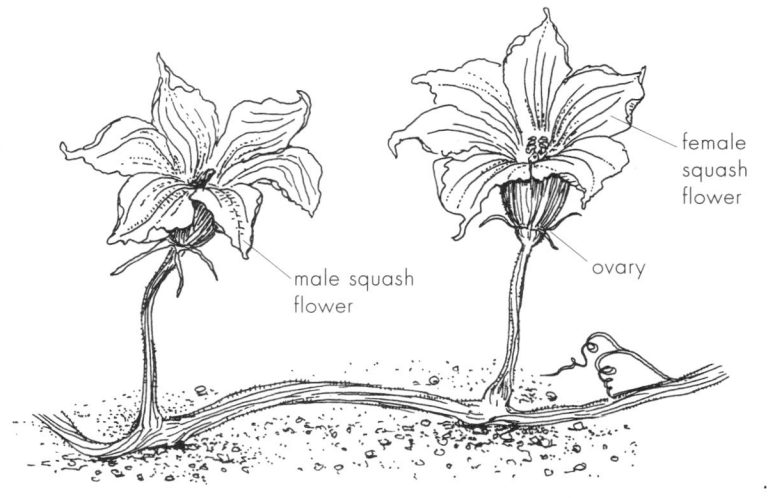

female squash flower

male squash flower

ovary

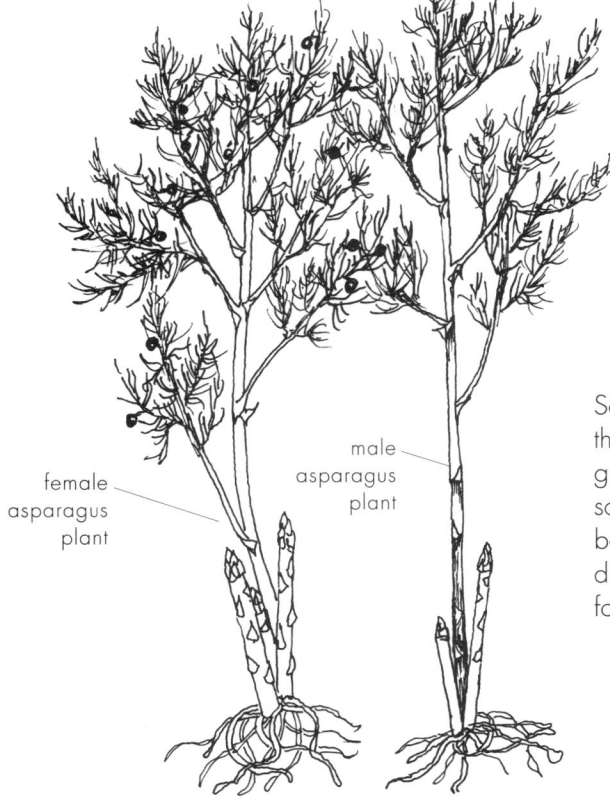

female asparagus plant

male asparagus plant

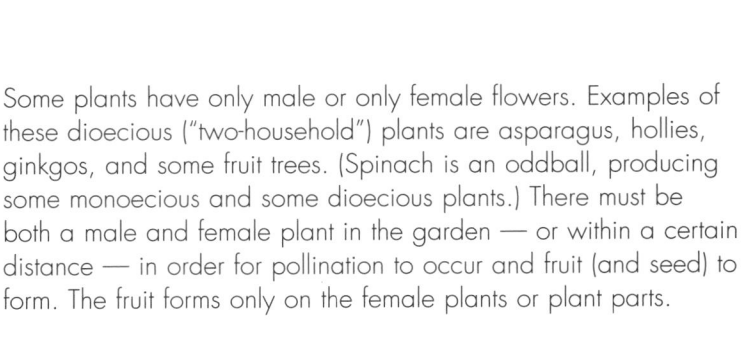

Some plants have only male or only female flowers. Examples of these dioecious ("two-household") plants are asparagus, hollies, ginkgos, and some fruit trees. (Spinach is an oddball, producing some monoecious and some dioecious plants.) There must be both a male and female plant in the garden — or within a certain distance — in order for pollination to occur and fruit (and seed) to form. The fruit forms only on the female plants or plant parts.

Attracting Pollinators

Nature is manipulative when it comes to getting plants pollinated. Flowers are designed in come-hither colors and shapes that are irresistibly seductive to bees, butterflies, moths, and other winged pollinators. Some flowers are brightly colored, others are sweetly fragrant, and still others have petals marked with "nectar guides" that lead an insect to the center of the flower.

Some flowers are highly engineered to attract just the right pollinator. Pendulous, tubular, red flowers, for instance, are enticing and easily accessible to the hovering hummingbird with its needlelike beak. A few flowers have the odor of rotten meat, intended to attract flies as pollinators. Certain flowers have a reputation as "butterfly flowers" because their bright red or orange color is appealing to butterflies.

No special tricks are needed for wind-pollinated plants such as corn. The flowers don't have to be colorful or fragrant, as they are in insect-pollinated plants; in fact, the flowers of wind-pollinated plants are usually small and inconspicuous. However, even wind-pollinated plants are optimally designed; the anthers are usually exposed and the pollen grains lightweight and abundant, so that a passing breeze can pick them up and carry them easily to the nearest accommodating stigma.

The Anatomy of a Seed

All flowering plants are classified as either monocotyledons or dicotyledons. The primary difference is in the seed itself. Dicotyledons have two cotyledons (seed leaves), while monocotyledons have one seed leaf. Most common seed plants are dicotyledons and include everything from beans to maple trees. Some common monocotyledons are grasses, corn, onions, asparagus, daylilies, and hostas.

A seed is made up of an embryo, food-storage tissues, and a seed covering. The embryo is the undeveloped plant that is formed from the union of a male and female cell during fertilization. The embryo begins putting out shoots and roots once germination occurs.

The seed covering is an important part of the seed. It protects the embryo from damage and helps keep it safely dormant until all conditions are right for germination. The seed covering may consist of a seed coat, the endosperm, and sometimes the fruit of the plant. There may be an outer and inner seed coat, the outer coat being hard, dry, thickened, and brownish, and the inner coat being thin, transparent, and membranous.

In dicotyledons the food-storage tissues of a seed are contained in the seed leaves, while in monocotyledons food is usually stored around the leaves. The embryo draws on these food-storage tissues for nourishment as it develops.

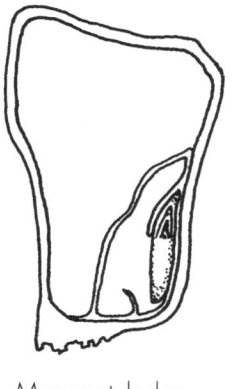

Monocotyledon

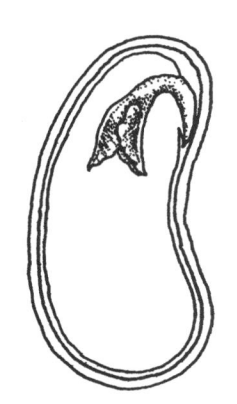

Dicotyledon

MASTER GARDENING TIP

Gymnosperms, such as pines and ginkgos, can have many cotyledons.

Monocotyledon

- Germination: Embryo with one cotyledon
- Leaves: Parallel veins
- Flowers: Parts usually in threes

Dicotyledon

- Germination: Embryo with usually two cotyledons
- Leaves: Netlike pattern of veins
- Flowers: Parts usually in fours or fives

The Miracle of Germination

Once seeds have ripened within their protective pod, fruit, or husk, they enter a state of suspended animation (dormancy), until all conditions are right for germination. This is the moment when a plant's embryo breaks its dormancy and begins to grow. The seed coat ruptures, and leaf and root shoots emerge. Thus, germination is not the beginning of a new plant, but rather a continuation of plant growth after a dormant period. Most plants require certain amounts of moisture, light, and temperature before the seed can germinate.

Water

When a seed is mature, its water content is at a low level, and little if any growth can take place. Before the embryo can begin growing again, it must absorb water. The water causes the seed to swell and its coat to soften and weaken so that the embryo can break through. Water also helps the embryo digest its stored food reserves. Respiration increases, and growth resumes.

But too much water can be harmful. Seeds also need oxygen to germinate, so submerging a seed in water will not help it to germinate. You can be sure seeds have the air they need to grow by planting them at the correct depth in a loose medium that is moist but not soggy.

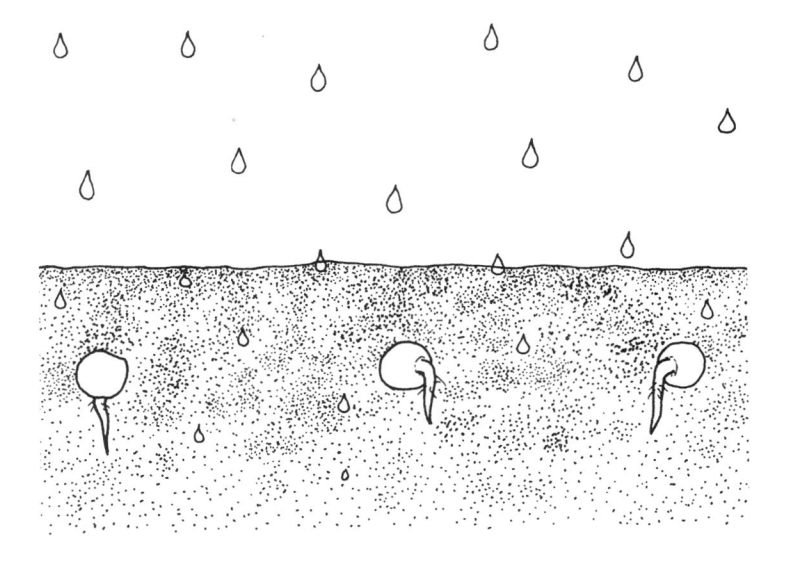

The Correct Temperature

Temperature is another critical factor in germination. Most seeds germinate well at a soil temperature of 70° to 75°F, but there are some that require cooler or warmer temperatures to germinate. Very few seeds can tolerate extreme heat or cold. After seeds have germinated, a somewhat cooler (60°–65°) environment is usually recommended. In general, the soil should be warmer than the surrounding air.

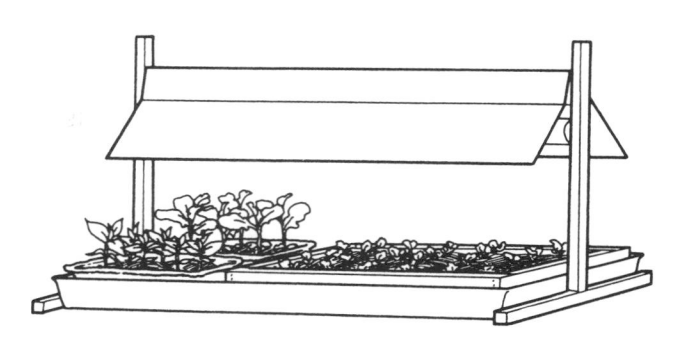

Light or Dark?

Light conditions can also influence germination. Some seeds require light to germinate, and they must be covered with a thin layer of soil, or not at all, so that light can reach them. Others need darkness to germinate; they should be covered with enough soil to exclude light, or the growing container should be covered with newspaper or some other opaque material that still allows some air circulation. Many vegetable seeds are light neutral and will germinate in either light or dark.

Chilling

Some plants, especially those from warm or tropical climates, are not picky about when their seeds can germinate. The moment the seeds are ripe, a little moisture sends them on their way. But most hardy plants that are native to temperate or cold climates must go through a period of chilling before their seeds will break dormancy.

The process goes like this: Seeds are produced at the end of the growing season. The flowers wither and die, the fruit swells and ripens, and the seeds within mature until they are ready to be dispersed. If the seed were to drop to the ground and germinate immediately, it would be disastrous for future generations of the plant. The dropping temperatures of fall and winter would soon destroy the fragile seedlings. These plants have a built-in mechanism for blocking germination until the cold has passed and warm weather has arrived.

When taken out of nature and sown by human hands, these seeds still need the period of cold before they will germinate. When propagating such plants from seed, the period of artificial chilling is called stratification (see chapter 1).

The Right Soil

Seeds also need certain soil conditions to germinate. The mix must be friable, loose, and moist but not too wet. Too much organic matter in the soil may produce an overabundance of carbon dioxide, which can retard germination. Seed-starting soil does not have to be rich in organic matter or nutrients. Leaf mold may contain chemical compounds that inhibit germination, depending on the types of leaves that make up the leaf mold. Salty soil, such as that found by the ocean, can prevent germination by drawing moisture from the seeds. Purchase a good soilless mix or make your own (see page 12).

Understanding plant vocabulary, page 41

Preventing cross-pollinating, page 43

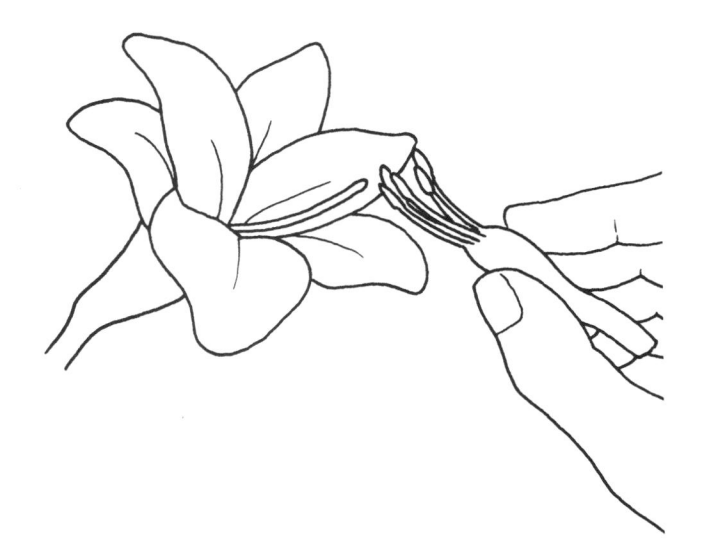

Hand-pollinating, page 45

Selecting Plants for Seed Saving

S eed saving is not, as I used to believe, simply a matter of pulling off a few seedpods and stuffing them in a bag to store in the basement until spring. Anyone who believes that is likely to find oneself (as I did) watering flats of seed-starting mix for weeks on end, searching in vain for some sign of plant life. There is much involved in saving seeds properly, and it all begins with selecting the right plant. You don't need to have a scientific background to be a successful seed saver, but you do have to practice a basic scientific technique: namely, observation. As you tend your garden and watch over your plants, you get to know them, to notice and wonder why some have richer color or more vigorous growth than others. You also develop preferences, and by saving seeds from the plants you most admire, you can satisfy your preferences in future seasons by growing even more of those special plants in your garden.

In This Chapter

- What Makes a Good Parent Plant?
- Family Tree of a Garden Flower
- Questions to Ask When Saving Seeds
- Isolating Plants to Prevent Cross-Pollination
- Hand-Pollination

MASTER GARDENING TIPS

"Coming True" from Seed

The first thing to know about seed saving is that not every plant in your garden will grow well from seed. Some hybrid varieties, for instance, will not produce viable seeds (capable of germinating). Others will produce seeds that germinate, but the offspring may not resemble the parent plant in any way. It is said that these plants do not come true from seed. The term "come true" means that the seedling plant has the same characteristics as the parent plant.

As an example, let's take a plant whose most outstanding trait is its double red flowers. This plant is said to come true if, when you collect and sow its seed, you end up with a bunch of new plants that also have double red flowers. On the other hand, if you collect and sow the seed, and months later you have a bed full of plants with smaller, single white flowers, then your red-flowered plant clearly did not come true from seed.

What Makes a Good Parent Plant?

If you've decided to collect seed from your own garden plants, you'll want to observe the plants throughout the growing season and select the best performers so that their genes will be passed on through the seed to the next generation. By continuing to select the best plants each year, you will eventually end up with a seed strain that is well adapted to your climate and conditions, that has the best flowers or fruit or leaf color, and that is pest- and disease-resistant. Here are some ideas for how to organize your selections:

- Keep a record of the traits listed at the right, in order to assess the overall performance of the plants you're observing. Don't look only at one characteristic; look at the entire plant. Just because a plant bears giant tomatoes doesn't mean you should collect its seed. What if it is also disease-prone or late to set fruit?

- Tag certain plants for observance, and make notes on their progress throughout the season. Don't pamper these plants — treat them like all the rest or you will defeat the purpose of selecting the plant that is the best performer under ordinary conditions. Mark your choices clearly, so that you don't accidentally deadhead the spent flowers before seed can form.

- "Rogue out" plants with undesirable characteristics. Roguing means weeding out plants that are weak or diseased, or that have other undesirable traits. If you're looking for early fruit production, pull out plants that are late to set blossoms. If you want only tall, statuesque plants, yank out the stunted and squat ones. If you see deformed leaves, spindly stems, or drab flowers, remove those plants from the group and concentrate only on the top performers.

Checklist of Possible Selection Characteristics

- ❑ Overall vigor
- ❑ Hardiness
- ❑ Ability to tolerate drought, wind, waterlogged soil, or other extreme conditions
- ❑ Disease resistance
- ❑ Resistance to insect pests
- ❑ Attractive plant shape
- ❑ Height
- ❑ Dwarf form (unless caused by drought or disease)
- ❑ Creeping or trailing form
- ❑ Double flowers
- ❑ Good flower color
- ❑ Larger flowers
- ❑ Early bloom time
- ❑ Fragrance
- ❑ Strong stems (especially for cutting flowers)
- ❑ Good leaf color
- ❑ Larger fruit
- ❑ Good fruit texture
- ❑ More flavorful fruit or other edible part
- ❑ Good or unusual fruit color
- ❑ Early- or late-bearing fruit (whichever is desired)
- ❑ Heavy fruit set
- ❑ Long storage life (for vegetables)
- ❑ Late to go to seed or bolt
- ❑ Good germination
- ❑ Large or small seeds (whichever is desired)
- ❑ Special qualities — absence of thorns, spines, strings, etc.

Family Tree of a Garden Flower

Every known plant has a unique scientific name. That unique name is a composite of its ancestral heritage: a family tree in the form of a name. This tree begins with the **family,** a group of plants that share some distinctive genetic characteristics, but cannot interbreed. The family is divided into smaller groups called **genera** (**genus,** singular), plants that share more genetic characteristics than those in the family, but are still different enough from each other so they cannot interbreed. The genera are then divided into **species,** which consist of very closely related plants that sometimes interbreed and often share a common geographic range.

Sometimes the species contains a group of plants that differ from the rest in a distinct but minor way, such as the color of the flower. This natural mutation is called a **variety.** If the variety is cultivated, or further modified by breeding or selection and then cultivated, the plant is called a **cultivar.**

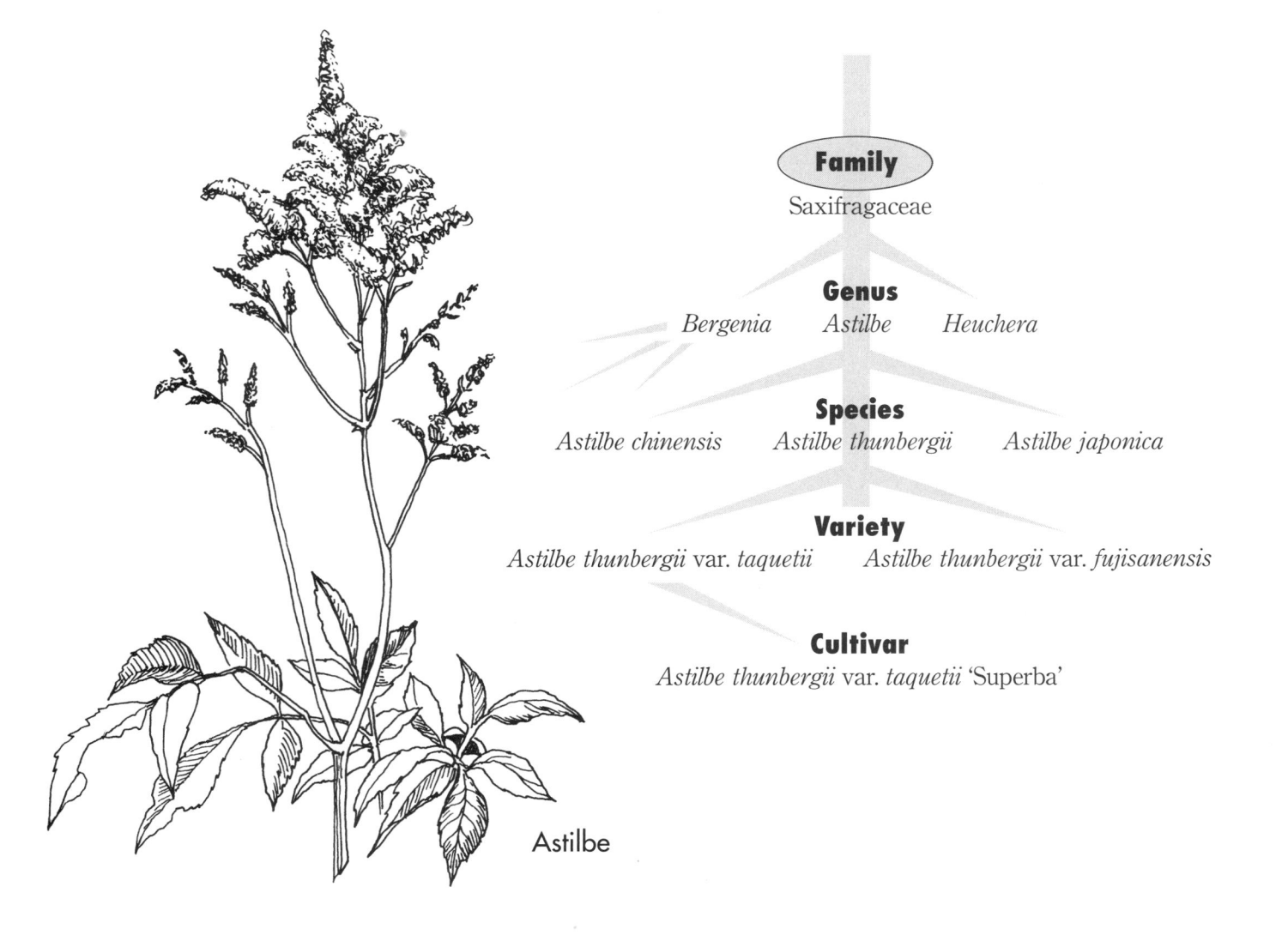

Family
Saxifragaceae

Genus
Bergenia   *Astilbe*   *Heuchera*

Species
Astilbe chinensis   *Astilbe thunbergii*   *Astilbe japonica*

Variety
Astilbe thunbergii var. *taquetii*   *Astilbe thunbergii* var. *fujisanensis*

Cultivar
Astilbe thunbergii var. *taquetii* 'Superba'

Astilbe

Questions to Ask When Saving Seeds

Here are some points to keep in mind as you plan to save seeds from your favorite plant.

- Is the plant a Hybrid, cultivar, variety, or species? _____

- If it is a Hybrid, cultivar, or variety, is it a seed strain? In other words, is it known to come true from seed? If not, is it worth experimenting with? _____

- If it is a species, is it self-pollinating or cross-pollinating? _____

- If it is cross-pollinated, are there any related species or varieties close by (or with the same bloom time) that might create a problem with unwanted crossing? _____

- If there is danger of unwanted crossing, can the selected plant be isolated or hand-pollinated?

_____

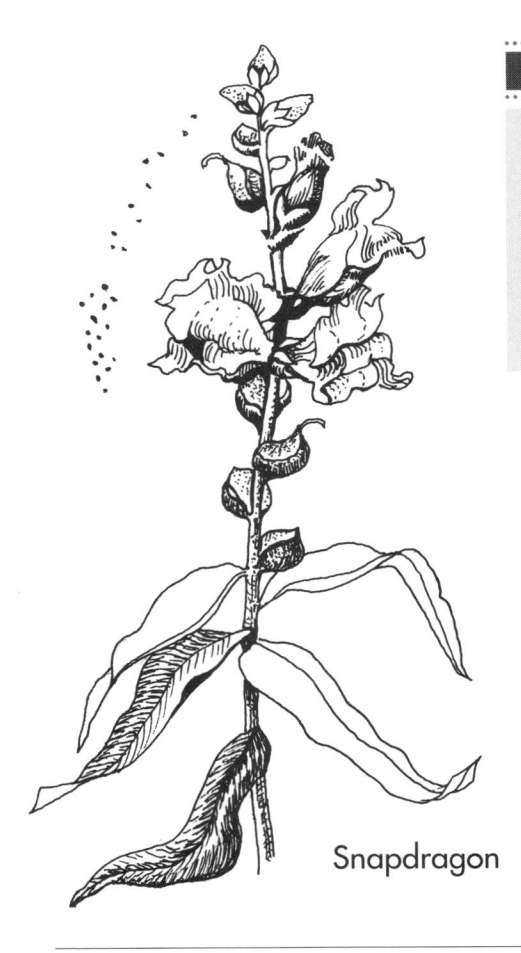

Snapdragon

HINT FOR SUCCESS

You can't (always) have your seed and eat it, too. When selecting vegetables for seed saving, remember that you may have to sacrifice the tastiest specimens in order to get ripe seed. For example, if you're selecting tomatoes, the fruit must remain on the vine until it's past its prime to produce viable seeds. This goes for most other vegetables, as well; exceptions include pumpkins and winter squash.

Self-pollinating plants like this snapdragon are the best choices for seed savers, because they accept their own pollen. Seeds from such plants will always grow into plants that resemble the parent since there is no genetic mixing going on. These are the best seeds to save when you're just starting out because they are most likely to come true. Examples of self-pollinating plants are legumes (peas, beans, sweet peas, lupines), tomatoes, peppers, eggplant, snapdragons, and lettuce. (Note that peas, beans, tomatoes, peppers, eggplant, and lettuce are partially cross-pollinated.)

Isolating Plants to Prevent Cross-Pollination

Gardeners can experiment with several techniques to protect plants from cross-pollinating with other plants of the same genus:

- Separate them by distance (see recommendations for specific plants).

- Isolate them by growing only one variety per year *or* planning your plantings so that different varieties bloom at different times.

- Enclose the plant within some kind of barrier that keeps pollen from being blown by wind or carried by insects onto the stigma.

You can protect both insect- and wind-pollinated plants from cross-pollination by covering them with a floating row cover or hot caps. The flowers must be covered just before they open, and the cover should be left in place until seeds have formed on the plant. Because you are preventing natural pollinators from doing their work, you will have to hand-pollinate all protected plants (see next page).

(see next page)

MASTER GARDENING TIPS

Storing Pollen

If your parent plants do not bloom at the same time, you may have to store the pollen of the early bloomer until the later one opens. Pollen doesn't keep well — a few weeks at the most, and sometimes only a few hours — so this is a risky venture at best, but if you have no choice, you may want to give it a try. Here's how:

1. Collect the pollen by shaking the flower over a small, dry container.
2. Label the container with the date and plant name.
3. Dry the pollen for a day or two directly under a hot light, or anyplace with a constant temperature of 90°F.
4. Store the dry pollen in the freezer until you are ready to use it. *Note:* Corn pollen cannnot be stored in a freezer; the grains will burst when frozen.

Hand-Pollination

Hand-pollination is when you take pollen from one plant and use it to fertilize the flower of another plant. In nature, this task is usually performed by wind or by insects. Hand pollination is a technique used by growers who artificially cross-pollinate in order to select characteristics from two different plants and attempt to combine them in a new plant. The basic technique, however, is equally applicable for seed savers who need to protect plants from cross-pollination through the use of floating row covers or other barriers.

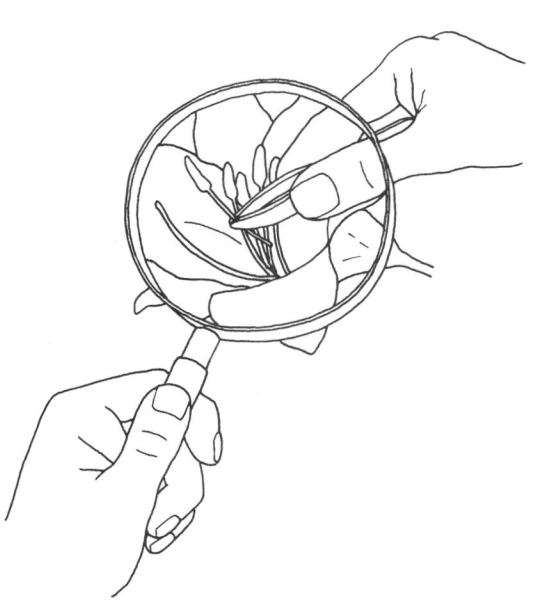

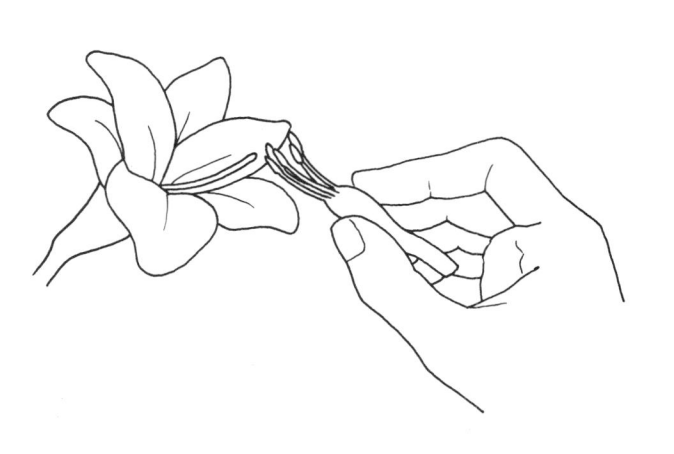

1 Remove the male parts (the stamens) of the flower with a small pair of tweezers. You may need a magnifying glass or hand lens to help you see the parts more clearly.

2 Rub the pollen-covered stamens against the pistils of several different female blossoms.

Or, transfer the pollen with a small watercolor brush, a cotton swab, your fingertip, or a pencil eraser. Be sure to wash your instrument of choice thoroughly after each use.

Preparing to Hand-Pollinate

► Whatever plants you choose, dissect a flower or two first to familiarize yourself with their structure and parts.

► The correct time to prepare for hand-pollination is just before the flowers are about to open.

► If you are hand-pollinating a plant that has separate male and female flowers, use pollen from several of the male flowers to avoid the reduced vigor that comes from inbreeding.

3 Tape the female blossoms shut, put plastic bags over them, or replace the floating row cover. Leave them that way until the petals wither and drop and the ovary begins to swell with ripening seeds. You will eventually have hybrid seeds to plant.

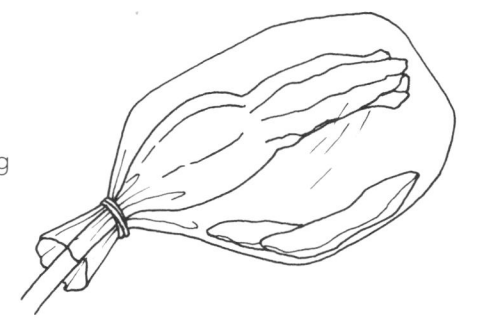

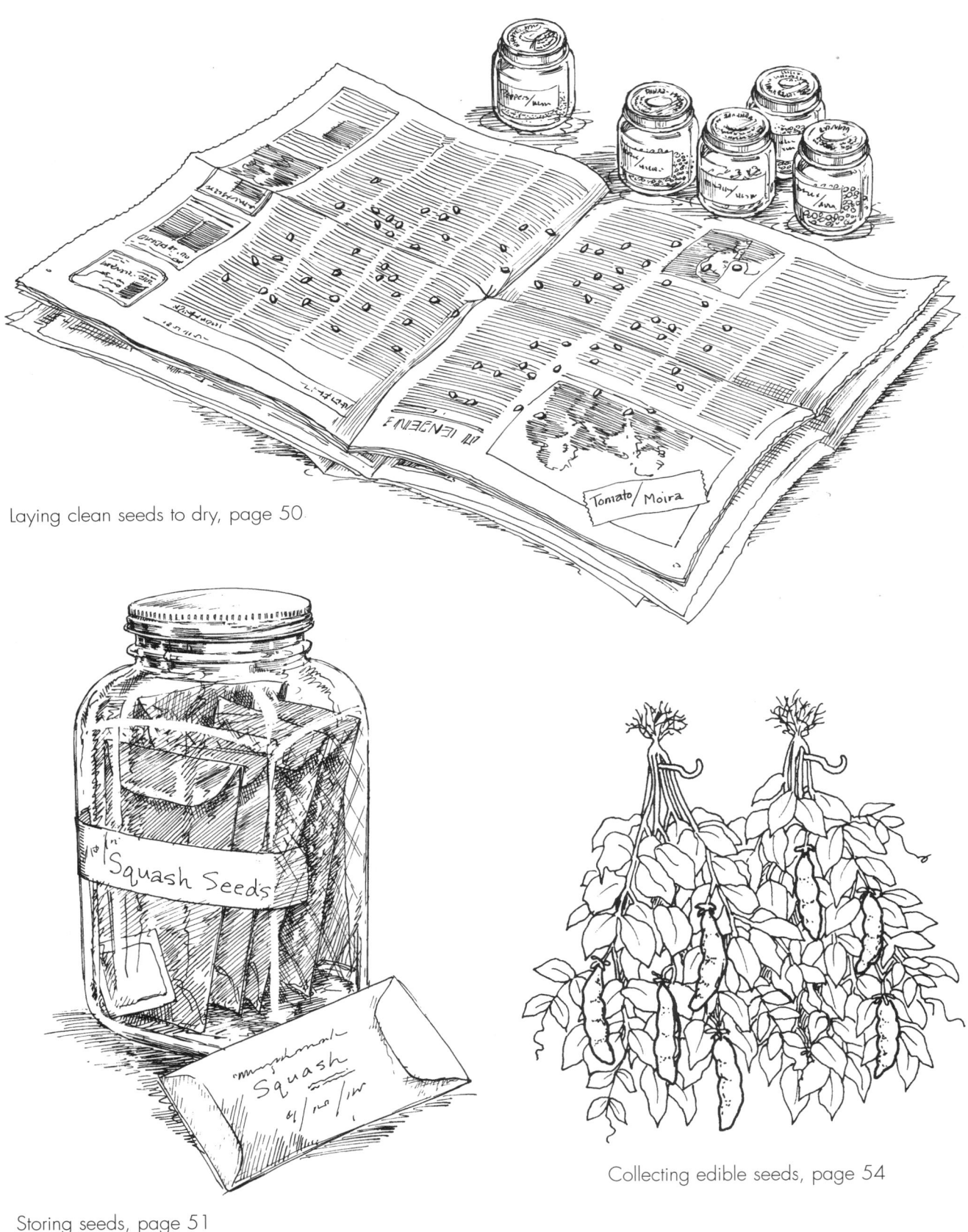

Laying clean seeds to dry, page 50.

Storing seeds, page 51

Collecting edible seeds, page 54

Collecting and Storing Seeds

I f you've gone to a lot of trouble to select the best plants for seed saving, you'll want to be sure the seeds you collect are harvested, cleaned, and stored correctly to preserve their viability. A seed that is viable has the ability to germinate. Seeds that have been collected at the wrong time, insufficiently cleaned, or stored under improper conditions may not be viable when you're ready to sow them. If you give seeds the treatment they need to survive, they will reward you with healthy, sturdy seedlings.

Methods for collecting seed vary, determined in part by the quantity of seed you need and the type of plant you are working with. Some seeds can easily be collected and removed from their pods by hand. With others, the entire plant must be cut down and threshed (beaten or flailed) to remove the seeds. Many seeds can simply be shaken free of their pods into a container.

In This Chapter

- Seed Dispersal
- Harvesting Seeds
- Cleaning Seeds
- Storing Seeds
- Collecting and Cleaning Seeds
- Seeds from Fleshy Fruits
- Collecting and Cleaning Edible Seeds
- Collecting Seed from the Wild

MASTER GARDENING TIPS

Some At-a-Glance Advice on Collecting and Storing Seed

▶ Determine the plant's method of seed dispersal, and time your harvest.

▶ After collecting seed, clean it and spread it out to dry.

▶ Be sure seed is thoroughly dry before storing; don't let it get damp after drying.

▶ Store seeds (or seed packets) in thoroughly dry glass jars or other sealed containers.

▶ Label all containers with variety and date.

▶ Store seeds in a dark, cool (or cold), dry place. The colder it is, the drier it should be.

Seed Dispersal

Every child has plucked dandelion seed heads in summertime, puffed on them, and watched the seeds float away on fluffy white parachutes. Like the wind, this gentle breath helps the dandelion disperse its seeds, ensuring the survival of future dandelion generations.

Wind, however, is only one of many vehicles plants use to disperse their seeds. Seeds come in many sizes and shapes with a variety of survival methods:

- Some (cockleburs) have hooked barbs or bristles, to hitch a ride on the fur of a passing animal.

- Some (maple) have wings or parachutes, to fly through the air.

- Some can float downstream to greener pastures.

- Some come in appetizing packages, to be eaten by birds or animals and later deposited in another location. Some, in fact, are so inviting to birds that you may have to cover the seed heads or otherwise protect them until it's time to harvest. Coneflowers and sunflowers are good examples.

Timing Considerations

Most seeds must be collected at a specific time. If harvested too soon, they may not have a fully developed endosperm to nourish the embryo in storage and allow it to finish maturing. If they are collected too late (assuming they have not already been eaten or blown away), they may have begun to rot and lose their viability. You'll probably have to check your plants daily so you don't miss that window of opportunity between underripe and overripe.

A few plants are easygoing about it: Their seeds can be collected early, if necessary, and will complete the ripening process in storage. Some plants have seeds that ripen at different times, so you'll have to visit the plant on several occasions if you want to catch all of its seed. Often these plants have flower spikes with blooms that open at the top first and work their way down (or vice versa); the seed pods ripen in the same order.

MASTER GARDENING TIPS

Some Advice on When to Harvest Seeds

▶ With flowering plants, the seeds are ready for harvest when they are dry, a few weeks after the flowers fade and the petals drop.

▶ With plants that bear seed within an edible fruit, the fruits should be allowed to remain on the plant a week or two beyond the time they would normally be picked for eating.

Harvesting Seeds

To find the seeds, watch the flowers. If they have been fertilized, they will quickly wither and fall away after blooming, leaving a seed head, pod, follicle, fruit, or other container for the seeds. Each seed will have a different way of telling you when it's ready. Some seeds will rattle in their pods when they are ripe. Most will change from light-colored to dark.

Except for those that are encased in fruit, seeds should be dry before being harvested. Collect the seeds on a sunny day, if possible, when all dew and raindrops have evaporated.

If you're collecting from perennials, don't allow all of them to go to seed. The act of developing seeds weakens a plant and shortens its life, so choose a few plants for seed saving, and deadhead the rest.

Seeds of fertilized flowers will quickly wither and fall away after blooming, leaving a seed head, pod, follicle, fruit, or other container for the seeds.

MASTER GARDENING TIPS

Easiest Seeds to Save

▶ Larger seeds, like those of four-o'clocks, beans, peas, morning glories, and marigolds, are easier to collect and work with than small, fine seeds.

▶ Seeds of annuals are best for the beginning seed saver or the impatient gardener. Since the plants complete their entire life cycle in one year, you don't have long to wait to collect the seed and see the results.

▶ Perennials produce seeds every year, but only after they have reached full maturity.

▶ Biennials produce seed in their second year. Biennial vegetables usually must be stored over winter in the first year and replanted the following spring in order to bloom and produce seeds, so they are the most challenging for a beginner.

Cleaning Seeds

After being harvested, seeds should be cleaned and dried before they are stored. This is important because any plant debris left on or around the seeds in storage may harbor fungi, insects, or moisture that can destroy your seeds. Moisture can cause the seed's metabolism to speed up when it should be slowing down to hold the seed dormant. All of these things can cause the seed to lose viability, and your efforts at plant selection and seed harvesting will be wasted. See descriptions of specific plants for instructions on cleaning.

Small seeds should be dry enough in 8 to 12 days; larger seeds may take a few days more. After the drying treatment, immediately place the seeds in their storage containers; do not expose them to moisture or humidity once they have finished drying.

Even if the seeds look dry when you collect them, spread them out on newspapers or screens indoors for at least a week to continue drying.

MASTER GARDENING TIP

Covering Seeds

Some seeds should be planted immediately after harvesting in order to germinate well, usually because they have low viability and/or a high moisture content. You can identify the seeds with high moisture content by their size and texture; they are generally large and leathery. Many tree seeds belong to this group.

HINT FOR SUCCESS

Another way to dry seeds is to seal them in a jar with a packet of silica gel (available at camera stores), which absorbs excess moisture. The silica gel packet can be reused after being dried in a 250°F oven for 20 minutes.

Storing Seeds

Most seeds can be stored for at least a year and still germinate, as long as the storage conditions are right. The idea is to keep the seed in a delicate state of existence: It must be able to exchange gases and digest food, yet its metabolism must be working slowly enough to keep it dormant. You can control these processes and slow them down by manipulating storage conditions such as temperature and moisture.

Temperature

Temperature is critical because heat usually causes the embryo's metabolism to speed up. This in turn causes the embryo to use up its stored food too rapidly. Try to keep seeds consistently cold or at least cool; fluctuating temperatures can be fatal. The refrigerator, or any other place that stays consistently just above freezing, is ideal for storing most seeds. Seeds can also be stored in a freezer — the colder they are kept, the longer they will remain viable — but they must be completely ripe and very dry to be stored this way.

Moisture

Moisture may be an even more important factor. Since seeds begin to germinate when they absorb water, you can see why moisture is the death of seeds in storage (seeds of aquatic plants are an exception). Always dry seeds thoroughly before placing them in storage containers. In addition, make sure the containers themselves have no trace of moisture inside, and that moisture cannot enter them. Finally, place the seeds in their storage containers as soon as they are fully dried. Do not allow them to sit out after drying, or they may reabsorb moisture from the atmosphere. If this happens, drying them again will not help them regain their viability.

Don't forget to label everything throughout the whole seed-collecting process, from the time you select your plants, through all the stages of cleaning, drying, storing, and sowing. You don't want to confuse your hot pepper seeds with your sweet pepper seeds, or your cherry tomatoes with your beefsteaks. Mark each batch of seeds with the variety name and date collected, and any other information you might want to include. This also comes in handy when you want to exchange seeds with another gardener.

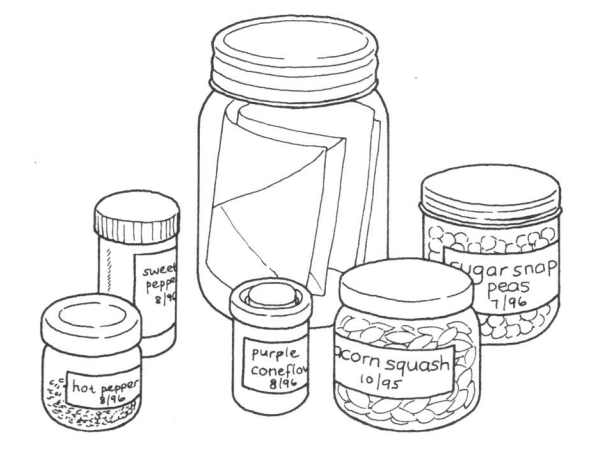

A variety of household containers can be used to store seeds. The container shouldn't be airtight (this would prevent gas exchange), but it should be securely closed to keep out moisture and pests. The following have been used for seed storage: screw-top glass jars, such as baby-food jars; paper or glassine envelopes labeled and sealed inside glass jars; plastic or metal film containers; prescription medicine containers; cans with metal lids.

Collecting and Cleaning Seeds

The process some plants use to scatter their seeds is called "dehiscence." Seeds are said to dehisce when they ripen and come free of the seed-bearing unit. Some cling to the mother plant until they are pulled out or forcefully dislodged. Others simply fall to the ground when ripe. In some cases, the plant has an ejection mechanism that catapults the seeds some distance from the plant when they are fully mature.

Timing is important when harvesting seed. Observe your plants carefully and note the time and method of seed dispersal. You'll soon get a good sense of when to collect seed from each plant. Some may escape if you don't collect them at just the right time. Others remain on the plant for so long that they may rot.

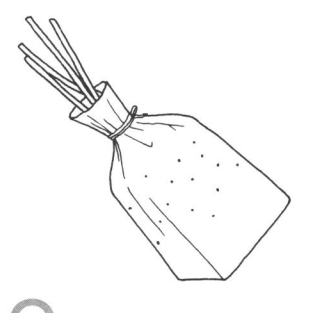

1 When seeds are thoroughly dry and seem about to scatter, cut off the seed heads with shears.

2 You can then lay them out on a light-colored surface in a warm, dry place for a week or so, or place them upside down in a bag and tie the bag shut until the seeds have released themselves. Be sure to leave a few small air holes in the bag.

3 When the seed heads are dry, separate out the individual seeds and remove any plant debris or chaff, especially green leaves and stems. The debris may be big enough to pick out by hand or you can sift or winnow the debris. For small seed, a kitchen strainer is useful.

Or, winnow out very light chaff from heavier seeds by pouring the seeds from one container to another while blowing on them or allowing a breeze to blow over them.

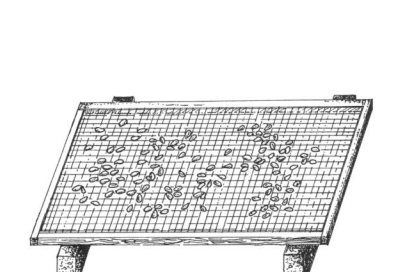

4 When the seeds are clean, they should be spread out indoors to continue drying for a week or so before being stored. (Seeds with beards or tufts should not be given this extra drying time.) Pick out and discard seeds that are more light-weight than the rest; these have usually lost viability and will cause problems by rotting in storage.

HINT FOR SUCCESS

A Seedsaver's Precaution

If you think you might not be able to get to the seeds before they disperse (which is very likely if they are the type to eject suddenly), you can let the nearly ripe seed heads mature in a bag tied to the plant over the seed head.

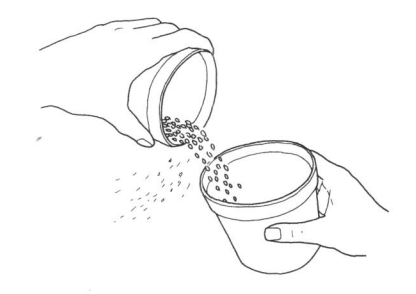

Seeds from Fleshy Fruits

If the seeds are carried within an edible fruit, the fruit should be left on the plant until it is slightly overripe (a few weeks after the normal harvest time). Don't let the fruit rot, though; the heat generated by decomposition may destroy the embryo within the seed. The seeds of some fruits, such as melons, winter squashes, and pumpkins, can be collected at the same time the fruit is harvested for eating.

HINT FOR SUCCESS

It's very important to remove all remnants of fruit pulp from the seeds before storing them, since this pulp often contains natural chemicals that inhibit germination. These inhibitors can delay germination for up to a year.

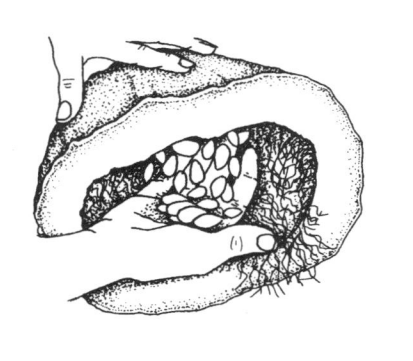

1 Cut open the fruit and scoop out the seeds. It's common for them have a considerable amount of pulp clinging to them.

2 Place the whole mass in a bowl or jar of water, and allow it to sit at room temperature. Stir the mixture occasionally to prevent mold from forming.

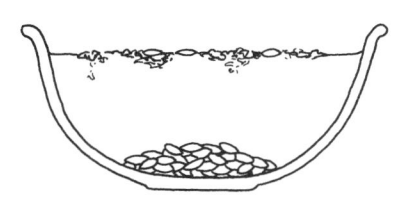

3 In two or three days, the pulp and lightweight (inviable) seeds will float to the top of the bowl or jar, and the viable seeds will remain at the bottom. Pour off the floating matter, then drain and rinse the good seeds.

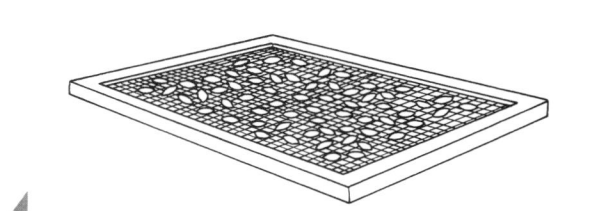

4 Lay out the seeds to dry for a week or two before storing them.

Collecting and Cleaning Edible Seeds

Edible seeds usually remain on the plant for a long time after maturing. It is generally good to collect edible seeds four to six weeks after the rest have been harvested for eating. Be sure to collect them before they fall on the ground or are eaten by birds and animals, and especially before the first hard frost, which may damage them. When these seeds are fully mature, they will be hard and dry.

1 Cut down the plants and lay them on screens or hang them upside down indoors to dry for a week or two.

2 Thresh the plants by beating or flailing them to remove the seeds.

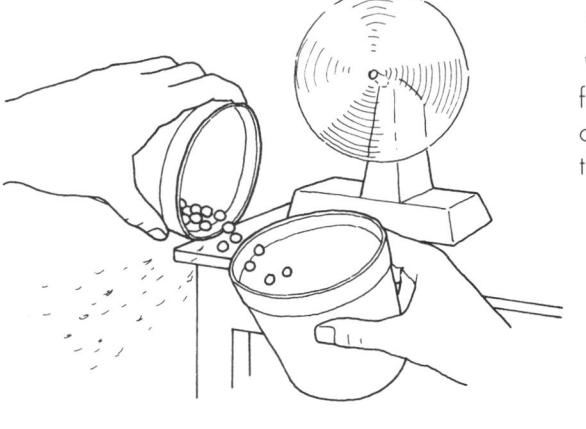

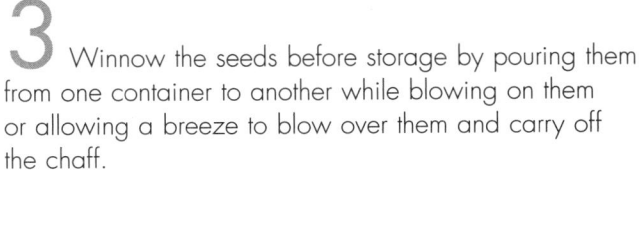

3 Winnow the seeds before storage by pouring them from one container to another while blowing on them or allowing a breeze to blow over them and carry off the chaff.

Collecting Seed from the Wild

You can start your own wildflower garden by collecting seed from certain plants. Knowing when to collect seeds requires patience and careful observation. Seeds are usually ready to be harvested about a month after the flowers bloom, although some plants hold their seeds longer. The seed must be mature before it is taken from the plant, or it may not germinate. Be sure pods and seeds are dry before collecting them. Berries should be on the later side of ripe. Refer to a good book on wildflowers for information about any pretreatment or special storage requirements for the species you select.

Keep careful records of what, when, and where you're collecting. Also note the growing conditions, so that you can try to duplicate them in your garden. One of the joys of growing wildflowers is that many annual species self seed, so once you begin your wildflower garden, you'll be able to rely on it year after year.

Mark plants you'd like to collect seed from with a tag or ribbon, and watch them closely throughout the season. If you are afraid you'll miss the moment, tie a small cheesecloth bag or piece of stocking over the ripening seeds. Be sure they can still get some light and air circulation.

MASTER GARDENING TIPS

Wild Seed Collecting: Dos and Don'ts

► If the plants are on private property, secure permission from the property owner before proceeding.

► Never take all the seeds from a colony of wildflowers. Leave enough so that the plants can reseed themselves and increase the colony for next year.

► Do not collect seed if there are only a few plants in the group. Take seed only from large, flourishing colonies.

► Check with your local wildflower society or conservation group if you're not sure whether it's appropriate to collect seeds from a particular plant.

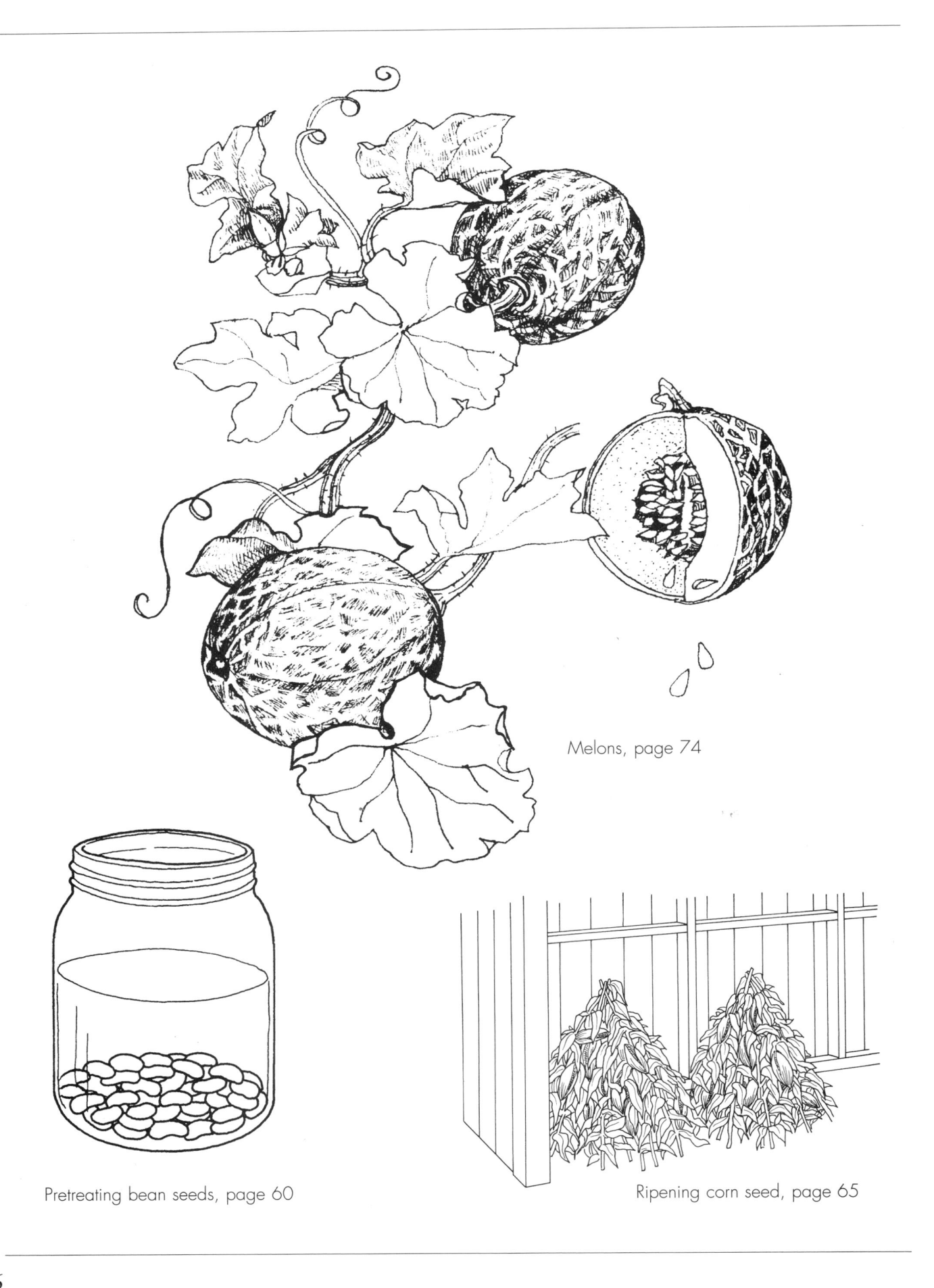

Melons, page 74

Pretreating bean seeds, page 60

Ripening corn seed, page 65

Annual Vegetables

Like all plants designated "annuals," annual vegetables are those that complete their entire life cycle (grow, bloom, set seed, and die) in the course of one growing season. There is a caveat to this: They will only *complete* their life cycle if they have *time* to complete it — that is, if the growing season is long enough. In cold regions with short growing seasons, annual vegetables may have to be started indoors in late winter to adequately extend the season, and transplanted into the garden when it is safe to do so. Most can be started this way, although some (like corn, peas, beans, and summer radishes) don't like to be transplanted and should be seeded directly outdoors.

Annual vegetables are usually easy to grow and collect seed from. Seeds from beans, corn, peas, and squash, for instance, are large and easy to handle, and make excellent first projects for beginning seed savers. Once you begin growing varieties that thrive in your garden and are delicious to eat as well, you can produce pounds of produce for your family year after year at little to no cost.

For many of the plants in this chapter you will be given advice to avoid F_1 Hybrid cultivars and to choose instead open-pollinated varieties if you are planning to harvest the seed. F_1 Hybrids are the product of several generations of selective inbreeding resulting in a high degree of predictability about the plants that are grown from a set of specific parents. But the seed from that next generation will not reliably reproduce itself — "come true." Hybrids result when two genetically dissimilar plants are cross fertilized, usually by a gardener or horticulturalist. The result of this kind of managed cross fertilization can result in a cultivar. Hybrids have a valuable place in gardens, since the goal of the hybridizer is to produce plants with more resistance to disease, bigger and juicier fruits, and other desirable qualities. Open-pollinated plants have a much more diverse heritage, and many gardeners prefer them for a number of reasons.

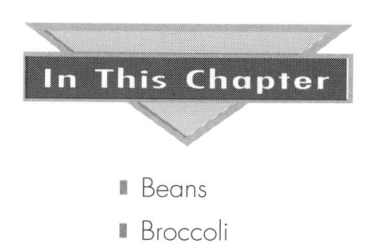

In This Chapter

- Beans
- Broccoli
- Corn
- Cucumber
- Eggplant
- Lettuce
- Melons
- Peas
- Pepper
- Radish
- Spinach
- Squash
- Tomato

Beans
Phaseolus vulgaris

Beans are a great choice for beginning seed savers. Although they may occasionally cross-pollinate if bees are in the neighborhood, they are generally self-pollinating. In fact, pollination usually occurs before the flower even opens. Since self-pollinating plants produce seeds that contain only the plant's own genetic material, they will always "come true" — in other words, their offspring will resemble the parent plant.

Even though cross-pollination is unlikely in beans, to be certain you don't mix up your bean genes — especially if you are raising a rare heirloom variety — you should plant different bean varieties at least 100 feet apart, if possible.

mature pod

seeds

MASTER GARDENING TIPS

▶ Never collect seed from a diseased plant, since the disease can pass on to subsequent generations through the seed. Beans are especially susceptible to anthracnose.

▶ The seeds of snap beans may germinate even if they are not fully ripe, but you'll get better results by allowing them to ripen completely before harvesting. Just be sure you harvest them before the first frost, since frost may injure the seeds.

▶ To see if a bean is dry enough for storage, bite down on it. If you can't dent it with your teeth, it's ready.

The edible part of the plant, the bean itself, is the seed. Select the sturdiest, strongest plants with the heaviest crop of beans. Though the beans on these plants may look tempting to eat, don't harvest them for food. Instead, allow the bean pods to hang on the plants until ripe enough to harvest for seed.

Optimum soil temperature for germination: 65° to 85°F

Germination time at optimum soil temperature: 7 to 10 days

Spacing/thinning (bush): 2 to 3 inches; thin to 8 to 10 inches

Spacing/thinning (pole): 7 to 8 beans around each pole; thin to the 3 or 4 strongest plants

Row spacing: 24 to 36 inches

Planting depth: 1 inch

Seed storage requirements: Paper or cloth bag; cool, dry area

Seed viability: 3 years

Harvesting the Seed

1 About six weeks after you've harvested your other beans for eating, the seed is usually ripe. If the seed rattles in the pod, the pods are brown and dry, and almost all the leaves have fallen from the plant, the seed is probably ready to harvest. Pull up the entire plant by the roots. Stack the plants loosely on screens or slatted shelves, or hang them upside down in a cool, dark, dry place for a week or two.

2 When the beans are hard and dry, remove them from the pods by hand or by threshing. To thresh beans, hold plants upside down inside a large trash can and whack them against the sides of the can. Another method is to put the plants inside a burlap bag and walk on them or beat them with a threshing tool (flail). When threshing the seeds, don't be too rough or you may damage the bean embryo and cause it to lose viability.

3 When the beans are out of the pods, winnow out the plant debris by pouring the beans from one container to another in a strong breeze; the chaff should blow away and leave the beans clean for storage.

4 When your beans are completely dry, store them in a jar or bag in a cool, dry area. Bean seeds should not be stored in tightly sealed containers; paper or cloth bags are often recommended. Polyethylene bags are also acceptable; they allow air to enter but not water. Healthy seed, stored properly, should remain viable for about three years.

Outdoor Sowing

1 Before sowing bean seeds, soak them for a few hours in tepid water to soften the seed coat. Dusting the seeds with a bacterial inoculant powder before planting will help them gather nitrogen from the atmosphere, resulting in healthier, more productive plants. Legume inoculant is available at many garden centers.

2 Sow beans directly in the garden; they don't care for transplanting. It's best to plant them after all danger of frost is past, when the soil is thoroughly warm. Bean seeds planted in cold soil will often rot before they can germinate. If you want a constant supply of beans, sow more seed every two or three weeks until late summer.

Coping with Weevils

Weevil grubs are often present in beans before harvest. After the beans are collected and stored, the grubs mature and eat through the seed coats, making the beans unsuitable for sowing. If you see small holes in any of the seed coats, you may have a weevil infestation. Try one of these remedies:

▶ Place the beans in a glass jar or metal container in an unheated building (like a detached garage or garden shed).

▶ Place beans in a glass jar or metal container in the freezer for up to a week.

▶ Spread beans thinly a cookie sheet, and kill the grubs by heating the beans in the oven (135°F for 1 hour).

Store seeds immediately in bags or containers to avoid reinfestation.

HINTS FOR SUCCESS

▶ For best results, plant seed with the "eyes" down.

▶ Pole beans will grow on a fence or trellis, or on tepee-shaped frames. Plant them on the north side of the garden so they don't shade other vegetables.

▶ Purple bean varieties, such as 'Royalty' and 'Royal Burgundy', can tolerate colder soil than can the green varieties.

▶ Beans will not produce healthy seeds if the soil has a zinc deficiency. To find out if your soil has enough zinc, use a soil-test kit for trace elements.

Broccoli

Brassica oleracea

Many varieties of broccoli are F$_1$ Hybrids. Look for open-pollinated seed if you are planning to harvest and save seed and choose early-bearing plants. Since broccoli is not self-pollinating but is cross-pollinated by insects, you'll need at least three plants, placed close together, for good seed set. Broccoli will cross with other brassicas, such as Brussels sprouts, cabbage, cauliflower, kale, and kohlrabi, so you should either raise only one of these plants each year or keep them well separated in the garden to avoid cross-pollination.

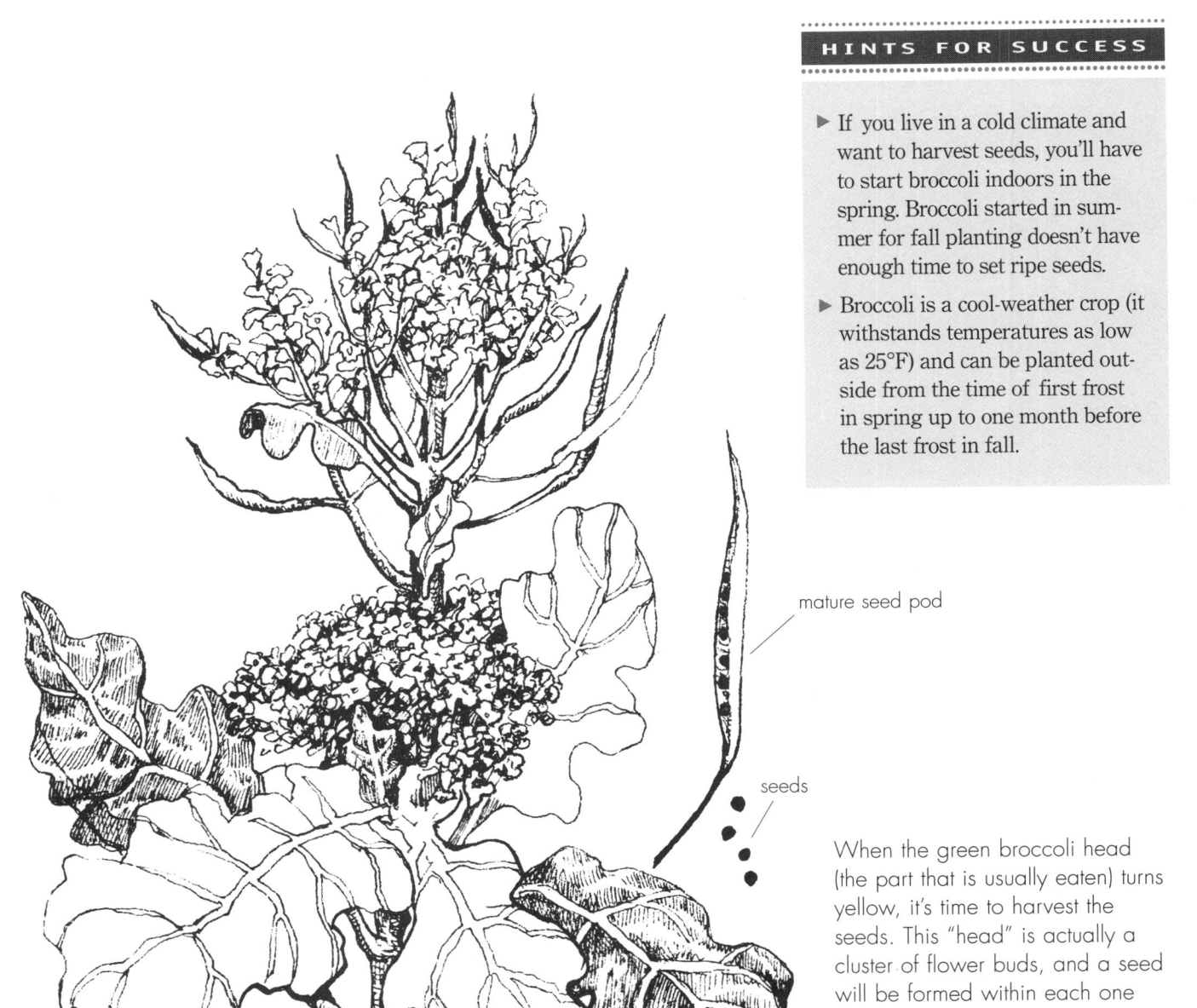

mature seed pod

seeds

HINTS FOR SUCCESS

▶ If you live in a cold climate and want to harvest seeds, you'll have to start broccoli indoors in the spring. Broccoli started in summer for fall planting doesn't have enough time to set ripe seeds.

▶ Broccoli is a cool-weather crop (it withstands temperatures as low as 25°F) and can be planted outside from the time of first frost in spring up to one month before the last frost in fall.

When the green broccoli head (the part that is usually eaten) turns yellow, it's time to harvest the seeds. This "head" is actually a cluster of flower buds, and a seed will be formed within each one after it blooms.

Optimum soil temperature for germination: 70° to 75°F

Germination time at optimum soil temperature: 10 to 14 days

Spacing/thinning: 12 to 18 inches; thin to 24 inches

Row spacing: 24 inches

Planting depth: ¼ to ½ inch

Seed storage requirements: Sealed containers; cool, dry area

Seed viability: About 5 years

Harvesting the Seed

1 When the seedpods are thoroughly dry on the plant, cut the entire plant to the ground and then hang it in a dry, well-aerated spot indoors for a week or two.

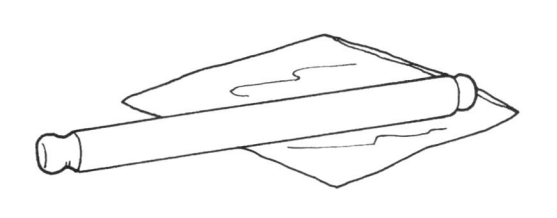

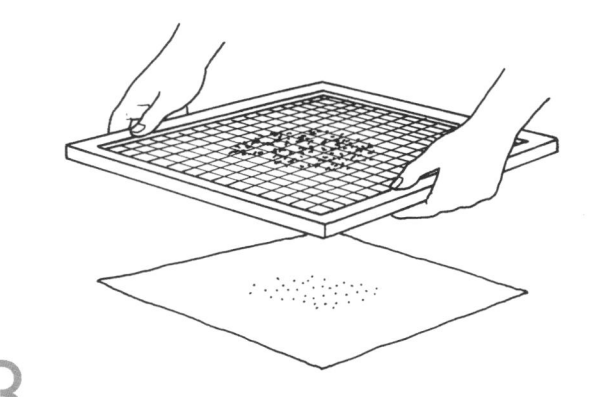

2 When the seeds are dry, remove them from the pods by placing the pods in a bag and crushing them with a rolling pin or with your hands.

3 Pass the seeds through a screen to clean them and remove the chaff, or they can be winnowed.

Indoor Sowing

Sow broccoli seeds in flats or containers indoors five to seven weeks before you plan to set them out in the garden. When the seedlings have four to five true leaves, transplant them into individual containers. The seedlings should be hardened off before they are planted outdoors in spring.

Corn
Zea mays

Because many varieties of corn are F_1 Hybrids, it may not be worth the time to collect their seed. Choose open-pollinated varieties if you are planning to harvest seed.

All kinds of corn — including sweet corn, popcorn, flint corn, dent corn, flour corn, and ornamental corn — cross readily with each other, so you must isolate the varieties if you plan to save seed. (If you are not saving seed, the cross-pollination should not be a problem.) Corn is wind-pollinated, so the distance downwind is important if you're concerned about cross-pollination. Although 250 feet is usually acceptable, to be absolutely safe, separate varieties by 1,000 feet.

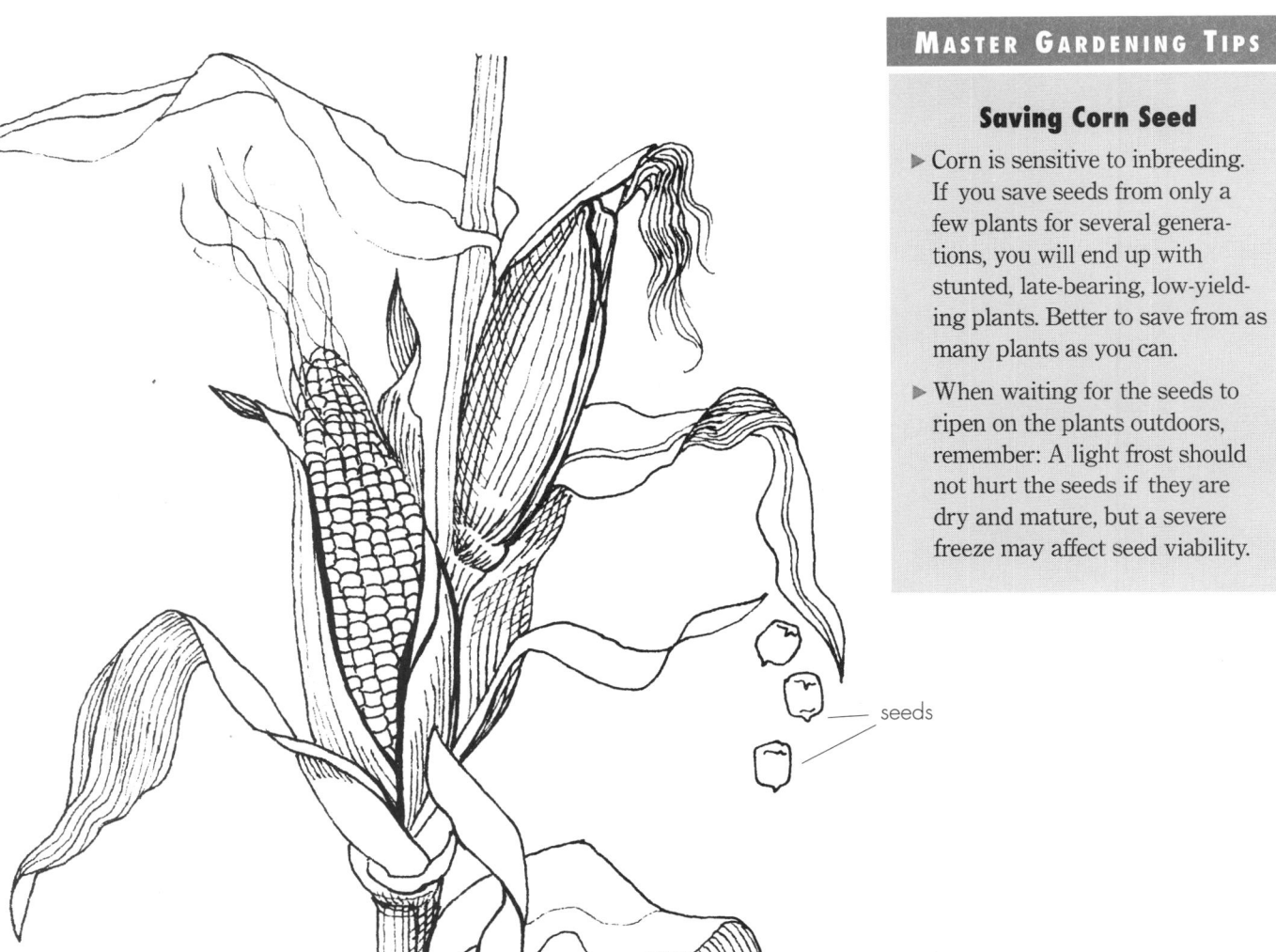

seeds

MASTER GARDENING TIPS

Saving Corn Seed

▶ Corn is sensitive to inbreeding. If you save seeds from only a few plants for several generations, you will end up with stunted, late-bearing, low-yielding plants. Better to save from as many plants as you can.

▶ When waiting for the seeds to ripen on the plants outdoors, remember: A light frost should not hurt the seeds if they are dry and mature, but a severe freeze may affect seed viability.

Inspect both plants and ears of corn when selecting those from which to save seed. Try to choose the fullest, most perfect ears from the earliest-bearing plants. You might also consider productivity and cold or drought tolerance.

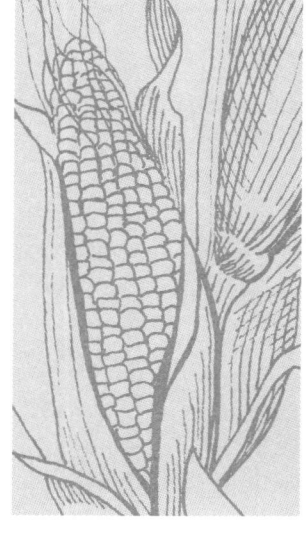

Optimum soil temperature for germination: 65° to 75°F
Germination time at optimum soil temperature: 5 to 7 days
Spacing/thinning (early): Rows: 4 to 5 inches; thin to 8 to 10 inches. Hills: 5 or 6 seeds per hill; thin to 3 plants.
Spacing/thinning (late): Rows: 4 to 5 inches; thin to 12 to 18 inches. Hills: 5 or 6 seeds per hill; thin to 2 plants.
Row spacing: Sow in blocks of at least 3 or 4 short rows, 2 to 3 feet apart. Hills should be 2 to 3 feet apart.
Planting depth (early): 1 inch
Planting depth (late): 2 to 3 inches
Seed pretreatment: Soak seeds in warm water for a few hours before planting.
Seed storage requirements: Store in paper or cloth bags in a cool, dry area.
Seed viability: About 2 years

Harvesting the Seed

1 Harvest seed corn about a month after picking the rest for eating. The seeds will continue to ripen on the cobs after harvest; simply peel back the husks, tie the ears together, and hang them in a well-ventilated place indoors for a few weeks.

2 If you are saving a large quantity of seed, cut the stalks to the ground and stand them up in shocks. After a few weeks, remove the husks and lay the cobs on racks in a warm, well-ventilated place until the kernels are hard. Be sure the corn is completely hard and dry, or it may heat in storage and lose viability.

Indoor Sowing

Corn does not transplant well, so indoor sowing is not recommended.

Outdoor Sowing

1 Since corn is a warm-weather crop, it should be planted after the last frost, or a week or two before for early varieties. Corn seeds tend to rot in cold soil (less than 50°F), so take care not to plant too soon. Native Americans planted their corn when oak leaves were the size of a mouse's ear.

2 Plant corn in blocks to ensure complete pollination and a well-developed set of kernels.

MASTER GARDENING TIPS

Pests of Corn

▶ Corn borers can be a menace to seeds. If you have problems with borers, soak the seeds for a couple of hours in a strong tea made from butterfly weed *(Asclepias tuberosa)* or English ivy *(Hedera helix)*. Seeds sown after mid-June should escape corn borer damage.

▶ Don't leave any stray kernels around when sowing seed for corn; the birds will find them — and then they'll find all the ones you planted, too.

Hybridizing Your Own Corn

Corn is monoecious, meaning it bears male flowers (tassels) and female flowers (silks) on the same plant. Kernels of corn are formed when pollen grains from the tassels are deposited on the silks of the same plant or a nearby plant. To hybridize your own seed corn, you can either hand-pollinate or let nature help out.

The Natural Approach

Plant two different varieties in alternating rows. Decide which variety will be male and which will be female (it doesn't matter which is which), and remove all the tassels from the "female" plants. These plants now cannot self-pollinate, so their silks will receive pollen only from the other variety. Then step back and let the wind do its job. When the female plants produce corn, it will be a hybrid of the two varieties. Save some of the corn for seed if you wish to grow the same hybrid next year.

Hand-Pollination

Use this trickier, but more precise, method if there is any chance of cross-pollination by other varieties in the neighborhood. First, look for ears on which the silks have not fully emerged. Cover them with paper bags, tied tightly around the cornstalk. When pollen appears on the tassels of the other variety, shake it into a bag and mix it together. Remove the paper bags from the protected ears and dust the pollen onto the silks of each ear. Replace the paper bags, label them, and leave them in place until the silks turn brown. After removing the bags, tie colored yarn around the hand-pollinated ears to keep them from being accidentally harvested for eating.

Growing the Best Corn

▶ Fertilize corn with plenty of nitrogen; healthier plants will produce better seeds.

▶ Sweet corn, especially the early extra-sweet varieties, has lower seedling vigor and disease resistance than other kinds of corn. Sweet corn also requires a rich soil to grow well.

▶ If you like to eat fresh sweet corn all summer (and you have a long growing season), make succession plantings 10 to 14 days apart. Better yet, plant early, midseason and late varieties at the same time, for different maturation dates. Another trick is to sow an early variety in midsummer and get one last harvest before frost.

▶ If you live in a cold area with a short growing season, and you plan to save seed, you may have to start your corn indoors to give it time to mature. Start seeds in warm soil about four weeks before you want to transplant. Once the seeds have germinated, the plants will grow well in cool soil, and you can transplant them outside after the last spring frost date.

How to Avoid Cross-Pollination

▶ To avoid unwanted cross-pollination, plant rows of sunflowers between corn varieties to provide a barrier and help reduce isolation distances.

▶ You can also avoid cross-pollination by planting different varieties at different times, so that pollen from one variety is not in the air when the silk of the other variety is developing.

Cucumber
Cucumis sativus

Many varieties of cucumber are F_1 Hybrids. Be sure to choose open-pollinated varieties if you are planning to harvest seed. Cucumbers are normally pollinated by bees, and they will cross-pollinate with other cucumber varieties but not with melons or squashes, as many people believe. If you're planning to save seed, keep cucumber varieties separated by at least 200 feet. Cucumbers are susceptible to mildew, scab, mosaic, and anthracnose; select plants that show resistance to these diseases.

Cucumbers are monoecious (male and female flowers on the same plant). The female flower is easy to distinguish by its ovary, a swelling beneath the blossom that looks like a little cucumber.

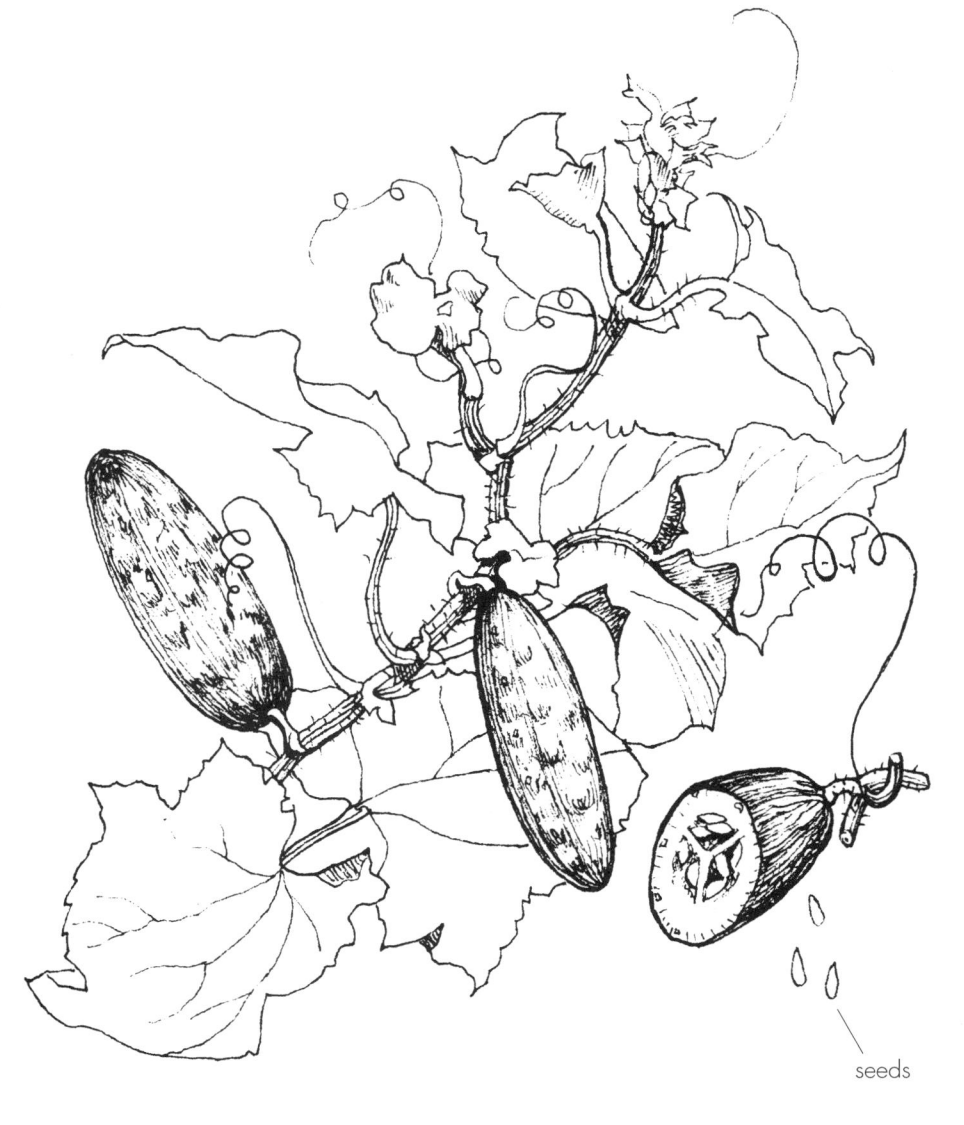

seeds

MASTER GARDENING TIPS

▶ Sometimes cucumbers set fruit without fertilization (parthenocarpy). This results in nearly seedless fruits, which can be great if you're eating the cucumbers but not so great if you're trying to collect seed.

▶ When thinning cucumber seedlings, it's better to pinch or snip them off than to pull them out by the roots, which may disturb the roots of their companions.

▶ Always provide seedlings with good air circulation, indoors and outdoors.

Leave seed cucumbers on the vine until they are fat and yellow, about five weeks after you've harvested the others for eating. Frost shouldn't damage the seeds, but be sure to pick the fruit before it rots.

Optimum soil temperature for germination: 65° to 95°F

Germination time at optimum soil temperature: 7 to 10 days

Spacing/thinning: Hills: 8 to 10 seeds per hill, 2 inches apart; thin to best 3 or 4 plants. Rows: 8 inches; thin to 12 to 24 inches.

Row spacing: 4 to 6 feet

Planting depth: ½ to 1 inch

Seed storage requirements: Store in airtight containers in a cool, dry place.

Seed viability: About 5 years

Harvesting the Seed

1 To prepare the seeds for storage, cut the cucumber in half lengthwise and scrape out the seedy pulp. Put the pulp, seeds and all, in a bowl of water to ferment. Stir frequently to prevent mold from forming. When the heavy, viable seeds sink to the bottom, drain and rinse them.

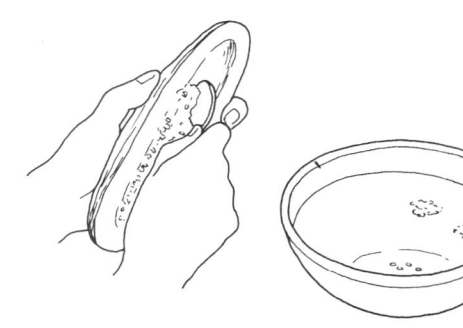

2 Let seeds dry on a screen for a week or two. Cucumber seeds often continue to ripen after storage.

Indoor Sowing

1 Cucumbers are best sown directly outdoors, but if you want an early crop, you can start seeds indoors three to four weeks before the last frost date. Because cucumber roots hate to be disturbed, start the plants in individual peat pots. Provide bottom heat during germination, and place the seedlings in a sunny, warm spot after they've emerged.

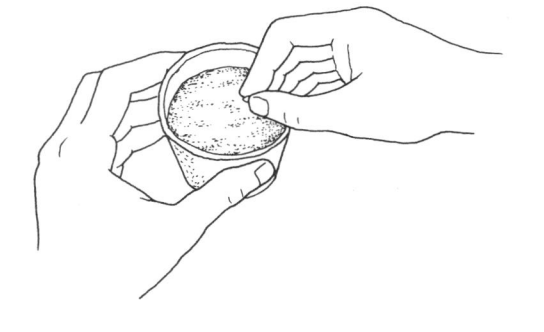

2 Harden them off before transplanting to the garden, and always cover them if frost threatens. Once they are set in place in the garden, they shouldn't be moved.

Outdoor Sowing

Cucumbers are a warm-season crop. If direct seeding outdoors, be sure all danger of frost has passed. If the nighttime temperatures fall below 40°F, the seed will rot before it can germinate. The seed germinates best at 90°F. Don't mulch the seedlings until the soil is thoroughly warm.

Eggplant
Solanum melongena var. *esculentum*

Many varieties of eggplant are F$_1$ Hybrids. Open-pollinated varieties are the best choice for seed savers. Eggplant is usually self-pollinated, but may also be cross-pollinated by insects. If you're concerned about cross-pollination, the best solution is to raise only one variety of eggplant per year. For seed saving, select early-bearing, productive plants with large, richly colored fruits. This tender warm-weather crop has the same cultural requirements as peppers.

seeds

MASTER GARDENING TIPS

▶ When hardening off eggplant seedlings, make sure they don't get chilled or dried out, or they may not fruit well later. Harden off very gradually.

▶ If you smoke or use tobacco in any form, wash your hands before handling eggplant seedlings, to avoid spreading tobacco mosaic disease. This applies to all members of the Solanaceae (tomatoes, potatoes, petunias, peppers, etc.). Also, don't grow eggplant where other members of the Solanaceae have grown if your garden had disease problems of any kind.

When the eggplant fruit turns from firm and glossy to dull and slightly puckered, the seed is ready to harvest. Simply wait until the fruit drops from the plant — another sure sign that the seed is mature. If the fruit is ripe enough to eat and there is frost in the forecast, cut the fruit from the plant and bring it inside to let the seeds finish maturing. It should take about two weeks.

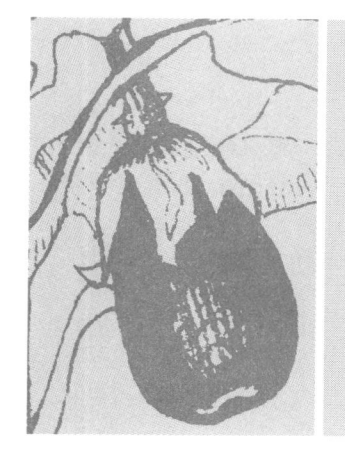

Optimum soil temperature for germination: 75° to 90°F

Germination time at optimum soil temperature: 10 to 15 days

Spacing/thinning: 3 inches; thin to 18 to 36 inches

Row spacing: 24 to 48 inches

Planting depth: ¼ inch

Seed storage requirements: Sealed container, in cool, dry area

Seed viability: About 5 years

Harvesting the Seed

1 To prepare the seeds for storage, cut open the eggplant, scoop out the seedy pulp, and place it in a bowl of water. Work it with your fingers until the viable seeds settle to the bottom of the bowl.

2 Drain off the remaining seeds and pulp, rinse the good seeds, and lay them out to dry on paper towels or screens.

Indoor Sowing

1 Start seeds indoors at least eight weeks before the last expected spring frost. Sow seeds in individual peat pots to minimize root shock when transplanting. Seeds can also be started in flats; when the seedlings are established, block out the flat by cutting a square around each seedling (simply run a knife through the soil midway between the plants in a grid pattern).

2 Provide bottom heat for a soil temperature of 70° to 90°F. The seed will not germinate if the soil is too cool.

Outdoor Sowing

If you prefer to sow them directly into the ground, wait until the garden soil is thoroughly warm and outdoor temperatures remain consistently at 65° or higher. Presprout the seeds by laying them out on damp paper towels and then rolling up the towels and placing them in a sealed plastic bag in a warm place. When the seeds germinate, they can be planted outdoors. The old rule of thumb for eggplant is to set it out in the garden when the oak leaves are fully developed.

Lettuce
Lactuca sativa

Since lettuce is self-pollinating, it will nearly always "come true" from seed, making it a good choice for seed saving. You can feel comfortable planting different varieties side by side, although to be absolutely sure no crossing occurs, it's best to plant another crop between the rows of lettuce.

Lettuce is a cool-weather crop, and it tends to bolt (go to seed) when the weather is hot. You'll know lettuce is beginning to bolt if you see a stalk rising from the center of the plant and the leaves begin to taste bitter. Since early bolting is an undesirable quality, save seed only from heat-tolerant, slow-to-bolt varieties. If you're growing head lettuce, you may have to encourage bolting by cutting an X into the top of the head, about 1 inch deep; this helps the stalk push up from the tightly packed leaves.

seeds

MASTER GARDENING TIPS

▶ Lettuce is an early crop for eating, but a long-season crop for seed saving.

▶ A single lettuce plant may yield as many as 30,000 seeds.

▶ Lettuce will bolt to seed when the weather is hot and days are long; if you have yard lights shining on the plants at night, they may be tricked into bolting.

▶ Although mulching keeps the soil nice and cool around the lettuce plants, it can also provide a hiding place for slugs, which love to eat lettuce.

▶ Head lettuce is less heat tolerant than is leaf lettuce.

When you have selected your seed plants, you must allow them to bolt. As the stalk grows, it will form a flower head with small yellow flowers that eventually change to feathery white tufts. Tucked inside are the tiny black or white seeds.

Optimum soil temperature for germination: 40° to 80°F

Germination time at optimum soil temperature: 3 to 10 days

Spacing/thinning (leaf): 1 to 3 inches; thin to 8 to 12 inches.

Spacing/thinning (head): 3 to 6 inches; thin to 12 to 18 inches.

Row spacing: 12 to 18 inches

Planting depth: ⅛ to ¼ inch

Seed storage requirements: Cool, dry area; sealed container

Seed viability: About 5 years

Harvesting the Seed

Lettuce seeds don't ripen all at once, so monitor the bolted plants closely for a month or two. Each time you see some seeds turning dark, shake the plant over a paper bag to catch them. Collected this way, seeds should be fairly clean and should not need much winnowing. Dry indoors for a week before storing.

Indoor Sowing

1 Head lettuce may have to be started indoors four to six weeks before planting outside to have enough time to produce good-size heads.

2 Sow seed in plugs or cells and keep the soil cool and moist. After two or three weeks, check the roots; if they are beginning to circle the plug, it's time to transplant outdoors or to a bigger pot. Harden off the plants for two or three days, then clip off all the outer leaves to make the plant sturdier and plant in the garden. Lettuce can be planted out as early as a month before the frost-free date in spring; just be sure to protect the plants if a severe frost is expected.

HINT FOR SUCCESS

Some lettuce varieties germinate better when the seed is exposed to light, at germination temperatures higher than optimum. At cooler temperatures, light does not seem to affect germination. In warm weather, cover seeds very lightly with fine soil to ensure good light exposure.

Outdoor Sowing

High temperatures cause lettuce seeds to go dormant. Older seeds are less sensitive to heat, so you could try "aging" your seeds for a few years (especially if you plan to sow in summer or live in a warm climate), or simply chill the seed in the refrigerator for about 24 hours prior to sowing.

Leaf lettuce grows quickly, so you can sow seed directly outdoors anytime from early spring (as soon as the ground can be worked) until midsummer. In areas with mild winters, start outdoors in fall for a winter crop; it will then produce seed in spring. Make succession plantings every two or three weeks.

Melons

Cucumis melo

Melons are normally pollinated by bees, and they will cross-pollinate with other melon varieties but not with cucumbers or squashes. If you're planning to save seed, keep melon varieties separated by at least 200 feet. Select early-bearing, disease-resistant plants (melons are susceptible to anthracnose) for seed saving.

Melons are monoecious (male and female flowers on the same plant). The first female flowers to appear are the ones most likely to set fruit.

MASTER GARDENING TIPS

▶ Melons are heavy feeders; mix fertilizer into the soil before planting.

▶ Watermelon is an altogether different genus and species — *Citrullus lanatus* — but has the same growing requirements as other melons.

seeds

When melons are ripe enough to eat, the seeds are ripe enough to collect and store. This means that you can eat your melon and save its seeds, too.

Optimum soil temperature for germination: 75° to 95°F

Germination time at optimum soil temperature: 5 to 7 days

Spacing/thinning: Rows: 3 to 4 inches; thin to 24 to 36 inches. Hills: 6 to 8 seeds per hill; thin to 2 to 3 plants.

Row spacing: Rows: 5 to 6 feet. Hills: 4 to 6 feet

Planting depth: ½ inch

Seed storage requirements: Cool, dry area; sealed container

Seed viability: About 5 years

Harvesting the Seed

Scoop out the seeds, thoroughly rinse off any pulp sticking to them, and air-dry them for a week. Or, place the seeds and pulp in a bowl of water. The heavy, viable seeds will soon sink to the bottom of the bowl, and you can then strain off the remaining seeds and pulp. Be sure seeds are thoroughly dry before storing.

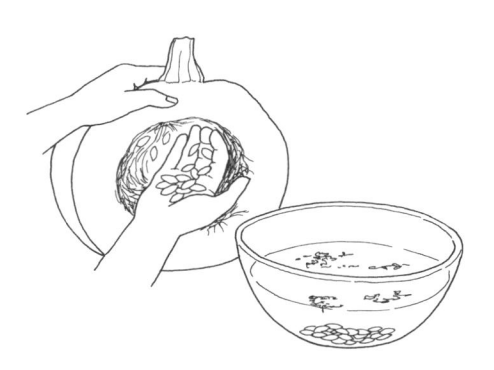

Indoor Sowing

If you live in a cold climate with a short growing season, start melons indoors three or four weeks (no sooner!) before transplanting outdoors. They will rapidly make the growth shown in the drawings below. Melons don't like to be transplanted, so start them in individual peat pots to avoid root disturbance when planting out. Sow two or three seeds in each pot, and thin to the strongest one or two plants. Keep the soil warm day and night; provide bottom heat if you can. Plant outdoors only when the ground is warm and there is no longer any danger of frost.

HINT FOR SUCCESS

Presprouting the seeds may help them get a head start. Lay the seeds out on a layer of damp paper towels, roll up the towels, and place the roll in a plastic bag. Seal the bag and keep it in a warm place until the seeds germinate. Then plant the seedlings in individual peat pots.

Outdoor Sowing

Melons can be direct-seeded outdoors, but the seeds may germinate unevenly if the weather is not consistently warm. After the last frost, when the soil is thoroughly warm, plant the seeds in hills. Use black plastic mulch to help heat the soil and conserve moisture, and cover the small plants with floating row covers (be sure to remove the covers when the plants begin to flower) or protect them with cloches or hot caps.

Peas
Pisum sativum

Peas offer a high success rate for beginning seed savers. Although they may occasionally cross-pollinate if bees are in the neighborhood, they are generally self-pollinating. Since self-pollinating plants produce seeds that contain only the plant's own genetic material, they will always "come true" — in other words, their offspring will resemble the parent plant.

Cross-pollination is unlikely in peas, but if you want to be sure it does not happen, sow different pea varieties 5 to 10 feet apart, and plant a tall barrier crop between them. Sugar peas generally don't cross with snap peas.

MASTER GARDENING TIPS

▶ Peas will not produce healthy seeds if the soil has a zinc or manganese deficiency. To find out if your soil has enough zinc and manganese, use a soil-test kit for trace elements.

▶ Peas need to be planted very early, while the weather is still cool. Because it's not wise to work the ground in early spring when it's wet and sticky, you might have to prepare a bed for peas the previous fall.

▶ Allow some weeds to remain when weeding around your pea plants; they help shade the roots and keep them cool.

▶ Peas don't like to be transplanted, so indoor sowing is not recommended.

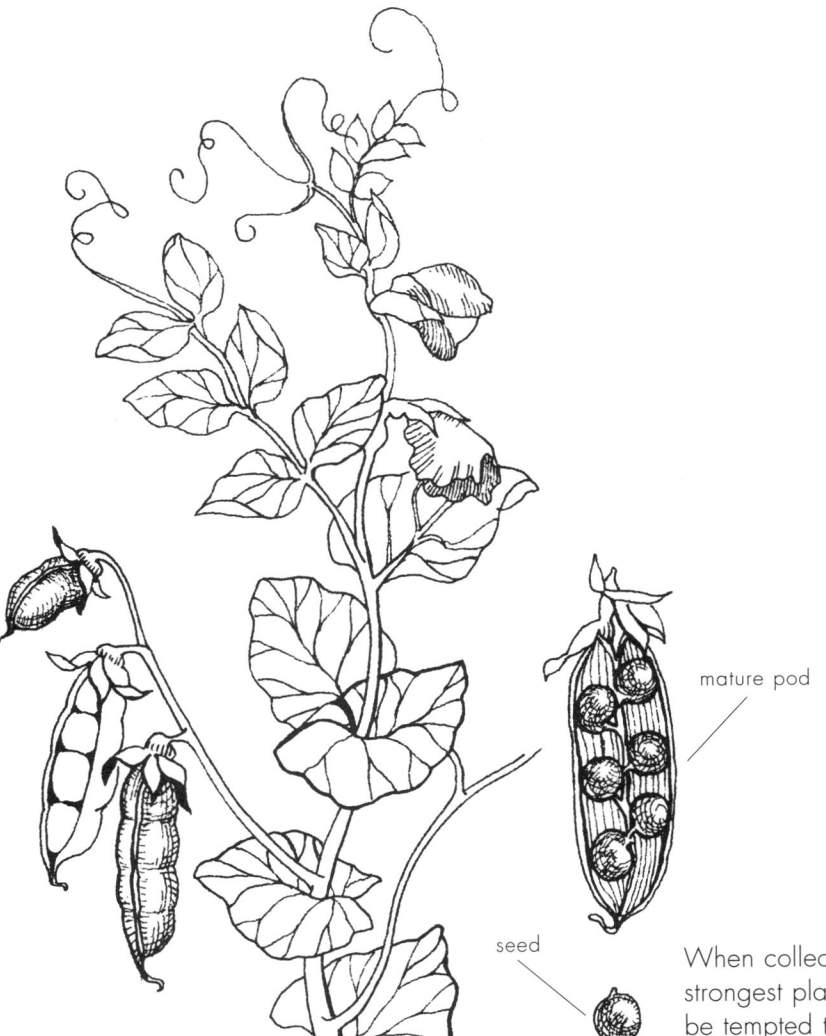

mature pod

seed

HINT FOR SUCCESS

To have an ongoing harvest of peas, make a second sowing three weeks after the first. Better yet, just sow early, medium, and late varieties all at once.

When collecting peas for seed, select the sturdiest, strongest plants with the heaviest crop of peas. Don't be tempted to harvest these peas for food; instead, allow the pods to hang on the plants until the seeds are ripe. Rogue out plants that are weak, discolored, or otherwise inferior.

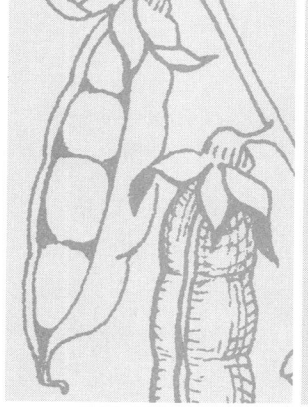

Optimum soil temperature for germination: 40° to 75°F

Germination time at optimum soil temperature: 7 to 20 days

Spacing/thinning: 1 inch; thin to 3 inches. Slight crowding doesn't affect pea production.

Row spacing: Plant peas in double rows (4 to 6 inches apart) or 3-foot-wide blocks.

Planting depth: 1 to 1½ inches

Seed storage requirements: Paper, cloth, or polyethylene bags; should not be stored in sealed container

Seed viability: About 3 years

Harvesting the Seed

1 Peas must be completely ripe in order to germinate well. Let the pea pods remain on the plants until the peas are thoroughly dry and rattling inside the pods, about a month after harvesting the others for eating. If the forecast calls for wet weather before the peas are dry, pull up the plants whole and stack them loosely in a well-ventilated area to continue drying. After a couple of weeks, remove the peas from the pods by hand or by threshing.

2 To thresh, hold plants upside down inside a large trash can and whack them against the sides of the can. Or put the plants inside a burlap bag and walk on them or beat them with a threshing tool (flail). Don't be too rough or you may damage the embryos and cause them to lose viability. When the peas are out of the pods, winnow out the plant debris by pouring the peas from one container to another in a strong breeze; the chaff should blow away and leave the peas clean for storage.

Outdoor Sowing

1 Before sowing peas, soak them for a few hours in tepid water to soften the seed coat. Dusting the seeds with a bacterial inoculant powder before planting will help them gather nitrogen from the atmosphere, resulting in healthier, more productive plants. Legume inoculant is available at many garden centers.

2 Sow peas outdoors in early spring, before the last frost. Poke your index finger down into the soil up to the first knuckle. Drop a pea seed in the hole, and do not cover it with soil. Late snows and spring rains will fall into the hole and give the pea the moisture it needs to begin germination.

Pepper

Capsicum annuum

Peppers are self-pollinating with perfect flowers (both male and female parts on the same flower), but the occasional bee may transfer pollen between varieties. To prevent this from happening, keep different varieties separated by at least 50 feet. Many pepper varieties are F_1 Hybrids. Look for open-pollinated varieties if you are planning to harvest seed. For seed saving, select the plants with the best fruits and no disease problems.

MASTER GARDENING TIPS

▶ Growing peppers in overly rich soil, or overfertilizing them with nitrogen, results in lush growth but fewer fruits.

▶ If you smoke or use tobacco in any form, wash your hands before handling pepper seedlings, to avoid spreading tobacco mosaic disease. This applies to all members of the Solanaceae family (tomatoes, potatoes, petunias, eggplant, etc.). Also, don't grow peppers where other members of the Solanaceae family have grown if the garden had disease problems of any kind in past seasons.

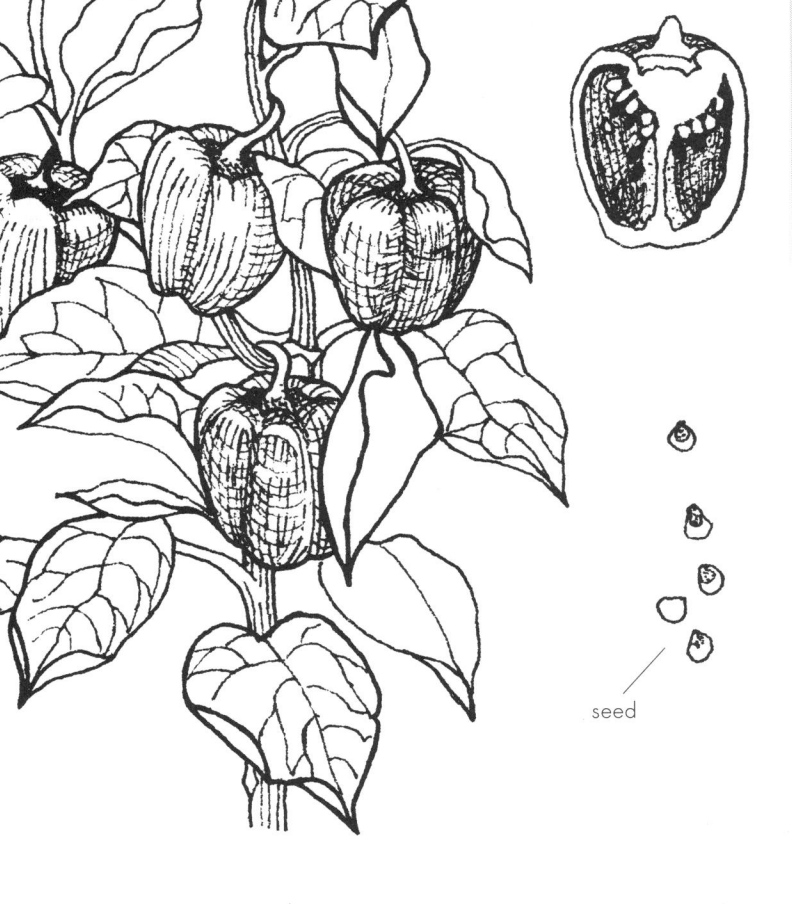

seed

When collecting seed, let peppers ripen beyond the eating stage. The seeds are ready when the fruit turns from green to red (or, in some cases, other colors) and begins to shrivel. The seed must be fully ripe or it may not germinate well. If you have a short growing season, and the peppers have not yet turned color when the first frost threatens in fall, bring the fruits indoors and let them finish ripening in a warm place.

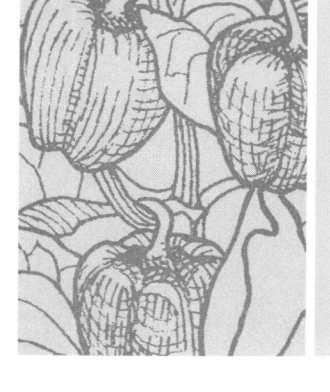

Optimum soil temperature for germination: 65° to 95°F

Germination time at optimum soil temperature: 10 to 15 days

Spacing/thinning: 4 inches; thin to 12 to 18 inches

Row spacing: 2 to 3 feet

Planting depth: ¼ inch

Seed storage requirements: Cool, dry area; sealed container

Seed viability: About 2 years

Harvesting the Seed

Cut open the pepper and remove the cluster of seeds. They should not have to be washed. Dry the seeds for two weeks before storing.

Indoor Sowing

1 In most areas, peppers must be started indoors 6 to 8 weeks before the frost-free date in spring (8 to 12 weeks, if you have a very short growing season). Sow shallowly in flats in a light seed-starting mix and cover with a fine sifting of peat or vermiculite. Water the flat from the bottom, if possible. Soil need not be very moist; pepper seeds will germinate in somewhat dry soil. The soil temperature must be kept consistently high to prevent slow germination or even rotting; provide bottom heat, if you can. Cover the flat with clear glass or plastic until the seeds germinate.

2 When the seedlings have their first true leaves, transplant them from the flat to individual pots. Near the last frost date, begin hardening them off gradually.

3 When the garden soil is warm and the weather is settled, transplant the peppers outside. Plant them a couple of inches deeper than they were in the flat. In cool weather, mulch around the young plants with black paper or plastic, or protect with cloches or row covers. If evening temperatures are still chilly, cover the plants at night, especially if they are in blossom. Very cool or very hot temperatures can cause the blossoms to drop. Protect young pepper plants from cutworms by placing paper collars around the base of the plants.

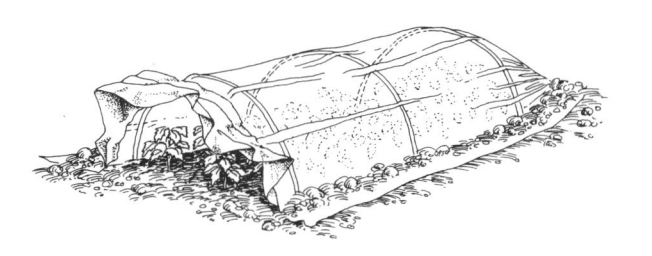

Radish
Raphanus sativus

Radishes are pollinated by bees and will cross readily with other radish varieties, so you should allow only one variety at a time to flower in the garden, to prevent cross-pollination. Radishes may not be the best choice for beginning seed savers; they sometimes have trouble producing seed in hot or dry weather, and bees often bypass the small, inconspicuous radish flowers for other blossoms. Radish seeds germinate quickly and readily, however, and are often sown along with slow-germinating seeds (like carrots and parsley) to mark the planting row.

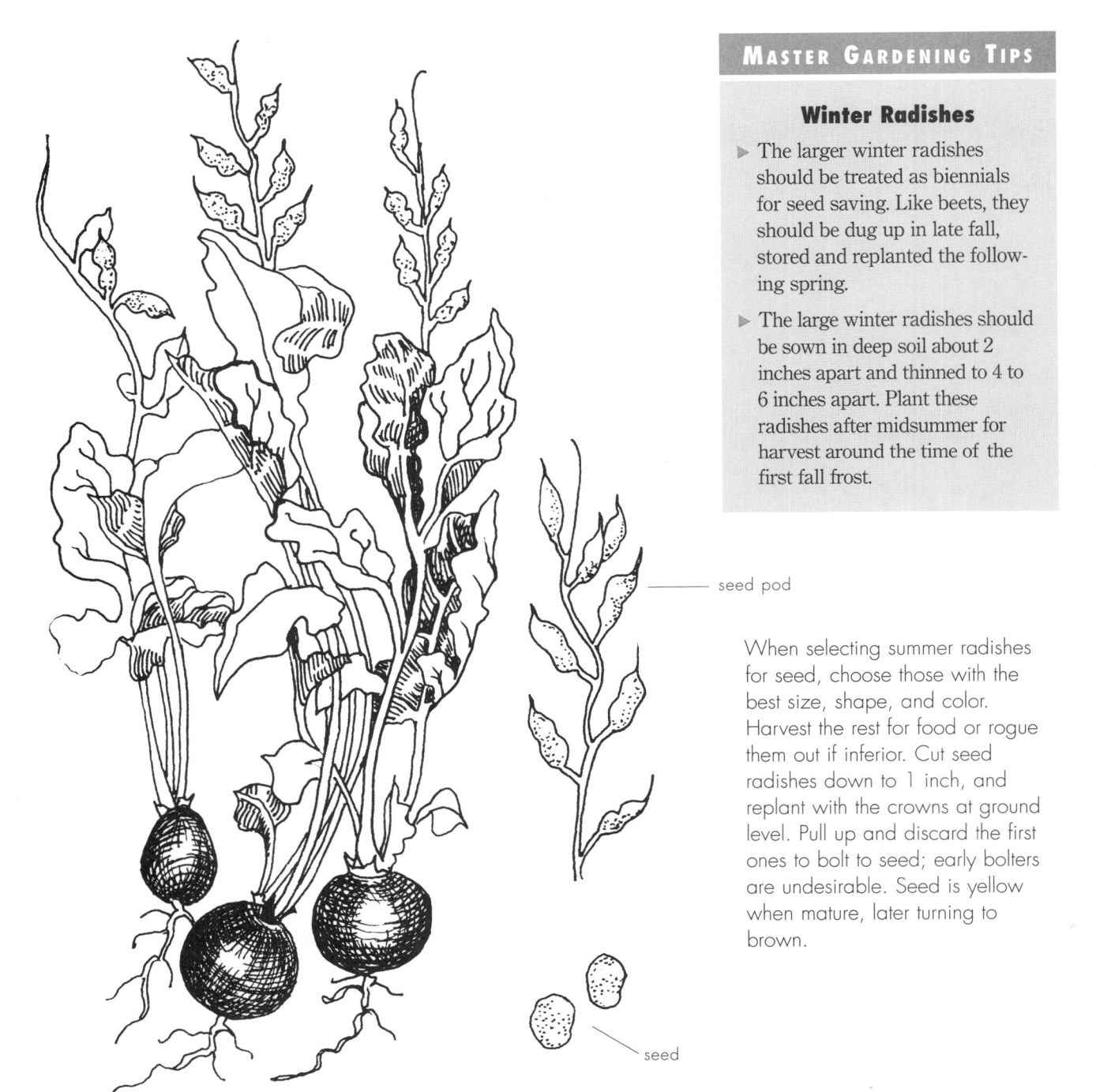

seed pod

seed

MASTER GARDENING TIPS

Winter Radishes

▶ The larger winter radishes should be treated as biennials for seed saving. Like beets, they should be dug up in late fall, stored and replanted the following spring.

▶ The large winter radishes should be sown in deep soil about 2 inches apart and thinned to 4 to 6 inches apart. Plant these radishes after midsummer for harvest around the time of the first fall frost.

When selecting summer radishes for seed, choose those with the best size, shape, and color. Harvest the rest for food or rogue them out if inferior. Cut seed radishes down to 1 inch, and replant with the crowns at ground level. Pull up and discard the first ones to bolt to seed; early bolters are undesirable. Seed is yellow when mature, later turning to brown.

Optimum soil temperature for germination: 45° to 90°F

Germination time at optimum soil temperature: 5 to 10 days

Spacing/thinning: ½ to 1 inch; thin to 2 to 3 inches

Row spacing: 8 to 18 inches

Planting depth: ¼ to ½ inch

Seed storage requirements: Sealed containers; cool, dry area

Seed viability: About 5 years

Harvesting the Seed

Familiar red summer radishes produce green seed-pods by midsummer. These pods will not split open when mature, so you needn't worry about the seed dispersing before it's collected. When the pods turn brown, pull up the plants and then stack or hang them in a well-ventilated spot to dry. Remove the seeds from the pods by hand, or put the pods in a bag and crush them.

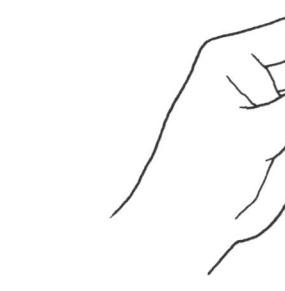

Outdoor Sowing

The small summer radishes are very easy to grow and should be direct-seeded outdoors. They are cool-weather plants; sow seed as soon as the ground can be worked in spring. Since radishes mature all at once and don't keep well, it's best to sow small amounts every two weeks or so for a continuous supply. For a fall crop, plant radishes in late summer or early fall.

Spinach

Spinacia oleracea

Spinach is wind-pollinated, so you may find it difficult to maintain the purity of a certain strain if there are any other varieties growing within a mile of your garden. The best thing you can do is grow only one variety at a time, and weed out undesirable specimens as they appear. Many varieties are F_1 Hybrids, and it may not be worth the time to collect their seed; check what kind you are growing before planning to harvest seed. Although most of the plants are dioecious (having either male or female flowers, but not both), some plants are monoecious (both male and female flowers are on the same plant). Spinach is a cool-weather crop and does not thrive in hot weather, so plant outdoors as soon as the ground can be worked in spring, or sow seed in late summer for fall harvest.

seeds

Spinach flowers, like those of many wind-pollinated plants, are inconspicuous and hard to identify. You'll know the seeds are almost mature when the spinach leaves begin to turn yellow, usually in summer. When selecting plants for seed saving, choose the leafiest ones that are latest to bolt. Hot weather and long days cause spinach to bolt to seed quickly; pull out early-bolting plants and discard.

Optimum soil temperature for germination: 45° to 75°F

Germination time at optimum soil temperature: 7 to 20 days

Spacing/thinning: 1 inch; thin to 4 to 6 inches

Row spacing: 12 to 18 inches

Seed depth: ½ inch

Seed storage requirements: Sealed container; cool, dry area

Seed viability: About 5 years

Harvesting the Seed

When spinach leaves yellow, pull up the plants and strip off the seeds with your hands. Dry the seeds thoroughly before storing.

Indoor or Outdoor Sowing

1 Soak the seeds overnight before planting, or presprout on damp paper towels sealed in a plastic bag kept in the refrigerator for a week or so.

2 Start spinach in flats indoors for later transplanting, or sow directly outdoors.

MASTER GARDENING TIPS

▶ Pick the oldest, largest leaves from spinach to help postpone bolting.

▶ In milder climates, you can even plant the seed in fall (well before the first frost), mulch lightly with straw or hay, and watch the young plants emerge the following spring.

▶ For a continuous supply, make small succession plantings every two weeks through mid-spring, and then start again when the weather turns cooler in late summer or early fall. Spinach is also ideal for sowing in cold frames for winter and early-spring harvest in cold regions.

HINT FOR SUCCESS

The seeds are sometimes susceptible to fungus; soaking them in a 3:1 bleach and water solution for 10 minutes before planting should help ward off fungal attack.

Squash

Cucurbita spp.

Choose open-pollinated squash varieties, rather than the more common F$_1$ Hybrids, if you are planning to harvest seed. Select the most productive plants with the tastiest fruits for seed saving. Squashes are normally pollinated by bees. They will cross-pollinate with other squash varieties but not with other cucurbits, like cucumbers and melons, and not with other squash species (a butternut with a zucchini for example). There are many varieties of squash in each species, so if you're planning to save seed, keep the varieties separated by at least 500 feet, or grow just one variety at a time. If they do happen to cross, the resulting fruit will be edible but not necessarily tasty. This information applies to both summer and winter squashes, as well as to pumpkins.

seeds

MASTER GARDENING TIPS

▶ Inbreeding is not a problem, so you don't have to save seed from several plants to get a good genetic mix. Next year's crop will be just as good as this year's, even if you saved seed from only one plant.

▶ When thinning squash seedlings, it's better to pinch or snip them off rather than to pull them out by the roots, which may disturb the roots of their companions.

▶ Radishes and potatoes planted along with squash may help deter squash borers and other insect pests.

With winter squashes and pumpkins, the seed is ripe when the fruit is mature and ready to be harvested. With summer squashes, however, the fruit must stay on the vine about eight weeks past the stage when it would be harvested for eating. Squash seed is generally collected around the time of the first fall frost.

Optimum soil temperature for germination: 70° to 95°F

Germination time at optimum soil temperature: 7 to 10 days

Spacing/thinning: Hills: 8 to 10 seeds per hill; thin to 3 plants (for vining varieties, a little more space). Rows: 4 to 8 inches; thin to 12 to 18 inches (give vining varieties a little more space).

Row spacing (Summer): Hills or rows, 3 to 4 feet

Row spacing (Winter): Hills: 4 to 5 feet. Rows: 7 to 8 feet (small varieties), 9 feet (large varieties).

Planting depth: ½ to 1 inch

Seed storage requirements: Cool, dry area; sealed container

Seed viability: About 4 years

Harvesting the Seed

1 Squash seeds will gain vigor if allowed to afterripen in the fruit. Removing and storing them can wait for a month or two. To prepare for storage, cut the fruit open, scoop out the seeds, and rinse off the pulp.

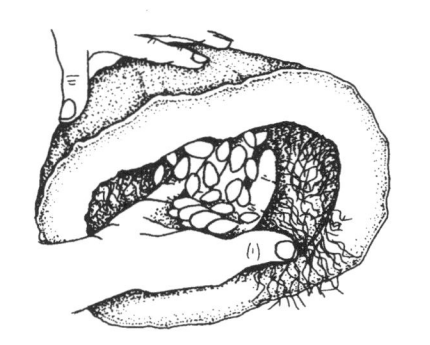

2 Spread out the good seeds to dry for a couple of weeks, cull out any flat ones (plump seeds are viable; flat are not), and store.

Indoor Sowing

Squash and pumpkins don't like to be transplanted, but if you have a short growing season or a cool, wet spring, you can sow seeds indoors in individual pots three weeks before planting out. Or lay the seeds on damp paper towels, roll up the towels, and seal them inside plastic bags. Store in a warm spot until they germinate, then plant up in individual pots until they can be transplanted outside. When you set them in the garden, plant them deeper than they grew in the pot.

Outdoor Sowing

Sow seeds directly outdoors about a week after the last frost. A second sowing in midsummer will make up for losses from pests.

Tomato

Lycopersicon lycopersicum

Tomatoes are a good choice for seed saving. Since they are self-pollinating, they will nearly always "come true" from seed. Because they can occasionally be cross-pollinated by insects, however, grow different varieties as far apart as possible (at least 10 feet).

seed

Save seeds from the fruits of several plants (at least three of each variety) for a larger gene pool. Select early-bearing, productive, disease-resistant plants with good fruits for seed saving. Harvest seeds when the fruits are fully ripe.

MASTER GARDENING TIPS

▶ *Determinate* varieties are sometimes referred to as bush tomatoes; they stop growing at a certain height and do not need staking. *Indeterminate* types are known as vining tomatoes since they continue to grow throughout the season and usually need support.

▶ If you smoke or use tobacco in any form, wash your hands before handling tomato seedlings, to avoid spreading tobacco mosaic disease. Also, don't grow tomatoes where eggplant, potatoes, petunias, or peppers have grown, if your garden had disease problems of any kind in past seasons.

▶ If you're planning to save seeds, beware of hormone sprays. These sprays sometimes are used to prevent blossom drop and help tomatoes ripen more quickly, but the resulting tomatoes are often seedless because the fruit was set chemically rather than by pollination.

▶ In cool weather, mulch around the young plants with black paper or plastic, or protect with cloches or row covers.

▶ Protect seedlings from cutworms by placing paper collars around the base of the plants.

Optimum soil temperature for germination: 60° to 85°F

Germination time at optimum soil temperature: 8 to 10 days

Spacing/thinning (determinate): 3 inches; thin to 12 to 24

Spacing/thinning (indeterminate): 24 to 36 inches

Row spacing: 3 to 4 feet

Planting depth: ¼ to ½ inch

Seed storage requirements: Cool, dry area; sealed container

Seed viability: About 4 years

Harvesting the Seed

1 Cut open the tomato and scoop out the seeds and pulp. Place in a bowl or jar and add a little water. Let sit at room temperature for two to four days and stir once a day to prevent mold from forming. Each day, pour off pulp and seeds that float to the top. The viable seeds will have sunk to the bottom.

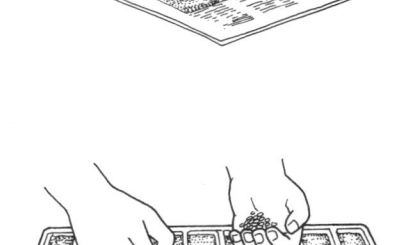

2 After four days, remove the viable seeds, rinse thoroughly, drain, and spread them on newspapers to dry for a week or two. Roll up the paper and seal in a container. When you're ready to sow the seeds, you can simply tear off a piece of paper with a seed on it and plant. The paper will quickly disintegrate.

Indoor Sowing

1 Tomatoes should be started indoors in most areas, about six to eight weeks before the last frost date. Sow seeds in flats or cells, providing bottom heat if possible, for a soil temperature of 70° to 90°F. Tomato seed will not germinate if the soil is too cool. The seeds germinate better in darkness, so cover the flats until the first sprouts appear.

Or lay seeds on damp paper towels, roll up the towels, and place them in a sealed plastic bag in a warm place. When they germinate, plant up in flats or individual pots. Transplant at least once into larger pots, setting them slightly deeper than they were before. Keep the seedlings fairly cool (about 60°F) to keep them from getting leggy.

2 When the garden soil is thoroughly warm and outdoor temperatures remain at 65°F or higher, harden off seedlings and plant outside. Tomato plants should be planted deeper than they were in the pots, to allow additional roots to form along the stems. Make a long, shallow trench and lay the plant in it with the top leaves sticking out.

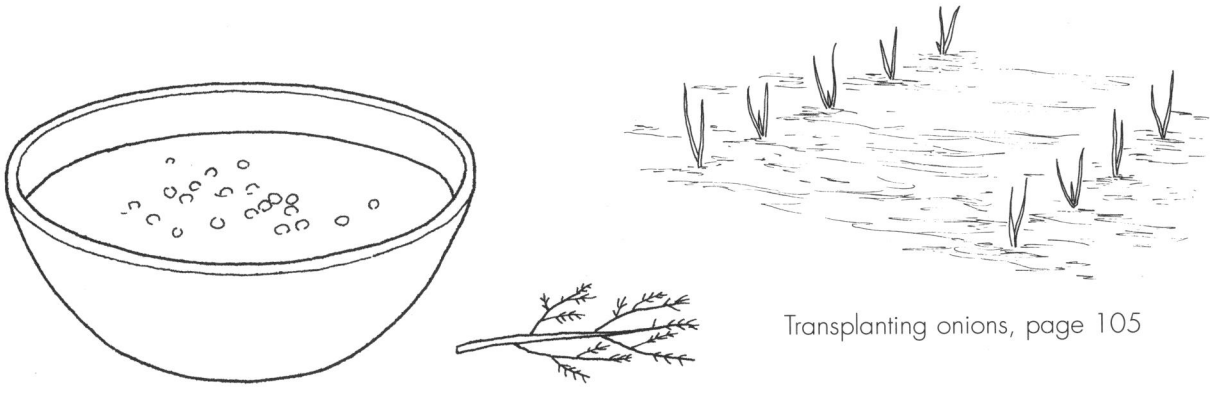

Cabbage, page 94

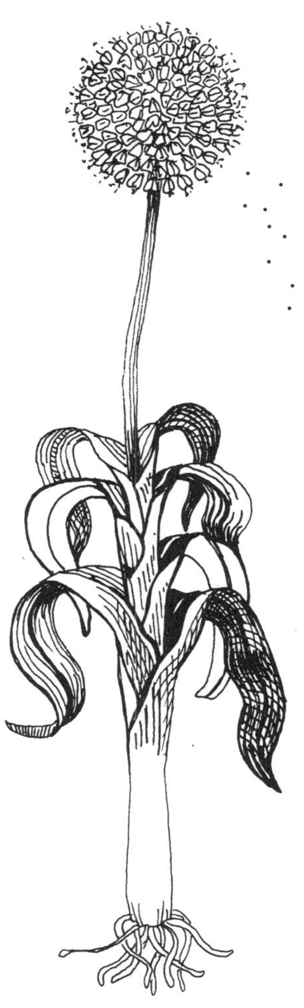

Leeks, page 102

Harvesting asparagus seed, page 91

Transplanting onions, page 105

CHAPTER·6

Biennial and Perennial Vegetables

Biennial vegetables are those that grow and produce a crop in the first year after planting, but don't usually flower and set seed until the second year. Their entire life cycle is completed in two growing seasons. Perennial vegetables, on the other hand, may take several years to produce the first crop, but they return year after year from the same root or crown. You should be able to collect seed from perennial vegetables every year once the plants are established.

Perennial vegetables, including asparagus and chives, are easy to save seed from, although an even more expedient way to propagate these plants might be simply to divide them. Saving seed from biennial vegetables, on the other hand, takes patience and some practice. Since biennials don't flower and set seed until the second year, the ones set aside for seed saving cannot be harvested for eating. Also, in cold regions of the country, biennials may not survive the winter unless they are protected, or even dug up, stored, and replanted the following spring to allow them to complete their growth cycle and set seed during the second season.

If you are planting perennial vegetables, set aside a special place in your garden and put extra effort into preparing the soil well. You won't want to disturb that area once the bed is established.

As with annual vegetables (see page 57), you'll see that we recommend using open-pollinated varieties for any seed-saving activities. Also, refer to information about specific plants to determine how the plant you're growing is pollinated. You will find advice on how to avoid unwanted cross-pollination on page 43. See also the box on heirloom plants on page 3 and the chart on Open-Pollinated Varieties on page 194.

In This Chapter

▪ Asparagus
▪ Beets
▪ Cabbage
▪ Carrots
▪ Cauliflower
▪ Chives
▪ Leeks
▪ Onions
▪ Parsley

Asparagus

Asparagus officinalis

Asparagus, a perennial vegetable, is pollinated by insects, but cross-pollination is rarely a problem because so few varieties are available. You will need both male and female plants to produce seeds. Only female plants will bear seeds, which are found inside red berries. Before flowering, you can tell male from female plants by the stalks. Female plants have thicker but fewer stalks, and males have thinner but more plentiful stalks. To save seed, select disease-resistant, high-yielding plants, and be sure you have both males and females.

MASTER GARDENING TIPS

▶ Asparagus self-seeds readily.

▶ Wild asparagus is not much different from the garden variety; try harvesting seeds from roadside plants to sow in your garden.

▶ Asparagus is usually grown from roots or crowns, but can also be grown from seed if you don't mind waiting one more year to harvest the spears (root-grown asparagus can be harvested in the second year).

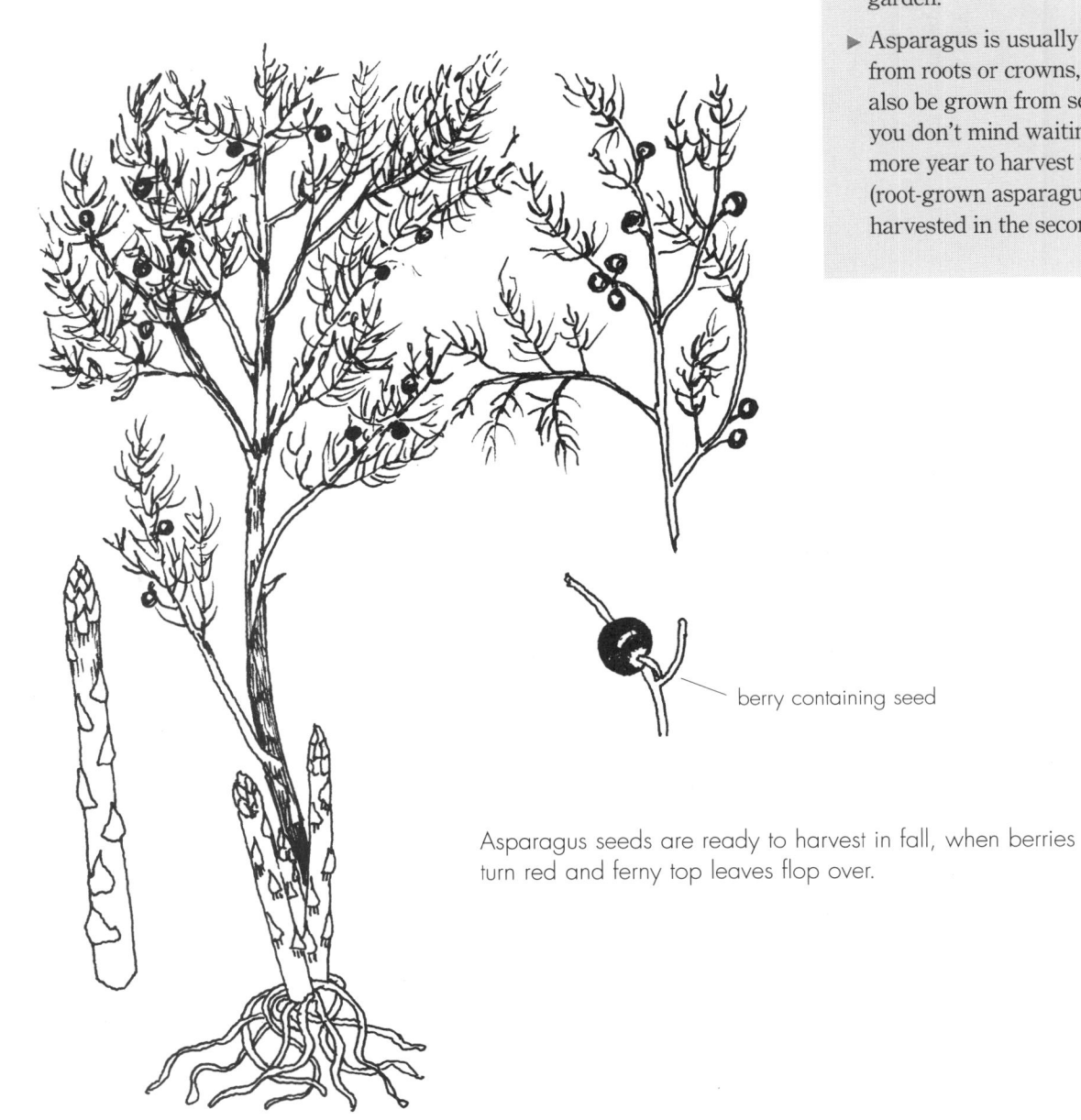

berry containing seed

Asparagus seeds are ready to harvest in fall, when berries turn red and ferny top leaves flop over.

SEED FACTS

Optimum soil temperature for germination: 60° to 85°F

Germination time at optimum soil temperature: 14 to 21 days

Spacing/thinning: Direct-seeding: 3 to 5 inches; thin to 12 inches

Sowing indoors: ½ inch; thin to 2 inches, transplant 12 inches apart

Row spacing: 48 to 72 inches

Planting depth: ½ inch

Seed pretreatment: To soften the tough seed coat, soak the seed for a day or two in lukewarm water, occasionally replenishing the water to keep it warm. Do this just before planting.

Seed storage requirements: Sealed container in cool, dry area

Seed viability: About 3 years

Harvesting the Seed

1 Cut asparagus top off and hang to dry.

2 Soak berries in water for an hour, until you can remove the fruit easily from the seed.

3 Spread seed on a tray and keep in a warm, dry, airy place until seeds are thoroughly dry. Store in a sealed container in a cool, dry area.

Indoor Sowing

You can start seeds indoors six to eight weeks before the last spring frost date. Despite their fragile appearance, the seedlings transplant well.

Outdoor Sowing

Asparagus seeds are usually sown directly in a nursery bed in spring in the North or fall in the South. In either case, transplant to a permanent growing area the following spring.

MASTER GARDENING TIP

Alternate Method for Removing Seed

Place berries in a bag and crush, then put pulp and seeds in a bowl of water until viable seeds sink to bottom. Drain off remaining seeds and pulp. When seeds are clean, spread them out to dry for about a week before storing.

Beets
Beta vulgaris

Since beets are biennial, they are tricky for beginning seed savers. They don't produce a seed stalk until the second year, so in most areas they must be dug up and stored after the first year, and replanted the following spring. Beets' lightweight pollen is carried long distances, and will cross with other members of the species, such as Swiss chard. If growing Swiss chard nearby, and you wish to save seed from your beets, don't let the chard flower at the same time the beets do.

Many varieties of beets are F_1 Hybrids; choose open-pollinated varieties if you are planning to harvest seed.

year 1

year 2

seed balls

Beet seeds are mature when brown. Beets produce a lot of seed. In fact, each "seed" is actually an aggregate of five or six seeds commonly called a seed ball.

MASTER GARDENING TIPS

▶ Six beet plants should provide plenty of seed, but you might want to store a few more in case some don't make it through winter storage.

▶ As beets grow, rogue out those that have poor leaf or root quality. Select only those with the best color, shape, and size, and don't save seed from a beet that bolts to seed the first year.

▶ Mix bonemeal into the soil before sowing to promote good root development.

▶ It is difficult to transplant beets, so avoid starting them indoors.

▶ Sow seed in summer so beets won't get too big by their first fall.

▶ Since the flowers don't always accept their own pollen, put in at least three plants.

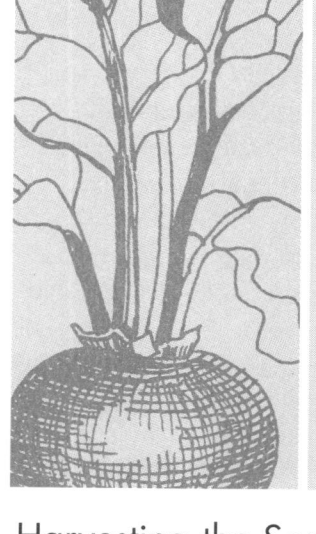

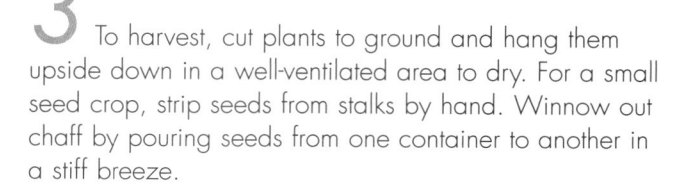

SEED FACTS

Optimum soil temperature for germination: 50° to 85°F

Germination time at optimum soil temperature: 5 to 20 days

Spacing/thinning: 1 to 2 inches; thin to 3 inches

Row spacing: 18 to 24 inches. For greens only, space rows 12 inches apart.

Planting depth: ½ inch

Seed pretreatment: Beet seeds have a germination inhibitor in their coats, which makes germination unpredictable. To dissolve this inhibitor and soften the seed coat, soak the seeds in water overnight before planting.

Seed storage requirements: Sealed container in cool, dry place

Seed viability: About 4 years

Harvesting the Seed

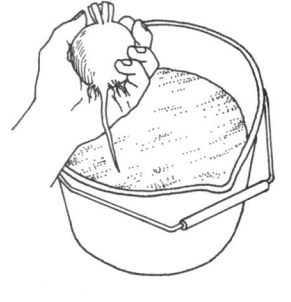

1 Select beets a couple of inches in diameter and dig up before first hard frost in fall. Cut leafy tops to 1 inch. Bury beets in damp sand or sawdust and store in a cool (40° to 50°F), humid place for the winter. In a mild climate, you can leave beets in the ground through winter and allow them to go to seed in the spring.

2 When soil can be worked in spring, throw out beets withered in storage and replant sound ones outdoors about 2 feet apart — the crowns just below the soil level. The plant will produce a tall, branched stalk loaded with tiny flowers.

3 To harvest, cut plants to ground and hang them upside down in a well-ventilated area to dry. For a small seed crop, strip seeds from stalks by hand. Winnow out chaff by pouring seeds from one container to another in a stiff breeze.

Outdoor Sowing

Sow them directly outdoors in early spring, a month before last expected frost. Press the seeds firmly into the ground to give them good contact with the soil; this helps germination. Beets tolerate light frost, but a severe freeze damages plants, causing them to bolt when weather warms up. Make a second sowing in mid- to late summer for beets to harvest in fall or to store over winter.

Cabbage
Brassica oleracea

Cabbage (a biennial) will cross with other brassicas like broccoli, Brussels sprouts, kale, kohlrabi, and cauliflower unless isolated. If you are planning to save seed, keep cabbage separated from other plants by 200 feet, or put a row of barrier plants in between varieties. You can also stagger your plantings so that different varieties bloom at different times, but you'll have to persuade your neighbors to do the same.

Many cabbage varieties are F_1 Hybrids; choose open-pollinated varieties if you are planning to harvest seed. Rogue out inferior plants before they bloom, so they don't pass their pollen to the good plants.

As a biennial, cabbage produces seed the second year; you must store plants over winter and replant in spring to save seed. Since cabbage flowers don't always accept their own pollen, select at least three plants to guarantee seed set.

brown seed pods

yellow seed pods

seeds

MASTER GARDENING TIPS

▶ When starting cabbage indoors, don't let the nighttime temperature rise above 60°F. Cabbage is a cool-weather crop and can't take the heat.

▶ Cabbage seed will germinate readily; it's likely that every seed you sow will sprout, so sow the seeds thinly in the flat, using tweezers. Otherwise, you may have to thin out more than you keep.

▶ Cabbage is a heavy feeder and requires consistent soil moisture. Mix manure or compost in the planting holes, and mulch the plants to keep the soil cool and moist.

In the second year, cabbage produces a very tall stalk with branches of yellow flowers that develop brown seedpods. When the pods turn yellow, the seed is ready for harvest.

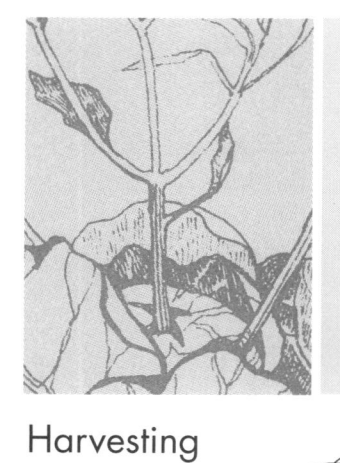

Optimum soil temperature for germination: 45° to 95°F

Germination time at optimum soil temperature: 8 to 14 days

Spacing/thinning: 2 to 3 inches; thin to 12 to 18 inches

Row spacing: 2 to 3 feet

Planting depth: ¼ to ½ inch

Seed storage requirements: Sealed container in cool, dry area

Seed viability: About 5 years

Harvesting the Seed

1 In the first year, select disease-resistant plants with firm, table-ready heads. Pull up with roots intact, trim off outermost leaves, and store plants in a cold (around 32°F), humid place with good air circulation.

2 When the ground can be worked early the next spring, replant the heads 2 to 3 feet apart, a little deeper than the year before. Each cabbage grows a 5-foot-tall flower stalk that should be staked. To help it emerge, cut a 1-inch-deep X into the top of the head after planting.

3 Watch as the brown seedpods turn yellow, so that you catch the seeds before dispersal. At this point, cut stalks and spread them out on a sheet to dry. Many seeds will spill onto the sheet; thresh out the rest by placing them in a bag and beating with your hands. Pass seeds through a screen to clean, or winnow them.

HINTS FOR SUCCESS

First-Year Storage Suggestions

▶ In mild climates, simply heap soil around the cabbage heads, covering about three-quarters of the way up, and leave them over winter.

▶ If you find any cabbage rotting in storage, throw it away immediately.

Indoor Sowing

Start early and midseason cabbage varieties indoors in flats, four to six weeks before transplanting. Transplant seedlings once into individual containers, then harden off and plant outdoors up to a month before last spring frost.

Outdoor Sowing

Sow late varieties directly in the garden, allowing enough time for the heads to mature before the first hard frost.

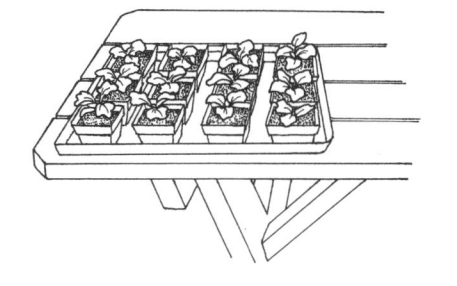

Carrots
Daucus carota var. *sativus*

Carrots, which are biennials, are insect-pollinated and will cross with other varieties in the same species. They also cross with the common roadside weed Queen Anne's lace, so if you plan to collect seed, mow any weedy areas before carrots bloom. Try to keep seed carrots separated from other varieties by 1,000 feet, if possible.

Many carrot varieties are F_1 Hybrids; choose open-pollinated varieties if you are planning to harvest seed. Throughout the growing season, rogue out any inferior plants with small or misshapen roots, and choose the healthiest looking carrots for seed saving.

▶ To mark the row while you're waiting for the carrots to germinate, sow radish seeds along the same row. The radishes germinate quickly and are ready to harvest long before the carrots.

▶ Bonemeal mixed into the soil before sowing will promote good root development.

▶ Be diligent about weeding around carrot seedlings; they have a hard time competing with weeds.

▶ Thin carrots soon after they come up, when they're only 1 or 2 inches tall. To avoid damaging neighboring plants, snip out unwanted seedlings with scissors rather than pulling them out. Thin more vigorously in heavy soil.

▶ For a continuous supply of carrots, make succession plantings every couple of weeks from spring until midsummer. Keep the soil moist to ensure good germination and healthy growth.

seeds

In the second year, flowers develop on a tall, branched stalk. Seed ripens from the top branches to the bottom. Harvest seed when seed heads turn brown in early fall.

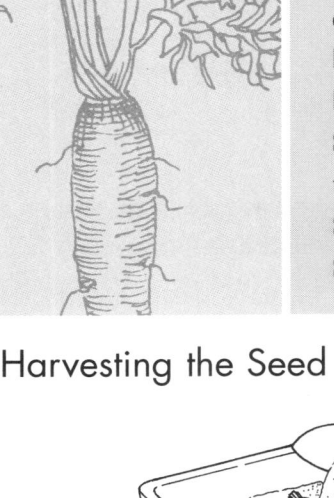

Optimum soil temperature for germination: 45° to 85°F

Germination time at optimum soil temperature: 7 to 20 days (or up to a month in cold soil)

Spacing/thinning: First thin to 1 inch; when the roots are "baby carrot" size, thin early varieties to 2 inches, later varieties to 3 to 4 inches.

Row spacing: 16 to 30 inches

Planting depth: ¼ to ½ inch

Seed pretreatment: To hasten germination, pour boiling water over seeds and soak until water has cooled. Or simply soak seeds overnight in water before planting.

Seed storage requirements: Sealed container in cool, dry area

Seed viability: About 3 years

Harvesting the Seed

1 Carrots produce seed the second year, so if you're saving seed, roots must be stored over winter and replanted in spring. Dig up roots before first hard frost in fall, and cut leafy tops to 1 inch. Bury carrots in a container of damp sand or sawdust and store in cold (around 32°F), humid place for winter.

3 Harvest seed when topmost seed heads turn brown in early fall. Seeds must be fully ripe in order to germinate well. Seed heads will begin to shatter two months after flowering, so tie bags over the seed heads to avoid losing any seed. To harvest seed, pull up plants, or just cut off seed heads, and lay out to dry. Rub off seeds when completely dry, and pass through a screen to clean and remove the chaff.

2 When soil can be worked in the spring, throw out withered carrots and replant sound ones outdoors in moist soil 1 to 2 feet apart. Set crown of carrot at or just below soil surface. Allow tops to grow and produce a tall, branched flower stalk. Flowers will develop, and seeds will ripen from top branches to bottom.

MASTER GARDENING TIPS

▶ In a mild climate, leave carrots in the ground through winter and allow to go to seed in spring.

▶ Beware of overplanting carrots: The seeds are fine, and it's hard to see how many you're sowing. Try mixing them with soil, sand, wood ashes, or dry coffee grounds to separate the seeds and make sowing easier.

Outdoor Sowing

Carrots should be direct-seeded in the garden — never transplant them. Sow seeds in deep, loose soil when all danger of frost is past and the ground can be well worked. Thin to 2 inches (see chart).

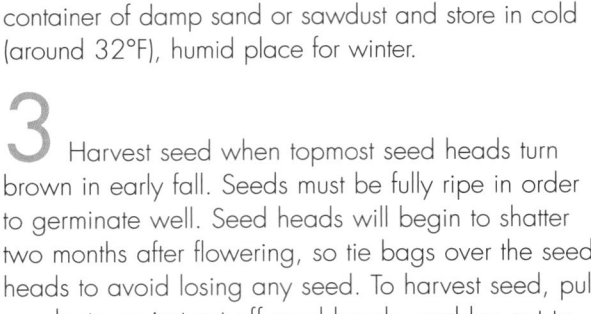

Cauliflower
Brassica oleracea

Cauliflower, which is a biennial, will cross with other brassicas like broccoli, Brussels sprouts, kale, kohlrabi, and cabbage unless it is isolated. If saving seed, try to keep cauliflower separated from these other plants by at least 200 feet, or put a row of barrier plants in between varieties to throw off pollinating insects. Or stagger your plantings so that different varieties bloom at different times. This technique will work only if you can cooperate with neighbors who may also be growing brassicas.

Many cauliflower varieties are F_1 Hybrids; choose open-pollinated varieties if you're planning to harvest seed. Select the healthiest, firmest heads for seed saving. Rogue out inferior plants before bloom, so they don't pass pollen to the good plants.

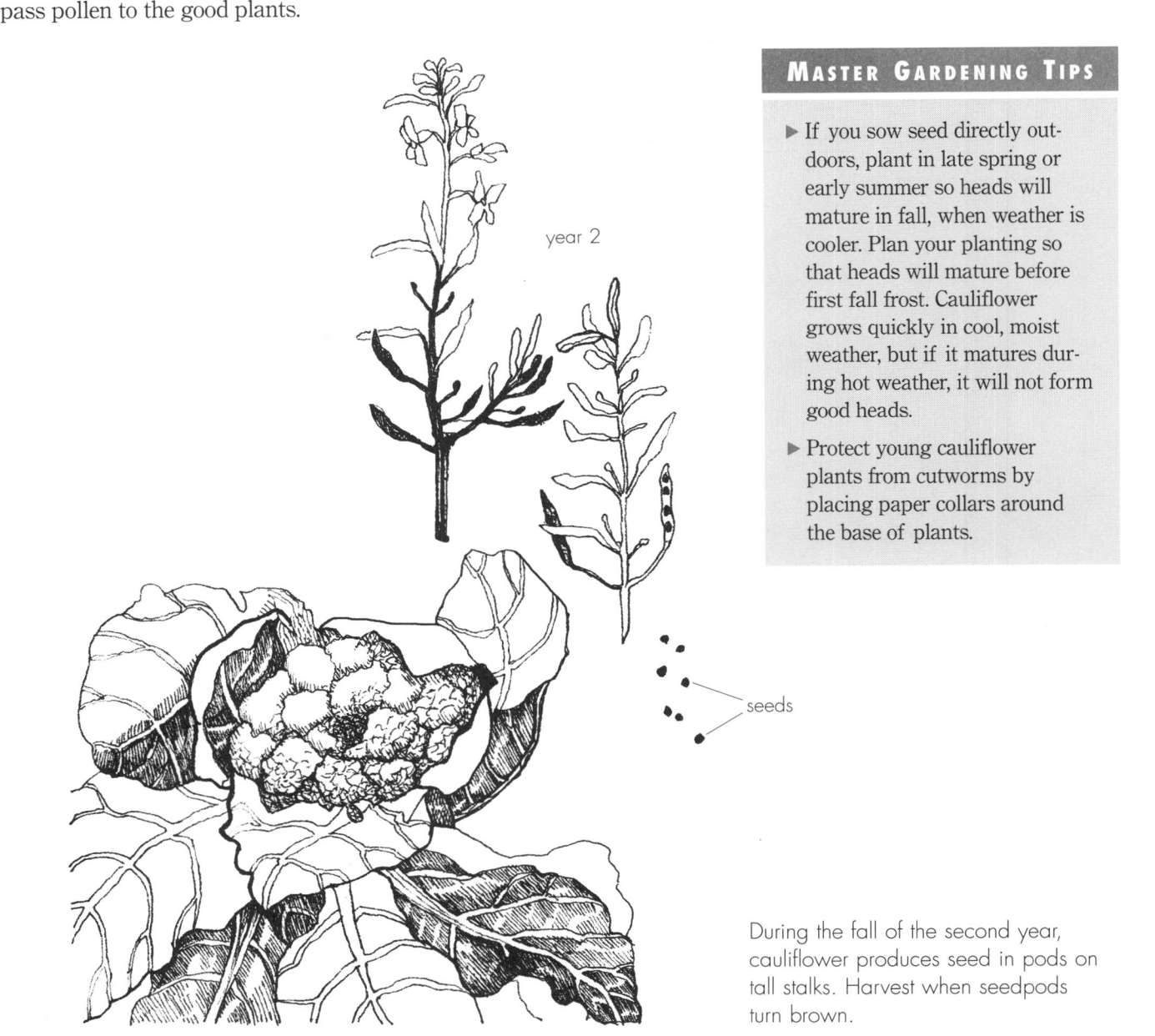

year 2

seeds

MASTER GARDENING TIPS

▶ If you sow seed directly outdoors, plant in late spring or early summer so heads will mature in fall, when weather is cooler. Plan your planting so that heads will mature before first fall frost. Cauliflower grows quickly in cool, moist weather, but if it matures during hot weather, it will not form good heads.

▶ Protect young cauliflower plants from cutworms by placing paper collars around the base of plants.

During the fall of the second year, cauliflower produces seed in pods on tall stalks. Harvest when seedpods turn brown.

year 1

SEED FACTS

Optimum soil temperature for germination: 45° to 85°F

Germination time at optimum soil temperature: 8 to 14 days

Spacing/thinning: 2 inches; thin to 18 to 24 inches

Row spacing: 2 to 3 feet

Planting depth: ¼ to ½ inch

Seed storage requirements: Sealed container in cool, dry area

Seed viability: About 5 years

Harvesting the Seed

1 Dig up cauliflower plants in early fall of the first year and store them over the winter in a cool place, roots up.

2 Set out plants 2 to 3 feet apart at last frost in spring. They will produce a tall stalk of yellow flowers, followed by seedpods.

3 Cut down stalks when the seedpods turn brown in fall, and lay out on a sheet to continue drying. Some seeds will spill out; thresh out the rest by placing seedpods in a bag and beating with your hands. Pass seeds through a screen to clean and remove the chaff, or they can be winnowed.

Indoor Sowing

Start early crops indoors in flats, five to seven weeks before transplanting to the garden. When seedlings have four or five true leaves, transplant into individual containers. Harden off before planting outdoors, no earlier than two or three weeks before last frost date. Water transplants daily, and keep shaded.

Outdoor Sowing

Start seed in a cold frame in early fall. After six weeks, transplant into individual containers and leave in a cool, protected growing area for the winter. Those that survive are the hardiest for seed saving.

Chives

Allium schoenoprasum

Chives, which are perennials, are pollinated by bees, but there's no need to worry that they will cross with onions or leeks. Select the healthiest, thickest plants for seed saving.

MASTER GARDENING TIPS

▶ For year-round harvest, grow chives in pots on a sunny windowsill, or dig up a clump in fall and bring it indoors to continue growing over the winter.

▶ Be sure to keep your chives well weeded. They have shallow roots and cannot compete with weeds for water.

▶ If you're planning to save seed, harvest only the outer leaves for the kitchen.

seeds

Chives produce a very ornamental, rounded, pinkish purple flower head. When tiny black seeds begin to appear, they are ripe to harvest. Seeds ripen gradually but the flower heads shatter readily, so be sure to watch them closely.

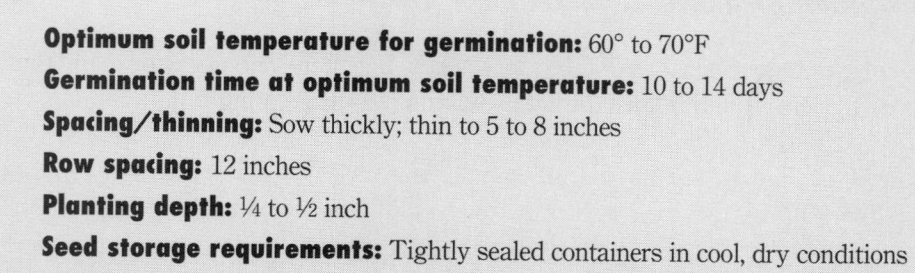

Optimum soil temperature for germination: 60° to 70°F

Germination time at optimum soil temperature: 10 to 14 days

Spacing/thinning: Sow thickly; thin to 5 to 8 inches

Row spacing: 12 inches

Planting depth: ¼ to ½ inch

Seed storage requirements: Tightly sealed containers in cool, dry conditions

Seed viability: About 2 years

Harvesting the Seed

Cut off seed heads when seeds blacken. Dry for several weeks, then rub off seeds with your hands.

Indoor Sowing

1 Chives can be started indoors in flats or individual pots eight weeks before transplanting outdoors. Seeds germinate better in darkness, so cover containers until first sprouts appear. You can grow pots of chives on a sunny windowsill indoors for culinary use year round.

2 If you started the seeds in flats, transplant them to pots when they're about 2 inches tall. Plant outside in early spring.

Outdoor Sowing

Chives can be direct-seeded outdoors as soon as soil can be worked.

Leeks

Allium ampeloprasum var. *porrum*

Leeks, which are biennials, are pollinated by bees, but they don't cross with onions or chives. To avoid cross-pollination of several different leek varieties, however, arrange plantings so different varieties don't bloom at the same time.

Leeks are very hardy, so they do not have to be stored over winter and replanted the next spring. Leave selected leeks in the ground over winter. In severe climates, hill up the soil around leeks, or mulch with hay. Large leeks can be stored in a root cellar, but they will generally do better in the ground over the winter.

During the fall of the first year, rogue out any inferior plants and keep the biggest, best ones for seed production.

umbel

seeds

During the second year, leeks produce a tall stalk with a ball of flowers (known as an umbel) at the top. The seeds that form inside papery capsules are ready to harvest when they being to show.

MASTER GARDENING TIP

Another Propagation Method

If you leave your leeks in the ground over the winter, they will develop small bulblets around the base in spring. These bulblets can be planted for a new crop of leeks.

Optimum soil temperature for germination: 70° to 75°F

Germination time at optimum soil temperature: 10 to 14 days

Spacing/thinning: ¼ inch; thin to 1 to 2 inches, later to 4 to 6 inches

Row spacing: 12 to 36 inches

Planting depth: ¼ inch

Seed storage requirements: Sealed container in cool, dry area

Seed viability: About 3 years

Harvesting the Seed

In fall, when you can see the seeds inside their capsules, cut off the entire seed head and place it in a bag to dry. When seeds are dry, rub the heads to remove them, and store in a container.

Indoor Sowing

1 For an early crop, sow seeds thickly in flats indoors 8 to 12 weeks before the last spring frost date. Seeds need warmth for germination, but once seedlings are visible, place them in a cool area with good light.

2 When the seedlings are about 3 inches tall, transplant into individual containers at least 10 inches deep (leeks develop deep roots).

3 As soon as frost danger is past, when young plants are ¼ to ½ inch thick, harden them off and transplant outdoors. Dig a 6-inch-deep trench and set the transplants in it, 4 to 6 inches apart. Be sure soil is deep and well worked, and avoid disturbing the roots when transplanting.

4 Fill in trench with loose soil. Only a few inches of leaves should be showing above ground; this keeps the edible (underground) part of leeks tender and white, while aboveground leaves turn green and tough.

Outdoor Sowing

5 Throughout the season, continue piling up soil around each plant, to exclude light and blanch as much of the stem as possible.

Sow as early as possible to give leeks enough time to mature. In mild climates, leeks can be planted in fall for winter harvest.

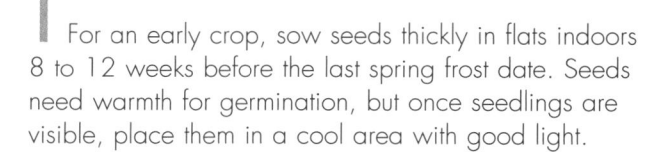

Onions

Allium cepa

Onions, which are biennial, are often grown from "sets," or small bulbs, but onions grown from seed are of better quality and less prone to disease. Onions flower and form seed in the second year of growth and are cross-pollinated by bees. To preserve the purity of a certain strain for seed saving, make sure you don't have different varieties blossoming at the same time. You can also separate the varieties by at least 100 feet, but this only reduces the likelihood of crossing; it doesn't prevent it. Onions will not cross with leeks or chives.

Many varieties of onions are F_1 Hybrids. Plant open-pollinated varieties if you're planning to harvest seed. During fall of the first year, rogue out any inferior plants and keep the biggest and best ones for seed production. Don't save seed from an onion that bolts the first year.

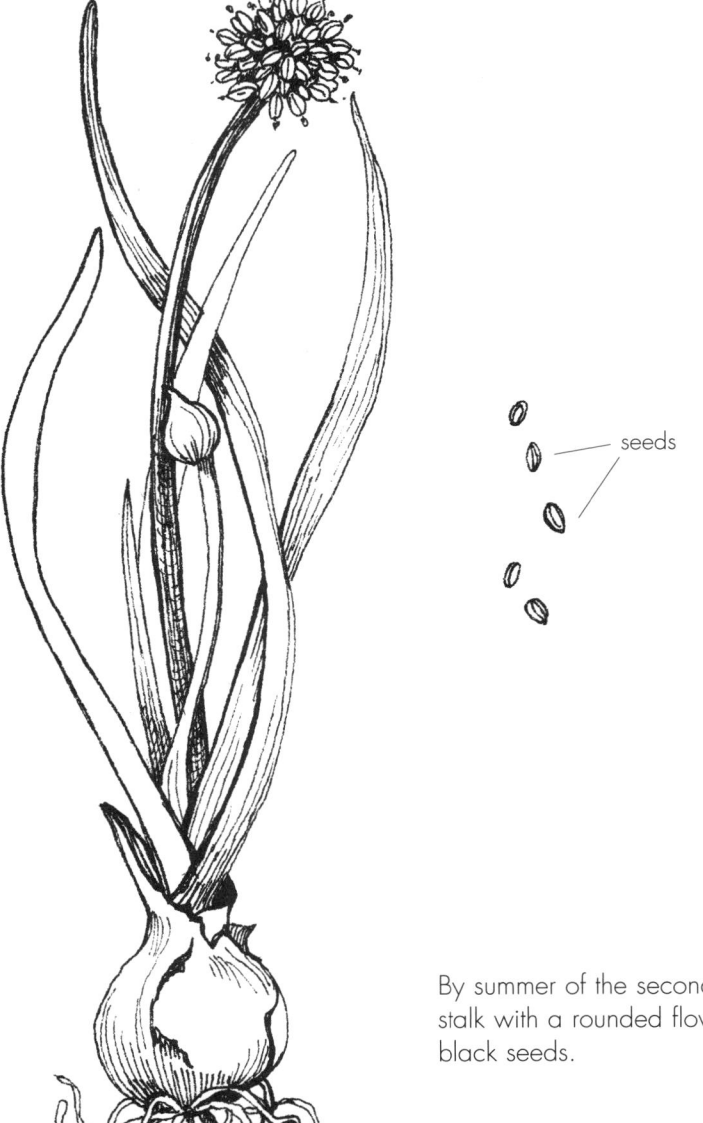

seeds

MASTER GARDENING TIPS

- ► Bunching onions *(Allium fistulosum)* have different sowing and seed-saving requirements from the globe onions discussed here.

- ► Be sure to keep your onions well weeded. They have shallow roots and cannot compete with weeds for water.

- ► Onions require a long growing season to form good bulbs, so if you have a short growing season, start them earlier — up to 14 weeks before transplanting outdoors.

- ► Keep an eye on onions in storage. Some, such as sweet onions, do not store well. Also, onions with thick necks do not keep well; use them for eating rather than seed saving.

- ► In a warm climate, leave onions in ground over winter.

By summer of the second year, each onion produces a tall stalk with a rounded flower head (umbel), which bears black seeds.

Optimum soil temperature for germination: 50° to 95°F

Germination time at optimum soil temperature: 5 to 14 days

Spacing/thinning: Sow thickly (2 to 3 seeds per inch); thin to 3 to 4 inches

Row spacing: 16 to 24 inches

Planting depth: ½ inch (¼ inch in heavy soil)

Seed storage requirements: Tightly sealed containers in cool, dry conditions

Seed viability: 1 to 2 years

Harvesting the Seed

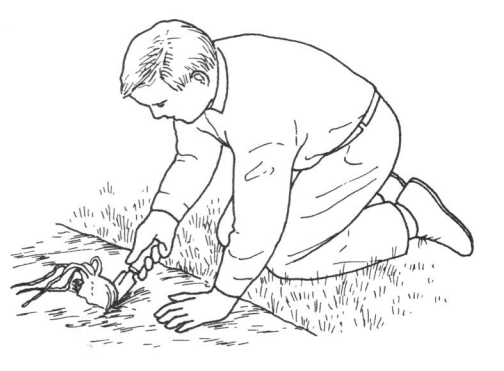

1 Dig up your best onions in fall of the first year and store in a cool (32° to 40°F), dry place over winter.

2 When ground can be worked in spring, replant onions 3 to 4 inches apart, covering bulbs with ½ inch of soil. Make a cut in the top of the onion before replanting to help the seed stalk emerge more quickly.

3 Harvest onion seeds by cutting off seed heads, drying for several weeks, and rubbing off seeds with your hands. Seeds ripen gradually but flower heads shatter easily, so be sure to watch them closely.

Indoor Sowing

Start fresh seeds indoors in flats four to six weeks before transplanting to the garden. Seeds germinate better in darkness, so cover flats until first sprouts appear. Harden seedlings off, and transplant outdoors no earlier than six weeks before last spring frost.

Outdoor Sowing

Onions can be direct-seeded in the garden in early spring. In most areas, you'll have to dig these up in fall and store over the winter, to be replanted the following spring.

Parsley
Petroselinum crispum

Parsley flowers and forms seed in the second year of growth and is cross-pollinated by insects. If you're trying to preserve the purity of a certain strain for seed saving, make sure you don't have different varieties blossoming at the same time. Don't save seed from parsley that bolts in the first year.

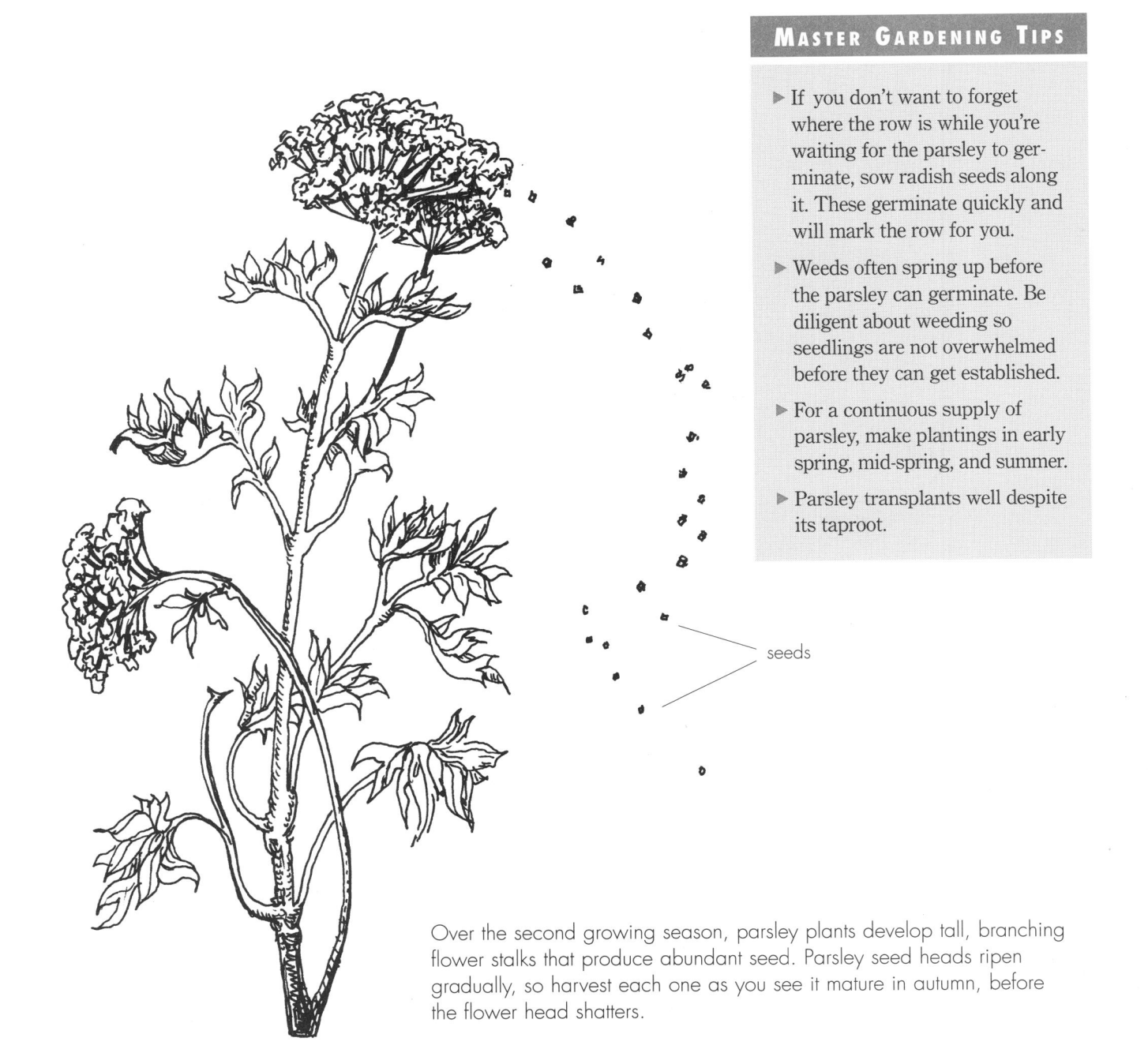

seeds

MASTER GARDENING TIPS

▶ If you don't want to forget where the row is while you're waiting for the parsley to germinate, sow radish seeds along it. These germinate quickly and will mark the row for you.

▶ Weeds often spring up before the parsley can germinate. Be diligent about weeding so seedlings are not overwhelmed before they can get established.

▶ For a continuous supply of parsley, make plantings in early spring, mid-spring, and summer.

▶ Parsley transplants well despite its taproot.

Over the second growing season, parsley plants develop tall, branching flower stalks that produce abundant seed. Parsley seed heads ripen gradually, so harvest each one as you see it mature in autumn, before the flower head shatters.

Optimum soil temperature for germination: 70° to 80°F

Germination time at optimum soil temperature: 21 days

Spacing/thinning: ½ inch; thin to 4 to 12 inches

Row spacing: 12 to 18 inches

Planting depth: ¼ inch

Seed storage requirements: Dry, cool conditions

Seed viability: 1 or 2 years at the most

Harvesting the Seed

Cut off seed heads, dry thoroughly, and shake inside a paper bag to release seeds. Rub off seeds when completely dry, and pass through a screen to clean and remove chaff.

Indoor Sowing

1 Parsley seed germinates very slowly because of a growth-inhibiting compound on the seed coat. Dissolve it by soaking seeds in warm water for two days just before sowing. Change the water a few times and rinse seeds before planting.

2 Sow seeds thinly in flats or individual pots, cover to exclude light, and firm soil. When seedlings are 1 inch tall, transplant outdoors, weather permitting.

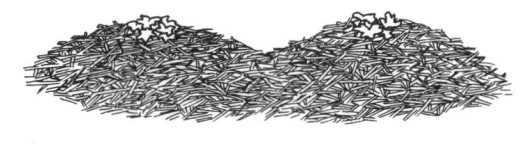

3 Select the best plants for seed saving, transplant them to a separate growing area (if necessary), and mulch lightly with leaves or hay after a couple of heavy frosts. Check the plants for new growth in spring, and remove the mulch when you see green leaves.

Outdoor Sowing

Sowing parsley outdoors in fall is not recommended due to its erratic and unreliable germination qualities, but if you wish to try it, be sure to soak seeds in warm water for 24 hours or freeze overnight to speed germination.

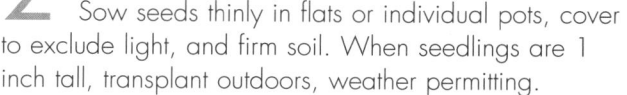

HINT FOR SUCCESS

In his book *Heirloom Vegetables*, Benjamin Watson suggests this method to speed up germination of parsley seed: Place planted (unwatered) flat in a large, sealed plastic freezer bag and set in freezer for one to three days of chilling. Remove bag from freezer but don't remove flat from bag until plants have begun to germinate. Water, and place under fluorescent lights or in a sunny window.

Marigold, page 116

Snapdragon, page 136

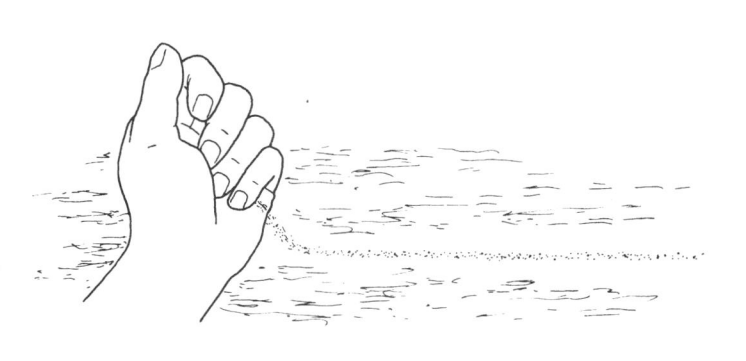

Sowing poppy seeds, page 129

Overwintering sweet pea seedlings, page 143

~ C H A P T E R · 7 ~

Annual Flowers

Annuals are those plants that complete their entire growth cycle in the course of one year. When you plant seeds for annuals, they will sprout, grow, blossom, set seed, and die before a year has passed, provided the growing season in your area is long enough. In cold regions where the growing season is short, seed for annuals should be started indoors in late winter, to get a head start on growth. Otherwise, the plants may not have enough time to form blossoms and seeds before frost comes again in fall.

Because they are easy to grow from seed and usually produce results so quickly — and often with a gratifying show of color — annuals are popular as bedding plants and cutting flowers in many gardens. Some will even reseed themselves and pop up in unexpected places the following year. Annuals usually produce a good amount of viable seed and are therefore a good choice for seed collecting. Unlike the seed of perennials, which often requires chilling before it will germinate, most annual seeds need no special treatment before sowing. However, many will not survive very cold temperatures, so you should wait until warm weather arrives before sowing them directly outdoors.

Some perennial plants can survive over the winter in only the warmest regions of the country, but they can be grown as annuals in colder regions. For all practical purposes, these plants, which are often termed tender perennials, can be treated as annuals. We have included some of those in this chapter: four-o'clocks, snapdragons, and flowering tobacco.

In This Chapter

- Bachelor's Buttons
- Cosmos
- Four-O'Clocks
- Marigold
- Morning Glory
- Moss Rose
- Nasturtium
- Pansy
- Petunia
- Poppy
- Poppy, California
- Pot Marigold
- Scarlet Sage
- Snapdragon
- Spider Flower
- Sunflower
- Sweet Pea
- Tobacco, Flowering
- Zinnia

Bachelor's Buttons
Centaurea cyanus

Bachelor's buttons are cross-pollinated by insects. If you want to pre-serve the purity of a certain strain for seed saving, grow only one variety at a time. Except for named varieties (hybrids and other cultivars), most bachelor's buttons will come true from seed. If a cross should occur, blue will be the genetically dominant color, followed by pink and then white. The plants frequently self-sow.

MASTER GARDENING TIP

Bachelor's buttons don't mind being crowded, but they produce bigger flowers if they have plenty of breathing room.

seed head

seeds

When the plant has finished flowering for the season, it is time to harvest the seed. Don't wait too long, or birds may beat you to it.

Optimum soil temperature for germination: 60° to 70°F

Germination time at optimum soil temperature: 7 to 10 days

Spacing/thinning: Space dwarf varieties 6 inches apart, tall varieties 12 inches apart.

Planting depth: ¼ inch

Seed storage requirements: Cool, dark, and dry

Harvesting the Seed

The seed heads shatter easily; so cut them off carefully, catching them in a bag so you don't lose any seeds. After separating the seeds, spread them out to dry for a week or two before storing.

Indoor Sowing

MASTER GARDENING TIP

In warm regions, sow bachelor's buttons in late summer or fall for winter or early-spring bloom.

1 Start bachelor's buttons indoors in flats 8 to 10 weeks before transplanting outdoors in late spring. For faster germination, sow the seeds in flats filled with moistened growing medium, and refrigerate for about five days.

2 Keep flats evenly moist. Transplant into individual peat pots when seedlings have two sets of true leaves. Set entire pot into ground when you plant outdoors.

Outdoor Sowing

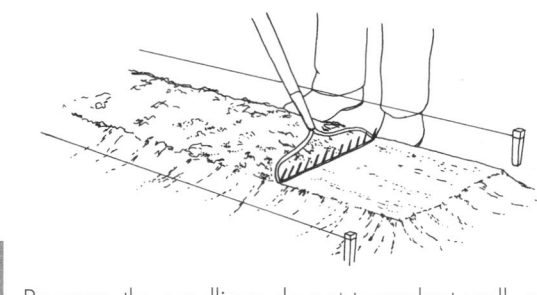

1 Because the seedlings do not transplant well, a more popular method is to sow the seeds directly outdoors several weeks before the last frost in spring. Prepare bed by raking smooth.

2 After sowing, cover the seeds with soil and firm it well. Make successive plantings to ensure continuous bloom.

Cosmos
Cosmos bipinnatus

Cosmos are cross-pollinated by insects, so grow only one variety at a time if you wish to preserve the purity of a certain strain for seed saving. If a cross should occur, dark colors will be genetically dominant over light colors. Another dominant trait is the color blotch at the base of the petals in some varieties.

MASTER GARDENING TIP

Klondike cosmos *(C. sulphureus)* will not cross with *C. bipinnatus,* so you can grow and collect seed from both cultivars the same season without fear of altering the purity of either strain.

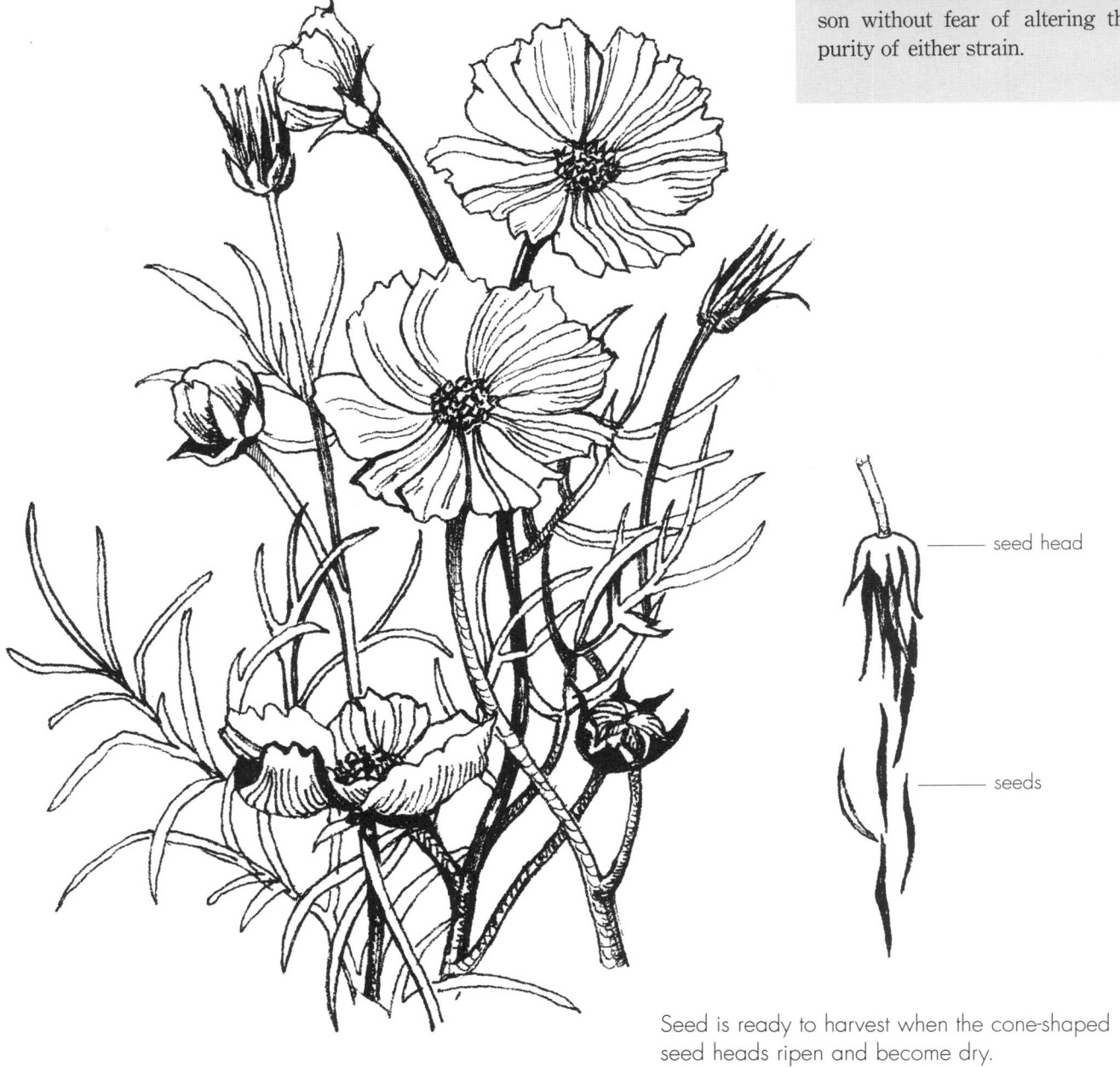

seed head

seeds

Seed is ready to harvest when the cone-shaped seed heads ripen and become dry.

Light requirements for germination: Seeds need light for germination.

Optimum soil temperature for germination: 70° to 75°F

Germination time at optimum soil temperature: 3 to 10 days

Spacing/thinning: Small varieties, 8 to 10 inches apart; tall varieties, 18 to 36 inches apart

Planting depth: ⅛ inch (or press lightly into the soil surface)

Seed storage requirements: Cool, dark, and dry

Harvesting the Seed

Cut seed heads from the plants and roll them between your hands or on a piece of paper to remove the seeds. After separating the seeds, spread them out to dry for a week or two before storing.

MASTER GARDENING TIP

Seed sown outdoors in fall may survive the winter to germinate in spring.

Indoor Sowing

1 Sow cosmos in flats indoors in spring for early bloom. Be sure to start them no more than four weeks before the last spring frost, or they will get too tall and will not transplant well.

2 Transplant into individual pots when seedlings have two or more true leaves.

Outdoor Sowing

1 Because cosmos seeds germinate easily, you should have no trouble sowing the seed directly outdoors in spring after danger of frost. Be sure to leave the seeds uncovered; exposure to light aids germination.

2 Tall species may need staking. All species should be watered during dry spells.

Four-O'Clocks
Mirabilis jalapa

Four-o'clocks are cross-pollinated by insects. If a cross should occur, tall forms will be genetically dominant over dwarf forms, but flower color cannot be predicted. Interestingly, a single four-o'clock plant may bloom in several colors. The flowers come in solid white, yellow, and pink, as well as bicolors and tricolors. The plants sometimes self-sow.

seed-bearing fruits

MASTER GARDENING TIP

There is no need to remove the leathery fruit encasing the seed; just sow the whole thing intact.

Easy to collect, four-o'clock seeds are contained in the large, black fruits nestled within the calyx after the flowers have faded. (I think they look like miniature hand grenades.) The seeds are ready to be harvested when the fruits tumble readily from the plant; you should not have to tug too hard to remove them.

SEED FACTS

Light requirements for germination: Seeds need light for germination.

Optimum soil temperature for germination: 70° to 80°F

Germination time at optimum soil temperature: 10 to 12 days

Spacing/thinning: Space small varieties 6 to 9 inches apart, medium varieties 12 to 18 inches apart, large varieties 24 to 36 inches apart.

Planting depth: Press lightly into the soil surface.

Seed storage requirements: Cool, dark, and dry

Harvesting the Seed

Four-o'clock seeds do not ripen all at once, so it's probably easiest just to pick the fruits out individually by hand. Or cut the plant stalks and let them dry indoors until the fruits fall out on their own. After harvesting, spread out the seeds to dry for a week or two before storing.

Outdoor Sowing

Sow seeds outdoors about a week after the last spring frost. In warm regions, sow seeds in autumn for spring bloom.

Indoor Sowing

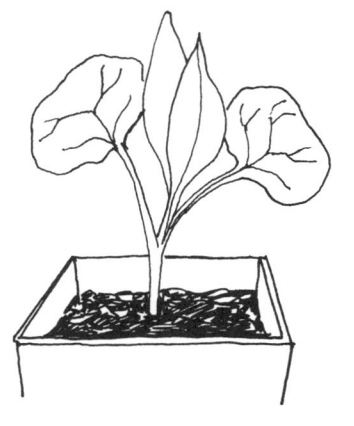

1 Start seeds indoors four to six weeks before the frost-free date. Sow in peat pots to avoid disturbing the roots when transplanting.

MASTER GARDENING TIP

Four-o'clocks may persist as perennials in the South. In the North, the tuberous roots can be lifted and stored over winter, like those of dahlias.

2 Set out seedlings as soon as possible after the last frost. Be sure to harden seedlings off before planting outdoors. Set edge of peat pots below ground level and water well.

Marigold
Tagetes spp.

Because marigolds are cross-pollinated by insects, you should grow only one variety at a time if you wish to preserve the purity of a certain strain for seed saving. If a cross should occur, double flowers will be genetically dominant over singles. Many varieties are hybrids, and so plants from saved seed will vary in color and quality.

MASTER GARDENING TIPS

▶ French marigolds (*T. patula*) are tetraploid, while American marigolds *(T. erecta)* are diploid. Crosses between these two produce a sterile triploid hybrid — a dwarf plant with large flowers. Seed collected from this hybrid will germinate poorly if at all.

▶ Seeds for triploids are expensive and have a relatively low germination rate.

seeds

Marigold seeds are ready for harvest when the seed heads dry and turn brown.

SEED FACTS

Optimum soil temperature for germination: 70° to 80°F

Germination time at optimum soil temperature: 3 to 5 days

Spacing/thinning: Space dwarf varieties 6 to 10 inches apart, medium varieties 12 to 15 inches apart, tall varieties 18 to 24 inches apart.

Planting depth: ⅛ inch

Seed storage requirements: Cool, dark, and dry

Harvesting the Seed

Cut the heads from the plant and rub off the seeds with your fingers. After separating the seeds, spread them out to dry for a week or two before storing.

Outdoor Sowing

You can sow marigolds directly outdoors in spring, when the soil is warm and the trees have leafed out. In the warmest parts of the country, marigolds can be direct-seeded outdoors at any time.

Indoor Sowing

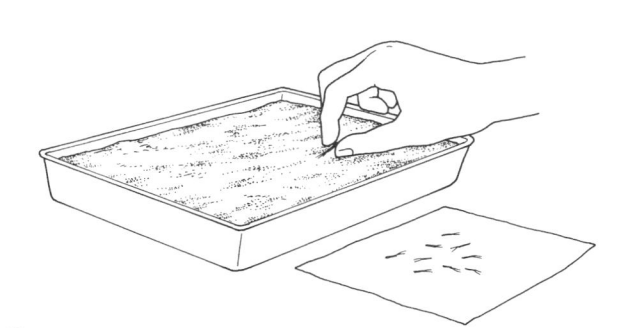

1 Start marigold seeds indoors in flats six to eight weeks before planting outdoors in spring (start late-blooming varieties a little earlier). The seedlings are somewhat susceptible to damping-off; keep the soil on the dry side and provide good air circulation.

2 When the seedlings are 1 or 2 inches tall, transplant them into larger containers, or set them out in the garden if all danger of frost is past.

Morning Glory

Ipomoea purpurea or ***I. tricolor***

Morning glories are cross-pollinated by insects. Grow only one variety at a time if you would like to preserve the purity of a certain strain for seed saving. If a cross should occur, double flowers will be genetically dominant over singles, but flower color cannot be predicted.

MASTER GARDENING TIP

Germination of morning glory seed may be erratic.

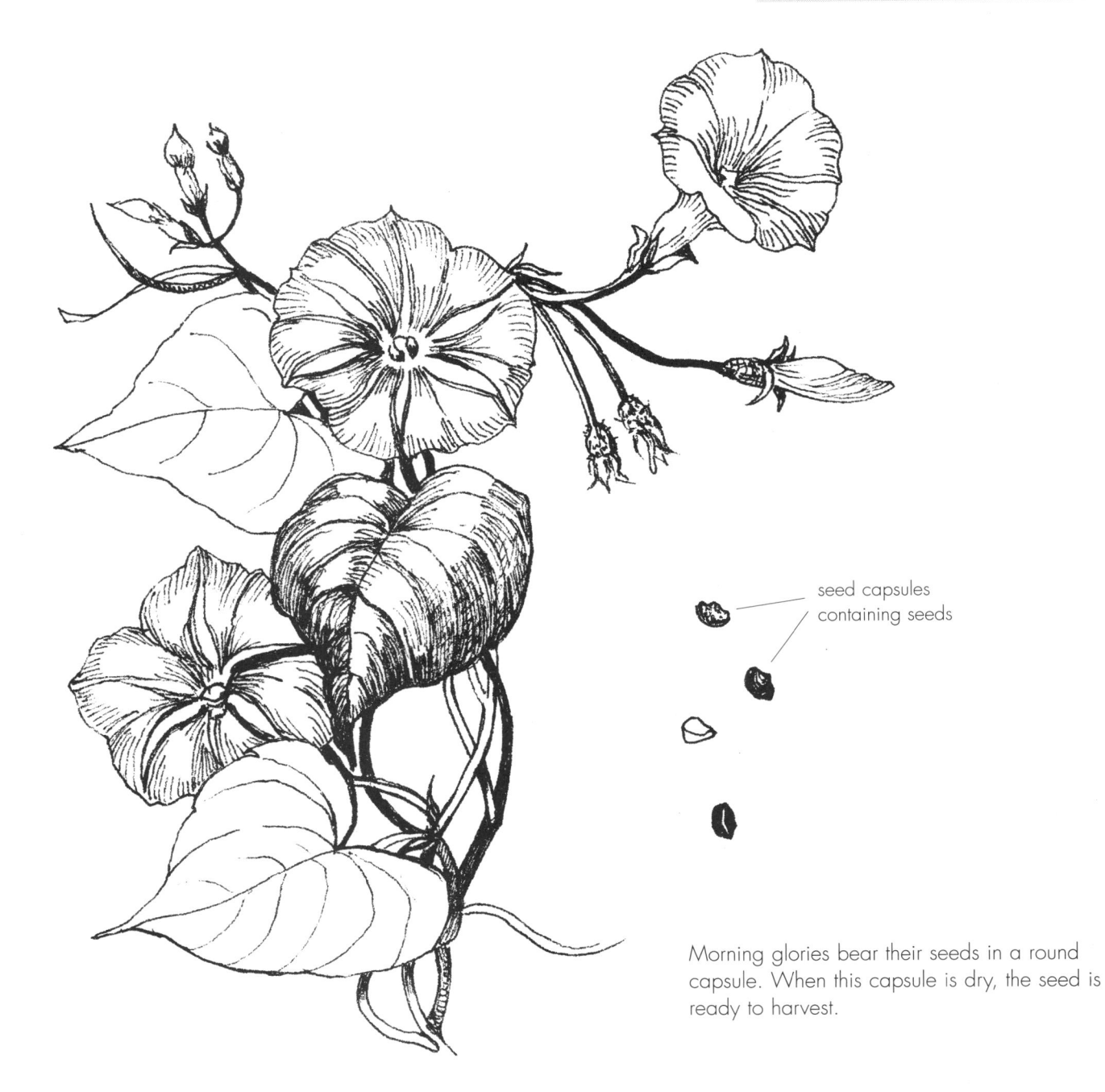

seed capsules containing seeds

Morning glories bear their seeds in a round capsule. When this capsule is dry, the seed is ready to harvest.

Optimum soil temperature for germination: 70° to 85°F

Germination time at optimum soil temperature: 5 to 21 days

Spacing/thinning: 8 to 18 inches

Planting depth: ¼ inch

Seed storage requirements: Cool, dark, and dry

Harvesting the Seed

Break open the round seed capsule and remove the seeds. Lay them out to dry for a week or two before storing.

Indoor Sowing

1 If the growing season is very short, morning glories can be started indoors in individual peat pots or Jiffy pellets (to avoid disturbing the roots when transplanting) four to six weeks before planting outdoors. The seed coat is very hard and must be broken down before the seed can germinate. Nick the seed with a file, and then soak it overnight in lukewarm water before sowing.

MASTER GARDENING TIP

You can also presprout the seeds by spreading them out on damp paper towels, and then folding up the towels and placing them in a sealed plastic bag in a warm place. When the seeds germinate, plant them in flats or individual pots.

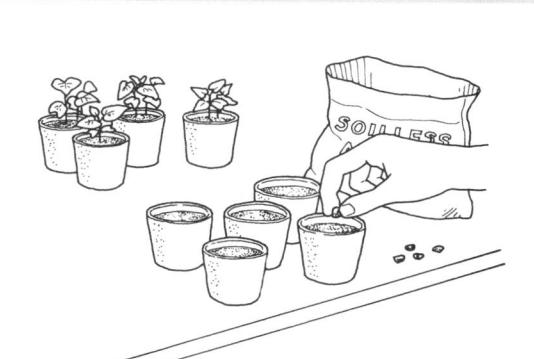

2 Sow three or four seeds in each pot and thin to the best two seedlings. Transplant the seedlings outdoors three to four weeks after the last frost, when temperatures remain above 45°F.

Outdoor Sowing

Morning glories are usually direct-sown outdoors a week or two after the last spring frost, when the soil is warm. They dislike transplanting, so sow them in the place they are to remain. Follow suggestions under indoor planting for how to break down the hard seed coat, or presprout seeds (see box above).

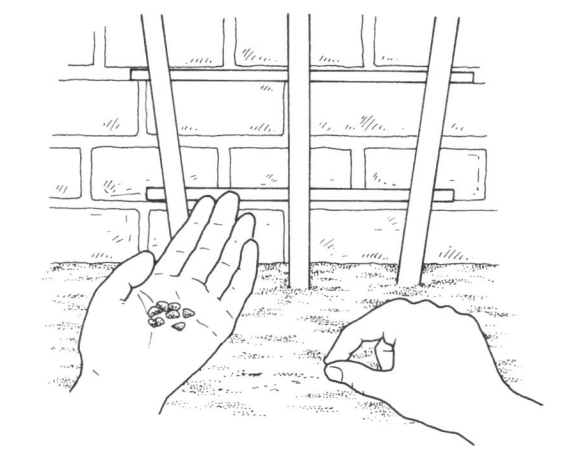

Moss Rose
Portulaca grandiflora

Moss rose is cross-pollinated by insects. If a cross should occur, single flowers will be genetically dominant over doubles, but flower color cannot be predicted. The flowers bloom in all shades of red, pink, yellow, orange, and white. The plants often self-sow.

MASTER GARDENING TIP

Moss roses bloom best in poor soil.

seed capsule

seeds

The tiny, dustlike seeds of moss rose are carried in a capsule and dispersed through the top of the capsule when ripe. Harvest the seed when the capsule is dry, before it shatters.

Light requirements for germination: Seeds need light for germination.

Optimum soil temperature for germination: 70° to 85°F

Germination time at optimum soil temperature: 7 to 21 days

Spacing/thinning: Thin to 6 inches apart.

Planting depth: Press lightly into the soil surface.

Seed storage requirements: Cool, dark, and dry

Harvesting the Seed

Carefully remove the seed capsule and shake the tiny seeds onto a tray. Let the seeds dry for a week before storing.

Outdoor Sowing

Sow the seeds directly outdoors after all danger of frost is past, when the soil is warm. The seeds are very tiny; some experts recommend mixing them with fine, dry sand to separate them and make sowing easier. Broadcast the seed-sand mixture over your prepared bed.

Indoor Sowing

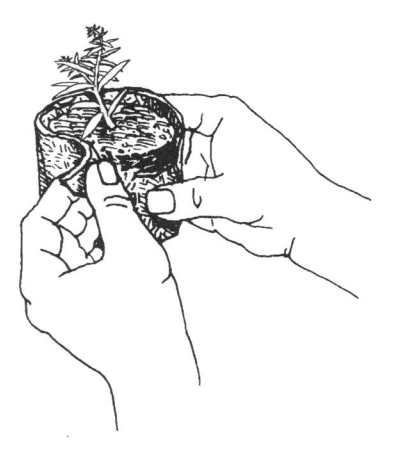

1 Moss rose can be started indoors six to eight weeks before setting out. Because seedlings are somewhat difficult to transplant, sow the seeds in peat pots, which can be set directly in the ground.

2 Harden off seedlings before setting them in the garden. Be sure top of peat pot is below ground level (tear off top edge if necessary), so that moisture isn't wicked away from plant through the peat.

Nasturtium
Tropaeolum majus

Breeders have developed many colors and forms of nasturtiums; unless you are growing them from commercially produced seed, the seedlings will be variable. Collect seed only from species and not from named varieties (hybrids and other cultivars), unless you wish to experiment. The plants sometimes self-sow.

MASTER GARDENING TIP

Heterosporium leaf spot is a seed-borne disease that affects nasturtiums.

unripe fruit

mature fruit

seeds

Nasturtium seeds are ready to harvest when the three-celled fruit that holds them is dry.

SEED FACTS

Optimum soil temperature for germination: 65° to 70°F

Germination time at optimum soil temperature: 7 to 14 days

Spacing/thinning: Space small or dwarf varieties 6 to 12 inches apart, medium or climbing varieties 12 to 20 inches apart, large varieties 24 to 36 inches apart.

Planting depth: ¼ inch

Seed storage requirements: Cool, dark, and dry

Harvesting the Seed

Remove the fruit from the plant and separate the cells. Each cell contains a seed, but do not try to remove the seed from its compartment. After harvesting, spread the seeds out to dry for a week or two before storing.

MASTER GARDENING TIP

In warm regions, sow the seeds outdoors in early fall for winter bloom.

Indoor Sowing

1 If the growing season is very short, nasturtiums can be started indoors in peat pots (to avoid disturbing the roots when transplanting) four to six weeks before planting outdoors. To facilitate germination, cover the pots with an opaque material like aluminum foil to exclude light. When germination begins, remove the covering.

2 Transplant the seedlings outdoors after all danger of frost is past. Be sure peat pots are completely beneath soil level, so that moisture isn't wicked away from plants.

Outdoor Sowing

Nasturtiums are commonly direct-sown outdoors in spring, when the soil is warm and the trees have leafed out. They dislike transplanting, so sow them in the place they are to remain.

Pansy
Viola spp.

Many varieties are hybrids, so plants from collected seed will vary in color and quality. Pansies are usually cross-pollinated by insects, but the flowers sometimes self-pollinate without opening. This often happens late in the season, and the resulting seed is viable. In case of cross-pollination, flower color cannot be predicted. The plants sometimes self-sow.

MASTER GARDENING TIPS

► Pansy anthracnose is a seed-borne disease that affects pansies.

► For faster germination, sow the seeds in pots filled with moistened growing medium and refrigerate for about two weeks.

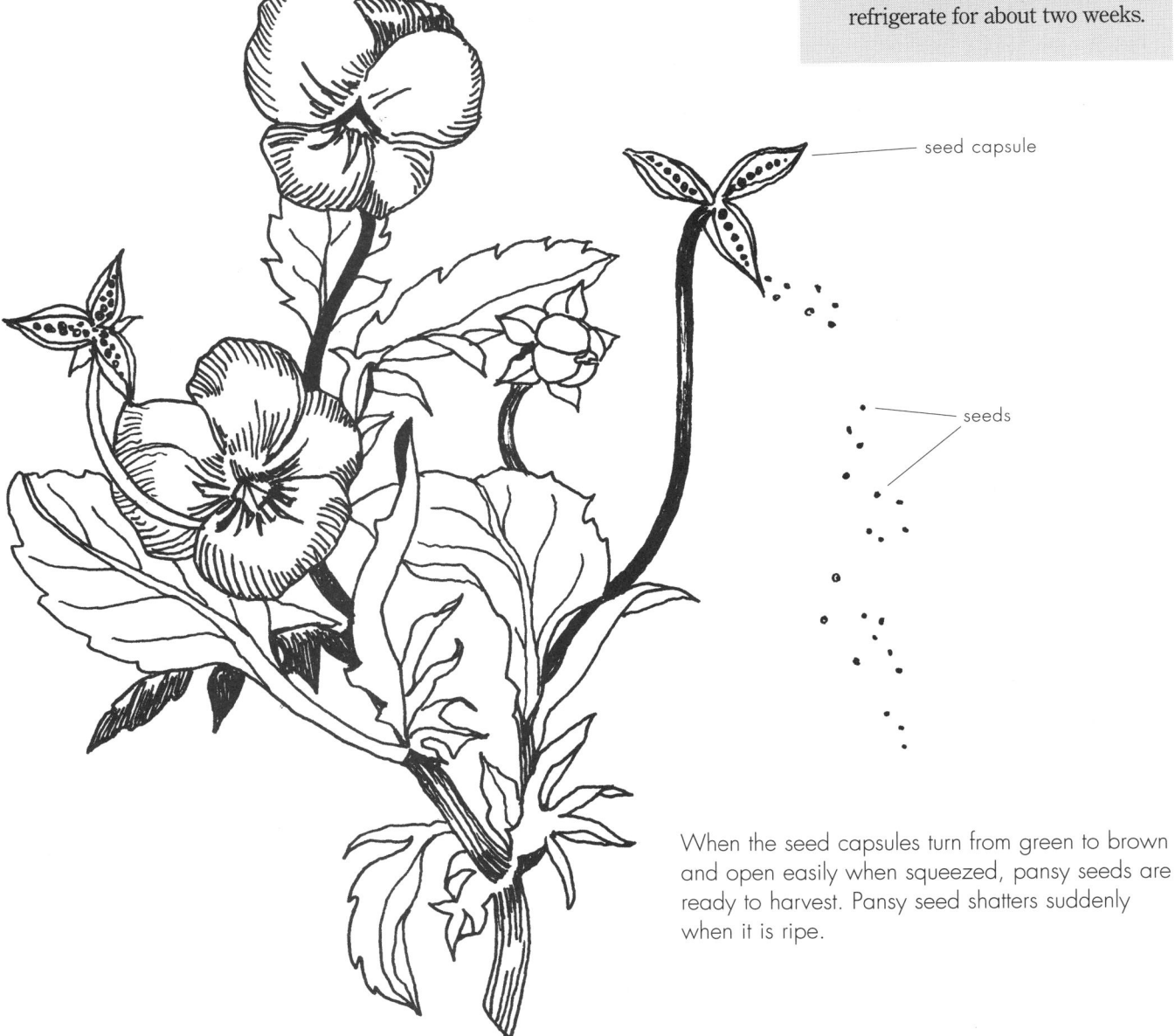

seed capsule

seeds

When the seed capsules turn from green to brown and open easily when squeezed, pansy seeds are ready to harvest. Pansy seed shatters suddenly when it is ripe.

Optimum soil temperature for germination: 65° to 75°F

Germination time at optimum soil temperature: 7 to 21 days

Spacing/thinning: 6 to 12 inches

Planting depth: ¼ inch

Seed storage requirements: Cool, dark, and dry

Harvesting the Seed

Pick the seed capsules and place them in a covered container until the seeds are released. After harvesting, spread out the seeds to dry for a week or two before storing.

MASTER GARDENING TIP

In warm regions, sow pansy seeds directly outdoors in early fall and mulch the plants lightly over winter.

Indoor Sowing

1 Start pansy seeds indoors 10 to 12 weeks before transplanting outdoors. Firm the soil gently, and cover the flat with an opaque material like aluminum foil to exclude light. When germination begins, remove the covering. Keep the soil temperature below 75°F (around 50°F is preferable), since pansies are cool-weather plants.

2 After hardening off, seedlings can be transplanted outdoors in early spring, up to a month before the last frost, or in late autumn, for fresh color until frost. In warm regions, pansies bloom throughout much of the winter.

Outdoor Sowing

Sow pansies outdoors in early spring.

Petunia
Petunia spp.

Many petunia varieties are hybrids, so you'll not be able to predict the colors and quality of plants from collected seed. Petunias can cross-breed with each other, even if they seem to be of different species (for instance, *P. grandiflora, P. floribunda, P. multiflora*), and their offspring will be variable. Double-flowered varieties usually do not produce seed, but they do have viable pollen that can be transferred to single-flowered forms. The plants often self-sow, and the resulting seedlings frequently revert to a wild, white-flowered form.

MASTER GARDENING TIPS

▶ Tobacco ringspot virus is a seed-borne disease that affects petunias.

▶ If you smoke or use tobacco in any form, wash your hands before handling petunia seedlings to avoid spreading tobacco mosaic disease. This applies to all members of the Solanaceae family (tomatoes, potatoes, eggplant, peppers, etc.). Also, don't grow petunias where other members of the Solanaceae have grown if there were disease problems of any kind.

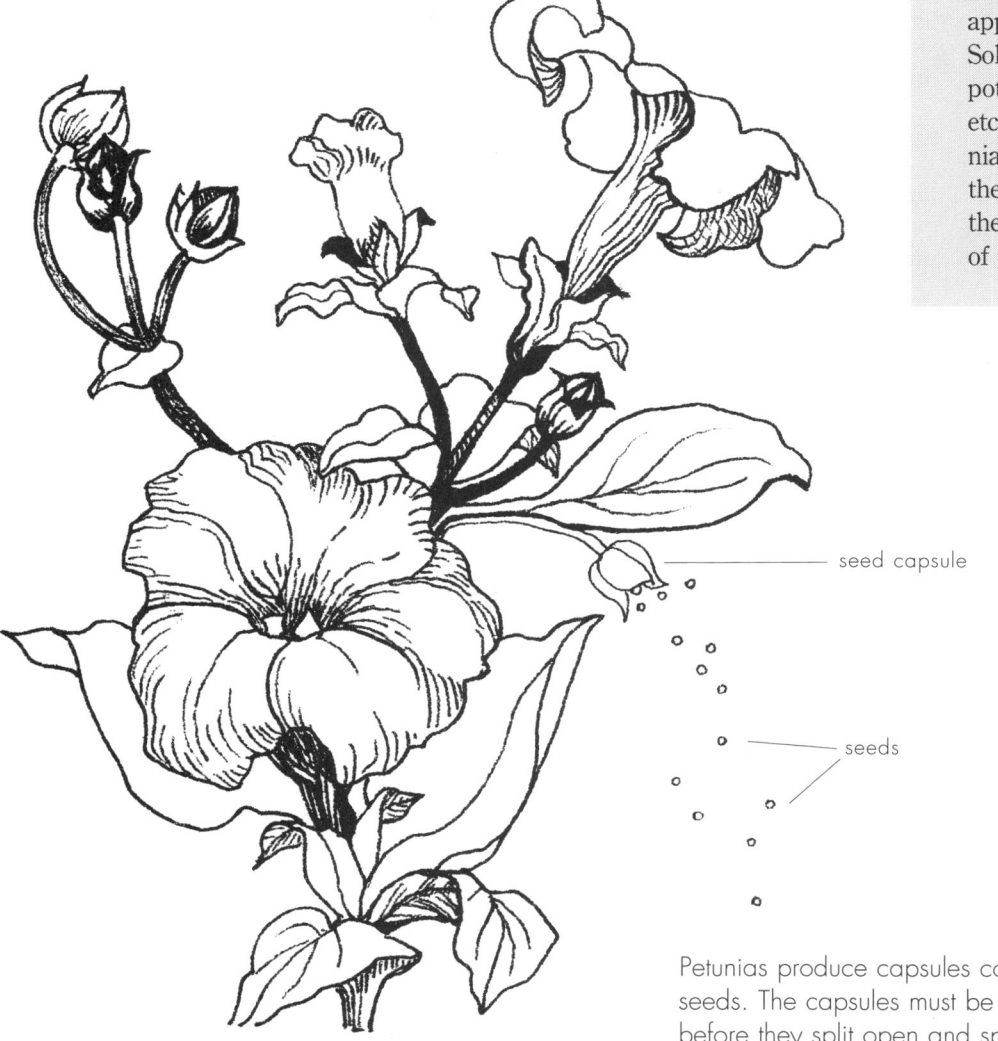

seed capsule

seeds

Petunias produce capsules containing hundreds of tiny seeds. The capsules must be removed from the plant before they split open and spill their contents.

SEED FACTS

Light requirements for germination: Seeds need light for germination.

Optimum soil temperature for germination: 70° to 80°F

Germination time at optimum soil temperature: 5 to 21 days

Spacing/thinning: 8 to 12 inches apart

Planting depth: Press lightly into the soil surface

Seed storage requirements: Cool, dark, and dry

Harvesting the Seed

Remove the seed capsules when they become brown and dry. Make sure the seeds are completely dry before storing.

Outdoor Sowing

Petunias can also be direct-sown outdoors after the last spring frost. Because petunias are so slow-growing, this is best done in warm regions only.

Indoor Sowing

1 Start petunia seeds indoors 10 to 12 weeks before transplanting outdoors; the seedlings (especially double-flowered forms) are slow-growing. Sow the seed thinly on the surface of the soil, and do not cover them. The seeds are very tiny; try mixing them with fine, dry sand to separate them and make sowing easier. Some gardeners find it useful to wear a magnifier (sold in craft stores).

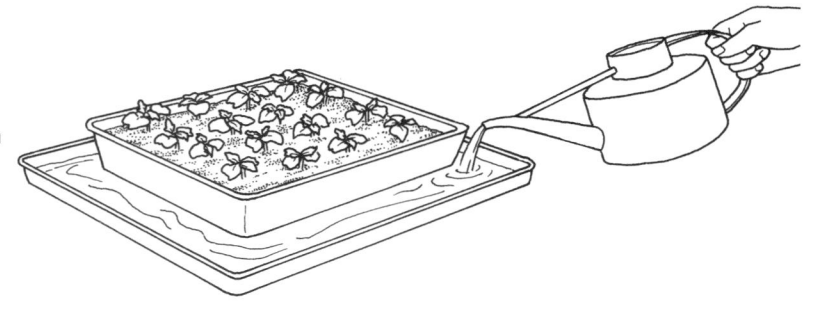

2 Petunia seedlings are susceptible to damping-off, so water the flats from the bottom and provide good air circulation.

3 When the plants have developed three or four sets of leaves, transplant them to individual containers. Harden them off after the last spring frost, and transplant outdoors when all danger of frost is past and the soil is warm.

Poppy
Papaver spp.

Poppies are cross-pollinated by insects. When crosses occur, single flowers are genetically dominant over doubles, but color cannot be predicted. There are many different color strains available, but if left to their own devices, corn poppies (*P. rhoeas*) eventually revert to single red flowers and opium poppies (*P. somniferum*) revert to single mauve flowers. If you're planning to save seed, you may have to rogue out unwanted color forms (before they can cross-pollinate) for several years before getting seed that produces the colors you want. The plants self-sow very freely.

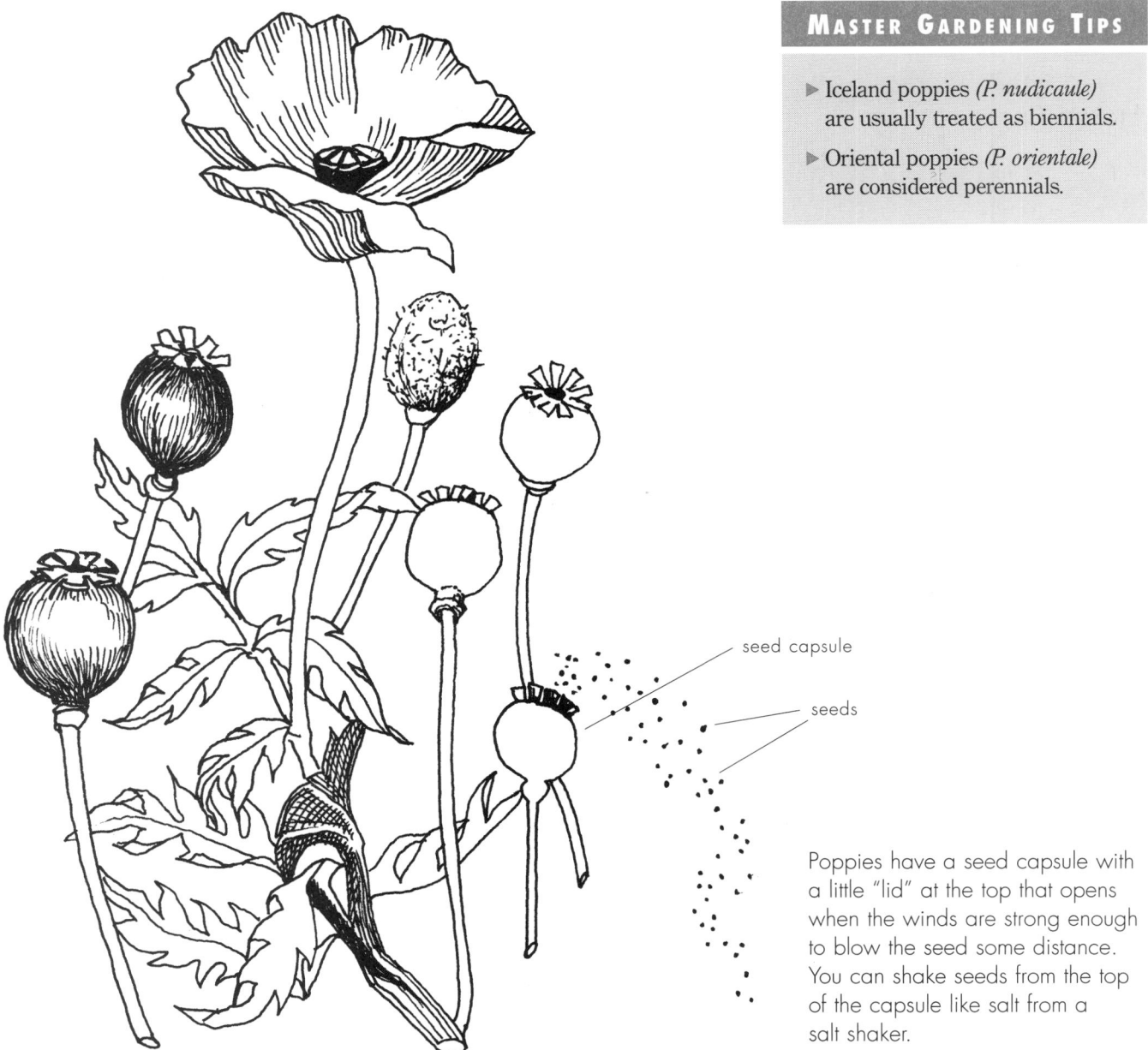

MASTER GARDENING TIPS

▶ Iceland poppies *(P. nudicaule)* are usually treated as biennials.

▶ Oriental poppies *(P. orientale)* are considered perennials.

seed capsule

seeds

Poppies have a seed capsule with a little "lid" at the top that opens when the winds are strong enough to blow the seed some distance. You can shake seeds from the top of the capsule like salt from a salt shaker.

Light requirements for germination: Seeds need light for germination.

Optimum soil temperature for germination: 60° to 70°F

Germination time at optimum soil temperature: 7 to 14 days

Spacing/thinning: Space small varieties 6 to 8 inches apart, large varieties 8 to 12 inches apart.

Planting depth: Press lightly into the soil surface.

Seed storage requirements: Cool, dark, and dry

Harvesting the Seed

To harvest the seeds before they are dispersed, cut down the flower stems when the capsules are dry but not yet open, and lay them inside a shallow box in a warm, dry place. As they continue to dry, the tops will open and you can then easily shake out the seeds into a bag or other container.

MASTER GARDENING TIPS

▶ In warm regions, sow the seeds only in fall. In fact, poppies self-sow so freely that you can sow seeds in the garden in the fall even in cold regions.

▶ Poppies prefer cool temperatures, so if your summers are cool, you can make succession plantings for a longer season of bloom.

Indoor Sowing

You can start seeds indoors in peat pots six to eight weeks before the last spring frost. I started my first batch of annual poppies this way, and they did extremely well after being transplanted to the garden. Hardening them off will help them adjust to the great outdoors if started inside. Plant the seedlings outdoors after the last frost.

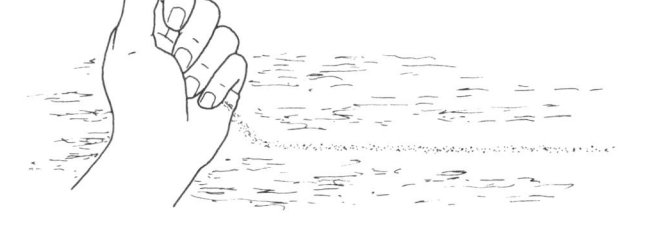

Outdoor Sowing

Poppies are easy to sow from seed. They don't like to be transplanted, so it's best to sow them in place outdoors in early spring, around the time of the last frost, or in late fall. The seeds are very tiny; some experts recommend mixing them with fine dry sand to separate them and make sowing easier.

Poppy, California
Eschscholzia californicum

California poppies are cross-pollinated by insects, so grow only one variety at a time if you wish to preserve the purity of a certain strain for seed saving. You may have to rogue out unwanted color forms (before they can cross-pollinate) for several years before getting seed that produces the colors you want. The flowers bloom in white, red, orange, and bicolors, but will almost always revert to orange if plants are grown from collected seed. Also, double-flowered forms eventually revert to single flowers. The plants often self-sow.

MASTER GARDENING TIP

Heterosporium leaf spot, or capsule spot, is a seed-borne disease that affects California poppies.

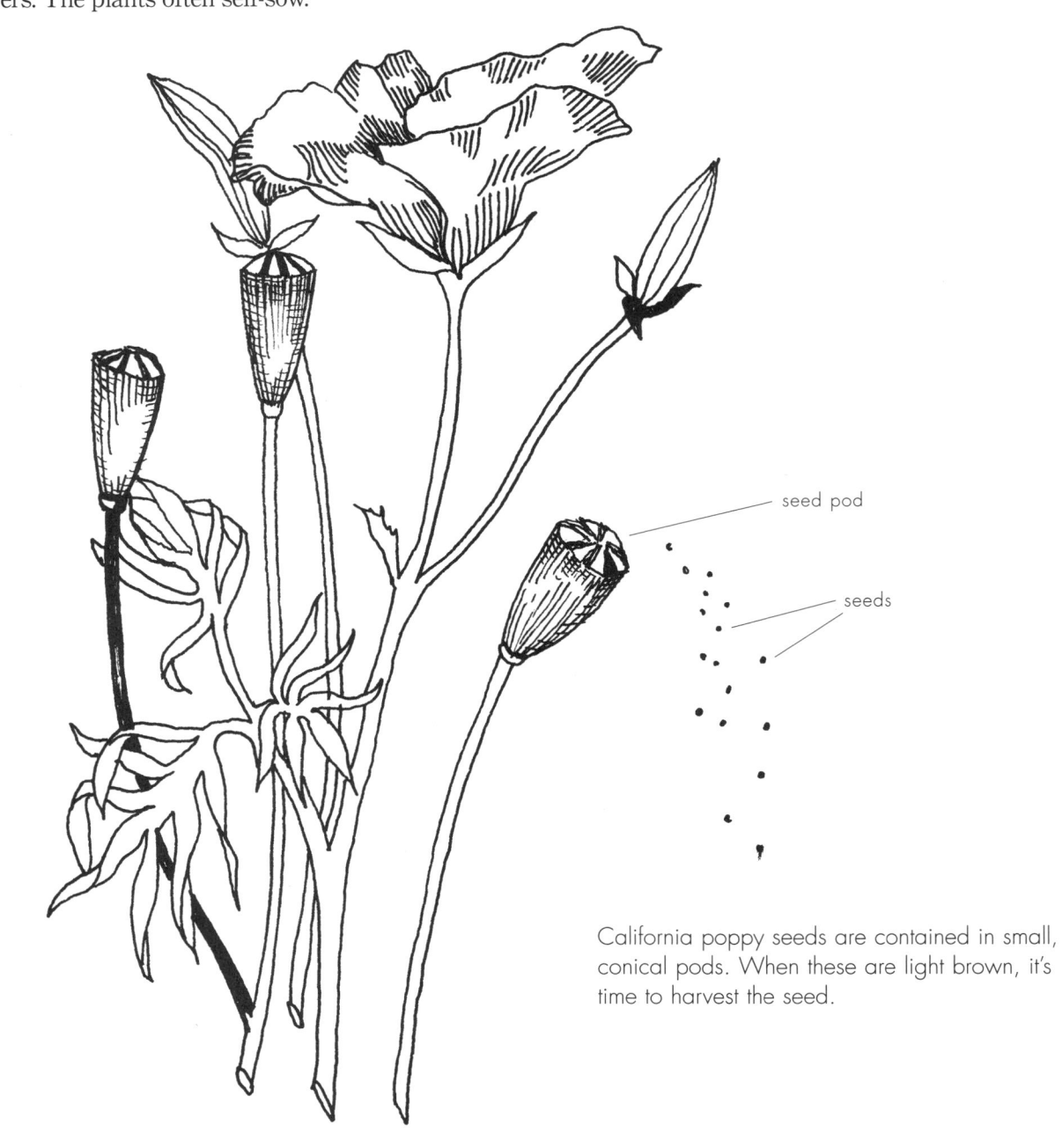

seed pod

seeds

California poppy seeds are contained in small, conical pods. When these are light brown, it's time to harvest the seed.

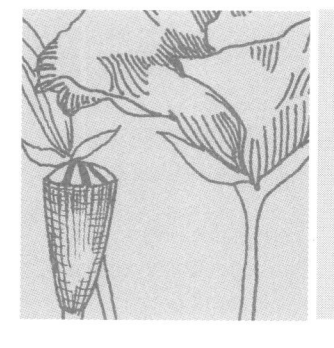

SEED FACTS

Optimum soil temperature for germination: 60° to 65°F

Germination time at optimum soil temperature: 14 to 21 days

Spacing/thinning: 8 to 10 inches

Planting depth: ¼ inch

Seed storage requirements: Cool, dark, and dry

Harvesting the Seed

When these seedpods turn light brown, remove them from the plants before they shatter and release the seeds. Make sure the seeds are completely dry before storing.

Indoor Sowing

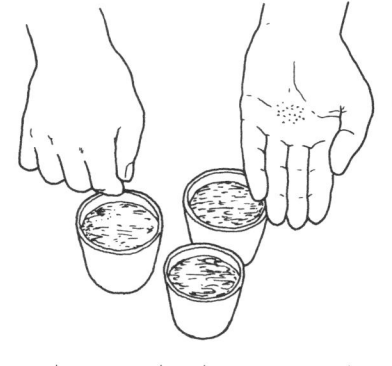

1 Seeds may be started indoors two to three weeks before the last spring frost. Sow them in peat pots to avoid disturbing the roots when transplanting the seedlings after the last frost.

3 Transplant seedlings outdoors after the last frost. set peat pots deeply, so that moisture isn't lost.

2 To avoid disturbing the tiny seeds, use a bulb-type sprinkler to water pots.

Outdoor Sowing

California poppies are commonly direct-sown outdoors after the last spring frost, or from autumn through early spring in warm regions. They dislike transplanting, so sow them in the place they are to remain.

Pot Marigold
Calendula officinalis

Pot marigolds are cross-pollinated by insects. You should grow only one variety at a time if you wish to preserve the purity of a certain strain for seed saving. Many varieties are hybrids, and it may not be worth the time to collect their seed; check what kind you are growing before planning to harvest seed. If you're going to save seed, select plants that are resistant to mildew.

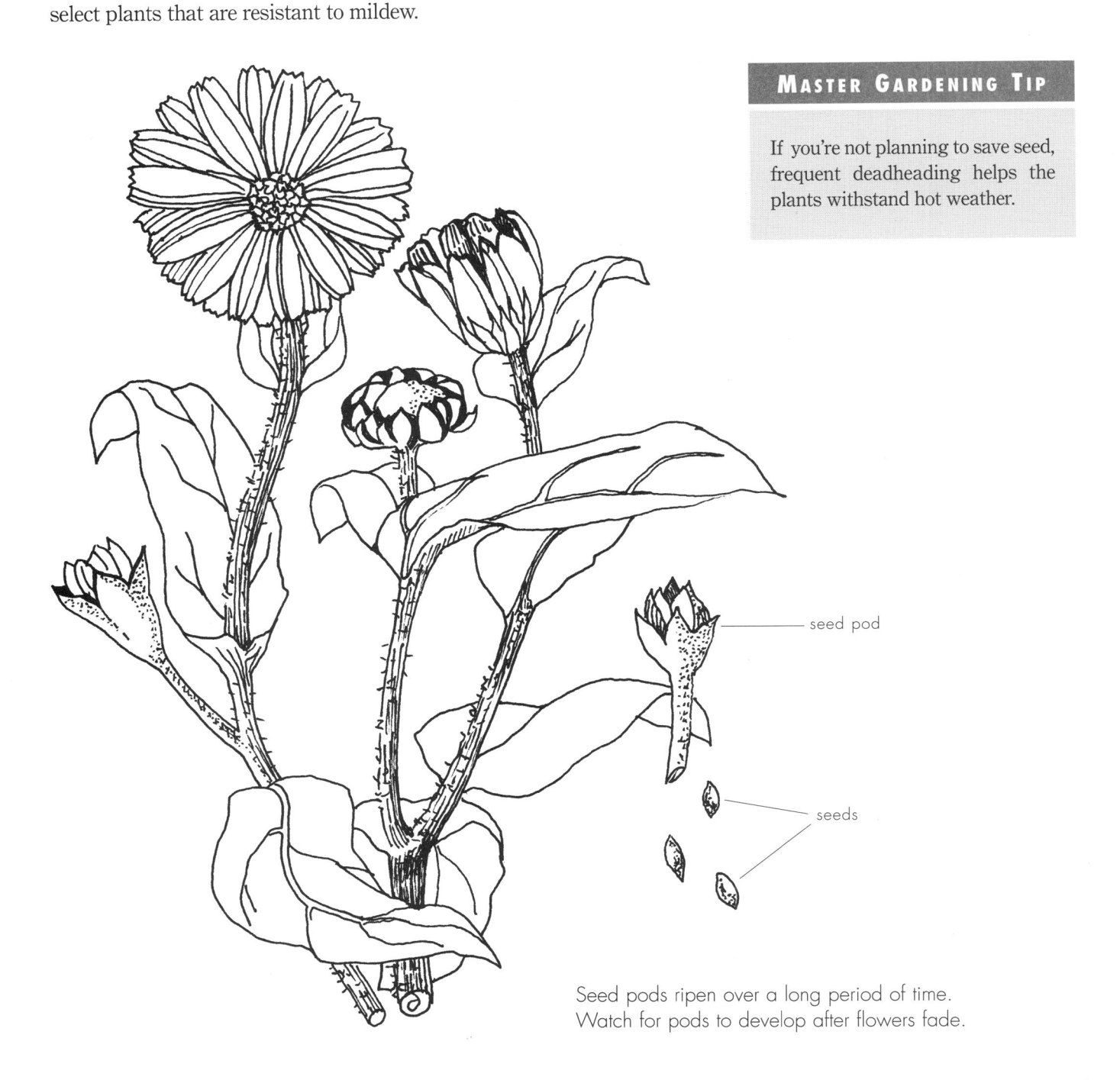

MASTER GARDENING TIP

If you're not planning to save seed, frequent deadheading helps the plants withstand hot weather.

seed pod

seeds

Seed pods ripen over a long period of time. Watch for pods to develop after flowers fade.

SEED FACTS

Optimum soil temperature for germination: 70°F

Germination time at optimum soil temperature: 4 to 14 days

Spacing/thinning: Space dwarf varieties 6 to 12 inches apart, tall varieties 18 to 24 inches apart.

Planting depth: ¼ inch

Seed storage requirements: Cool, dark, and dry

Harvesting the Seed

To harvest the seed before the seed pods shatter, cut the flowers off as they begin to fade. The seed may not be completely mature, but it will continue to ripen as it is dried for storage. Lay the flower heads out in a warm, dry place until they are thoroughly dry, then rub off the seeds by hand. Spread the seeds out to dry for another week or so before storing.

Indoor Sowing

1 Start seeds indoors six to eight weeks before the last spring frost. Firm the soil gently and cover the flat with an opaque material like aluminum foil to exclude light. When germination begins, remove the covering.

2 When the seedlings have two or three true leaves, transplant them to individual containers, or thin them in the flat by clipping out some of the seedlings with scissors.

3 Harden off the seedlings, and set them outdoors after the last spring frost.

Outdoor Sowing

Pot marigolds can also be direct-sown outdoors in early spring (just after pea-planting time), in early summer for fall blooms, or in fall to withstand the winter. Summer and fall sowing are recommended only in warmer regions.

Scarlet Sage
Salvia splendens

Because scarlet sage is cross-pollinated by insects, you should grow only one variety at a time if you would like to preserve the purity of a certain strain for seed saving. The flowers bloom in red, white, and purple. The plants sometimes self-sow.

MASTER GARDENING TIP

Scarlet sage seeds tend to be short-lived. Use fresh seed.

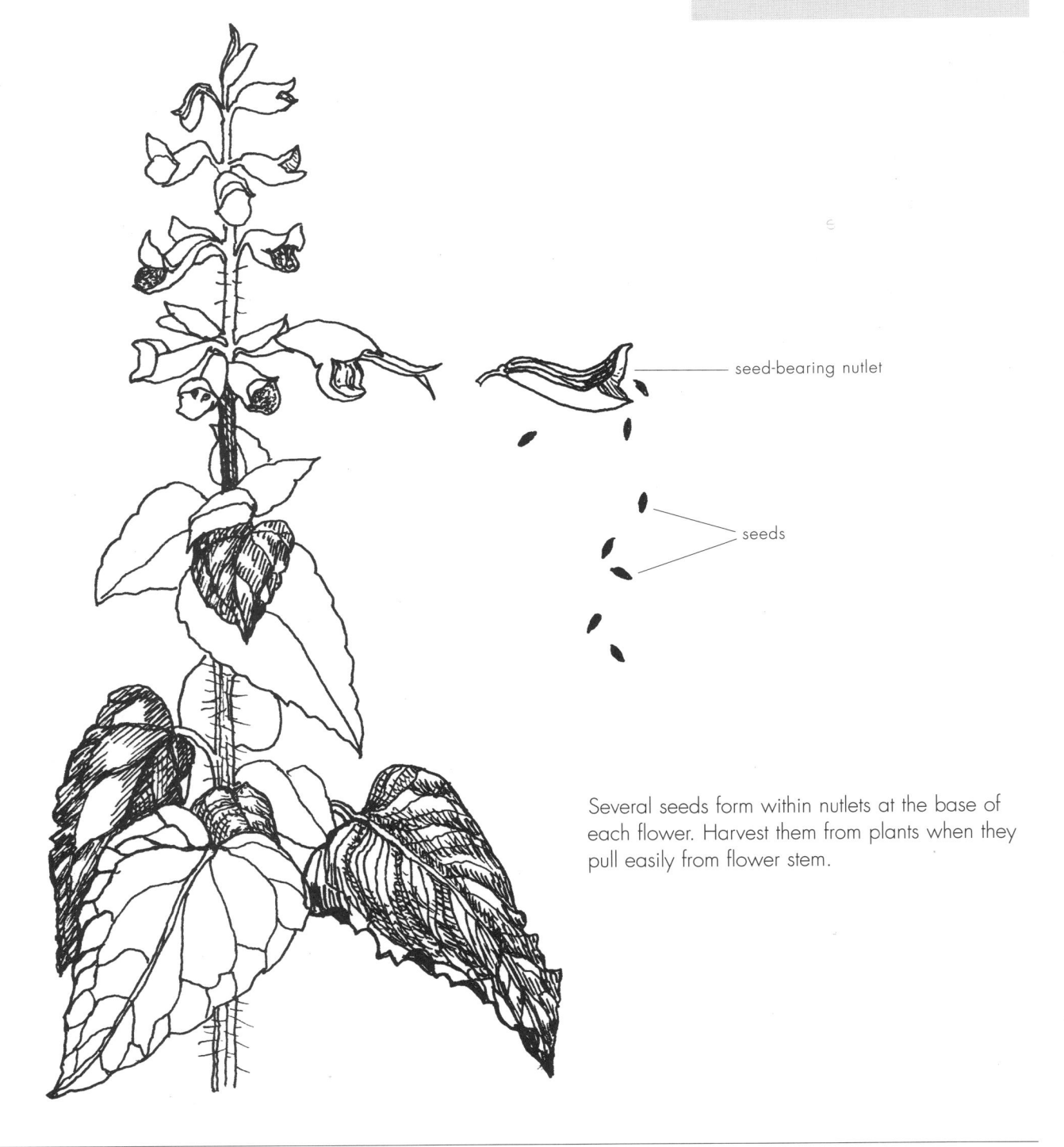

seed-bearing nutlet

seeds

Several seeds form within nutlets at the base of each flower. Harvest them from plants when they pull easily from flower stem.

SEED FACTS

Light requirements for germination: Seeds need light for germination.

Optimum soil temperature for germination: 65° to 75°F

Germination time at optimum soil temperature: 5 to 15 days

Spacing/thinning: 12 to 18 inches

Planting depth: Press lightly into the soil surface.

Seed storage requirements: Cool, dry area; tightly sealed container

Harvesting the Seed

When the nutlets are dry, harvest the seeds before they drop. Spread them out to dry for a week or so before storing.

Indoor Sowing

1 It's best to sow scarlet sage indoors in early spring, 10 to 12 weeks before the last frost. The seedlings are susceptible to damping-off, so water the flats from the bottom and provide good air circulation.

2 Transplant the seedlings outdoors when all danger of frost is past and the temperatures remain above 40°F.

Outdoor Sowing

Sow the seeds directly outdoors two weeks after the last frost.

MASTER GARDENING TIPS

In frost-free areas, sow scarlet sage in February or March. Provide good drainage.

Snapdragon
Antirrhinum majus

Snapdragons are self-pollinated, so different varieties usually do not cross. If a cross should occur, dark colors will be genetically dominant. Yellow is recessive. Many varieties of snapdragons are hybrids, so you will get a lot of variety in color and quality from plants sown from their seeds. Select plants that are resistant to fungal diseases. Self-sown seedlings will be the hardiest.

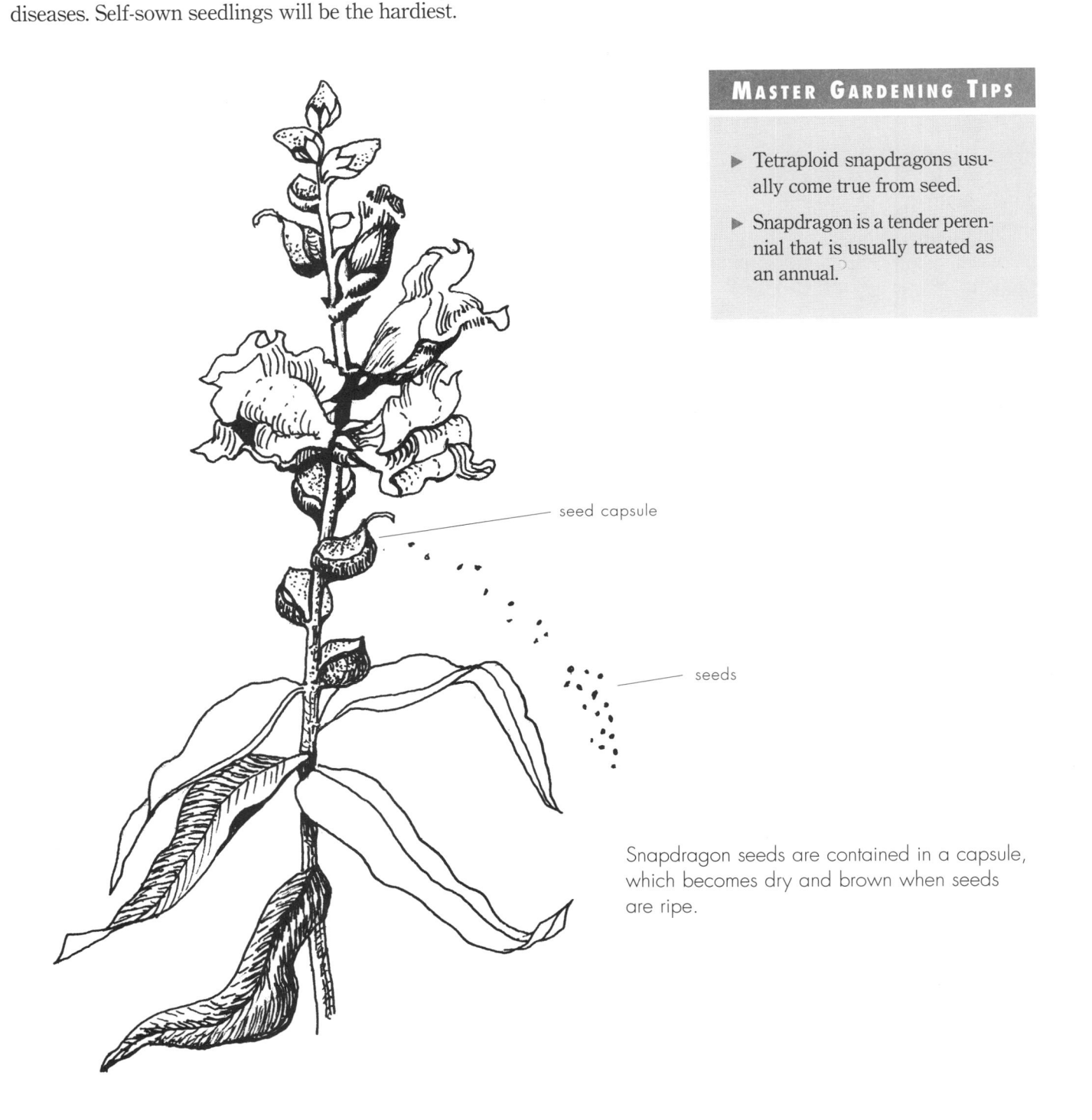

MASTER GARDENING TIPS

▶ Tetraploid snapdragons usually come true from seed.

▶ Snapdragon is a tender perennial that is usually treated as an annual.

seed capsule

seeds

Snapdragon seeds are contained in a capsule, which becomes dry and brown when seeds are ripe.

SEED FACTS

Light requirements for germination: Seeds need light for germination.

Optimum soil temperature for germination: 70° to 75°F

Germination time at optimum soil temperature: 7 to 21 days

Spacing/thinning: Space dwarf varieties 6 inches apart, tall varieties 12 inches apart.

Planting depth: Press lightly into the soil surface; do not cover.

Seed storage requirements: Cool, dark, and dry

Harvesting the Seed

When most of the capsules are ripe (dry and brown), cut them from the plants and shake out the tiny seeds. Make sure the seeds are completely dry before storing.

Indoor Sowing

1 Since snapdragon seedlings are slow-growing, they should be started indoors 8 to 10 weeks (or more) before the last spring frost. The seedlings are susceptible to damping-off, so water the flats from the bottom and provide good air circulation.

3 Transplant outdoors after the last frost. In warm climates, seedlings can be set out in fall.

Outdoor Sowing

Snapdragons should not generally be direct-seeded outdoors, unless you live in a warm region or you can plant seeds in a cold frame in late summer or early fall.

2 Grow the seedlings in a cool bright place after germination.

HINT FOR SUCCESS

For faster germination, sow the seeds in pots filled with moistened growing medium and refrigerate for two days.

Spider Flower
Cleome hasslerana

Spider flower is cross-pollinated by insects, so grow only one variety at a time if you wish to preserve the purity of a certain strain for seed saving. The flowers bloom in white, pink, and pale purple, and seedlings will be variable. The plants self-sow heavily.

MASTER GARDENING TIP

These tall plants are usually sturdy, but they may need staking in windy areas.

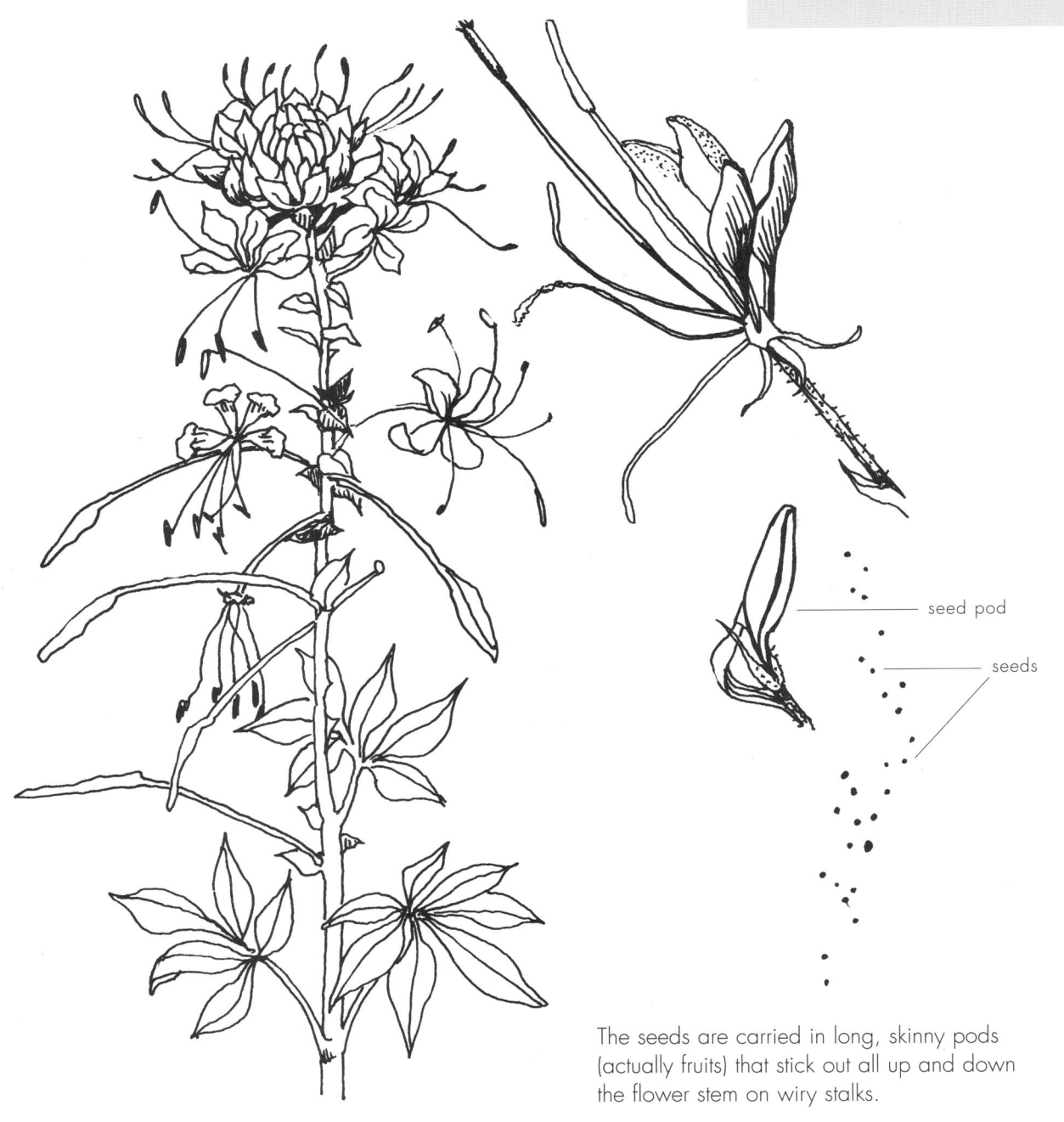

seed pod

seeds

The seeds are carried in long, skinny pods (actually fruits) that stick out all up and down the flower stem on wiry stalks.

SEED FACTS

Light requirements for germination: Seeds need light for germination.

Optimum soil temperature for germination: 70° to 75°F

Germination time at optimum soil temperature: 10 to 14 days

Spacing/thinning: 18 to 24 inches

Planting depth: Press lightly into the soil surface.

Seed storage requirements: Cool, dark, and dry

Harvesting the Seed

Snip the seed pods from the plant just before the pods shatter, and remove the seeds. Make sure the seeds are completely dry before storing.

Indoor Sowing

1 You can sow seed indoors six to eight weeks before transplanting outdoors. To speed germination, sow the seeds in pots filled with moistened growing medium, and refrigerate for about two weeks.

2 Harden off seedlings before setting them in the garden. Give them plenty of space; spider flowers are large plants.

Outdoor Sowing

Spider flower grows quickly and is usually direct-seeded outdoors after the last spring frost, when temperatures remain above 40°F. The seeds germinate best when daytime temperatures are warm and nights are cool.

Sunflower
***Helianthus* spp.**

Sunflowers are cross-pollinated by insects, so grow only one variety at a time, if you wish to preserve the purity of a certain strain for seed saving. You can also isolate varieties by at least 1,000 feet, if this is feasible. Collect seed only from species and not from named varieties (hybrids and other cultivars), unless you wish to experiment. The plants often self-sow.

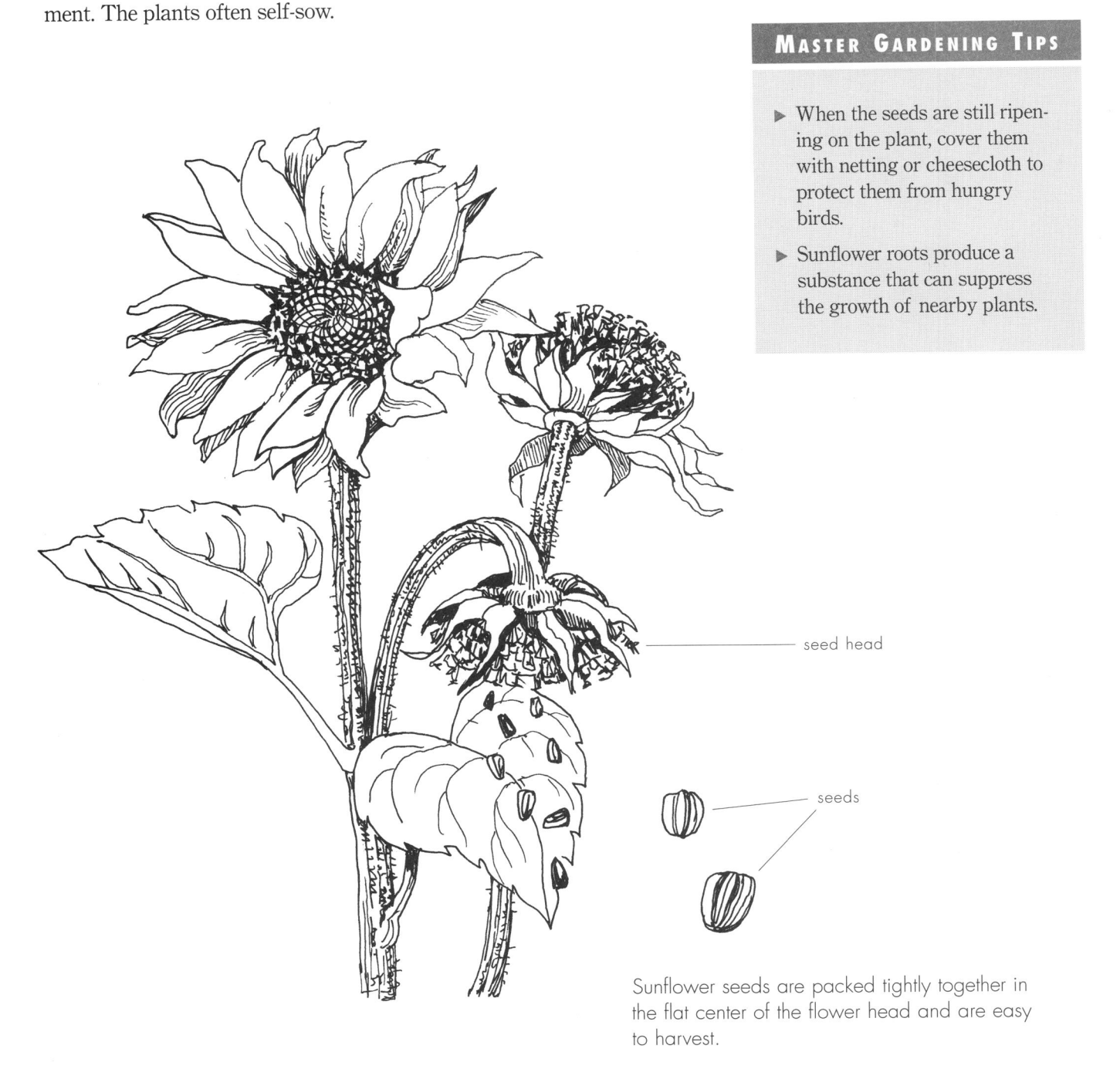

MASTER GARDENING TIPS

- ▶ When the seeds are still ripening on the plant, cover them with netting or cheesecloth to protect them from hungry birds.
- ▶ Sunflower roots produce a substance that can suppress the growth of nearby plants.

seed head

seeds

Sunflower seeds are packed tightly together in the flat center of the flower head and are easy to harvest.

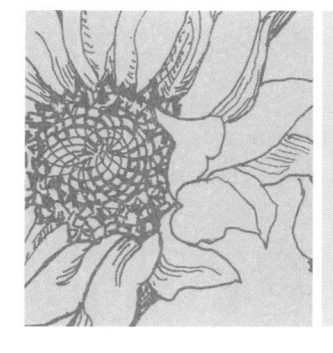

Optimum soil temperature for germination: 70° to 85°F

Germination time at optimum soil temperature: 10 to 14 days

Spacing/thinning: Space dwarf varieties 12 inches apart, large varieties 36 inches apart.

Planting depth: ¼ inch

Seed storage requirements: Dry, cool area; sealed container

Harvesting the Seed

1 Cut the head when the flower has withered and dropped its petals, then hang it up to dry for a few weeks in a well-ventilated place. To see if the seeds are ready, rub your hand over the seed head. The seeds fall off easily when ripe.

2 Spread out the seeds to dry for another week or so before storing.

3 Place sunflower seeds in a paper bag and seal the bag inside a glass jar; this protects against mice and weevils.

Indoor Sowing

For a really early start, sow seeds indoors three to four weeks before transplanting outdoors. Sunflowers don't much like being transplanted, so sow the seeds in peat pots to avoid disturbing the roots. Transplant the seedlings outdoors after the last frost. Place top edge of peat pots well below ground level.

Outdoor Sowing

1 Sunflowers grow quickly, so it's best to sow them directly outdoors in spring when the soil is warm, after all danger of frost is past. The seedlings are very sensitive to frost; they prefer heat and plenty of moisture.

2 Cover flowers and developing seed heads with netting or cheesecloth to make sure the birds don't get to your seeds first.

Sweet Pea

Lathyrus odoratus

Sweet peas are self-pollinated, so different varieties usually do not cross. Breeders have developed numerous colors and forms; inherited traits cannot be predicted when growing these hybrids from seed.

Sweet peas prefer cool, moist conditions, so they need to get an early start, before summer's heat sets in. In warm regions, you can sow them directly in the garden in fall, to bloom in late winter and early spring.

seed pod

seed

MASTER GARDENING TIPS

► Anthracnose and bacterial streak are seed-borne diseases that affect sweet peas.

► Dark-flowered sweet peas have harder, darker seed coats and take longer to germinate than light-flowered types, which sometimes rot before they can germinate. Try presprouting seeds of light-flowered types (see box on page 143).

► Feed seedlings with a 5-10-5 fertilizer when they are 4 or 5 inches tall.

The seeds are carried in pods, like those of garden peas. They are ready to harvest when pods are swollen, thoroughly dry, and beginning to break open.

Optimum soil temperature for germination: 55° to 65°F

Germination time at optimum soil temperature: 10 to 15 days

Spacing/thinning: Space vining varieties 6 inches apart, bush varieties 12 inches apart.

Planting depth: ½ to 1 inch

Seed storage requirements: In a jar or bag; cool, dry area

Harvesting the Seed

Let the pods remain on the plants until the seeds are thoroughly dry, then remove the seeds by hand and spread them out to dry for a few weeks before storing.

Indoor Sowing

1 For an extra-early start in spring, sow the seeds indoors 8 to 10 weeks before transplanting outdoors. Sow in peat pots to avoid disturbing the roots when transplanting the seedlings. Cover the pots with an opaque material like aluminum foil and remove covering after seeds germinate.

2 Harden off and transplant into the garden in early spring. Set peat pots deeply, so that the top edges of the pots are below ground level.

Outdoor Sowing

Sow sweet peas directly outdoors in early spring, as soon as the ground can be worked. Work plenty of organic matter (not manure) into the soil before planting. If you live where winters are not severe, sow them in fall in a cold frame where they can overwinter, then transplant seedlings in the garden in spring.

MASTER GARDENING TIPS

Pretreating Sweet Pea Seeds

Sweet peas (especially light-flowered types) benefit from pretreatment before planting. You may find that both soaking and scarifying (nicking the seed coat) enhance germination.

▶ Presprout light-flowered types: (1) lay seeds on damp paper towels, (2) fold up towel, and (3) place towel in a sealed plastic bag in a warm place. Seeds should germinate in three to five days.

▶ Nick the hard seed coat with a file before sowing. Make the cut to one side of the hilum (the scar where the seed was attached to the pod). Never cut into the hilum itself, or you risk damaging the embryo.

▶ Soak seed in warm water overnight before planting.

▶ Dust the seed with a bacterial inoculant powder (available at many garden centers). This helps them gather nitrogen from the atmosphere and results in healthier plants.

Tobacco, Flowering
Nicotiana spp.

Flowering tobacco is cross-pollinated by insects, so grow only one variety at a time if you wish to preserve the purity of a certain strain for seed saving. The flowers bloom in white, red, pink, and shades of yellow and green. Darker colors are genetically dominant over lighter colors. Collect seed only from species and not from named varieties (hybrids and other cultivars), unless you want to experiment. The plants often self-sow.

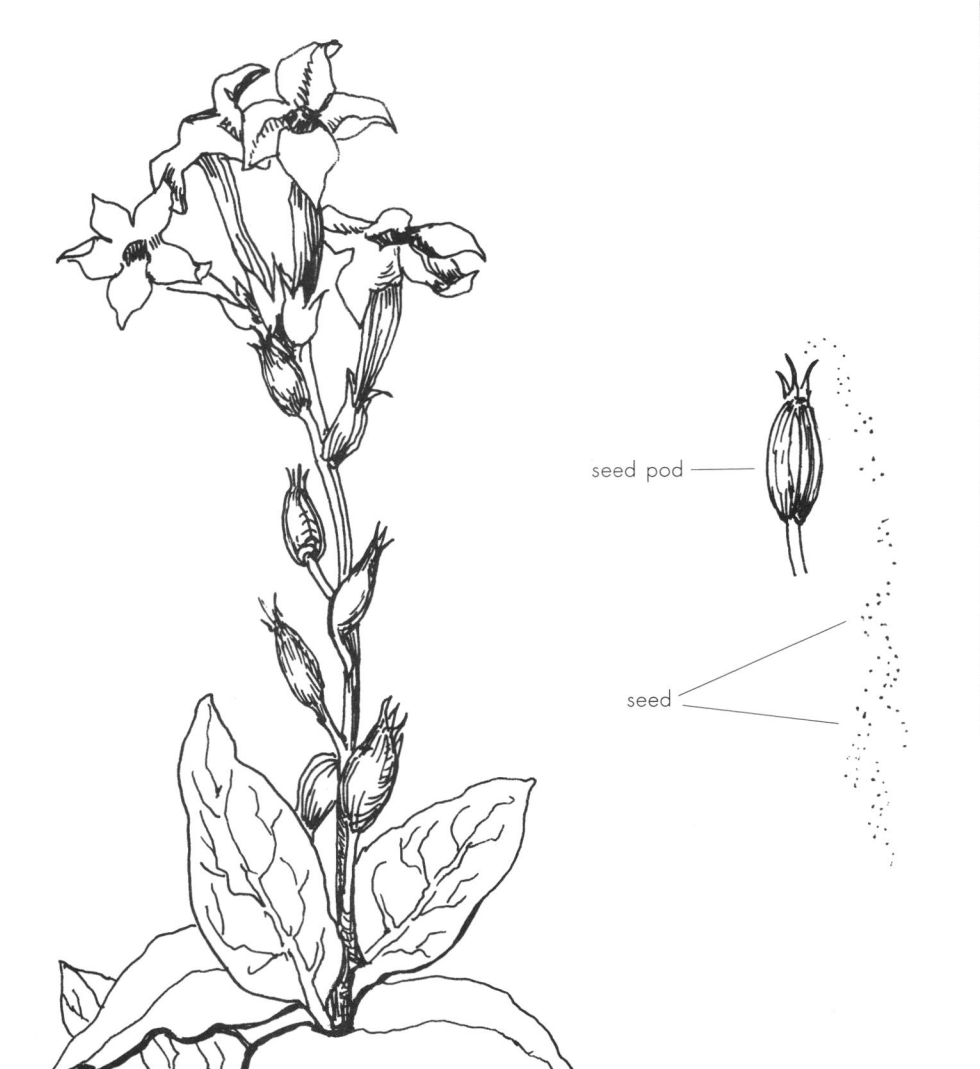

seed pod

seed

MASTER GARDENING TIPS

▶ If you smoke or use tobacco in any form, wash your hands before handling nicotiana seedlings, to avoid spreading tobacco mosaic disease. This applies to all members of the Solanaceae family (petunias, tomatoes, potatoes, eggplant, peppers, etc.). Also, don't grow flowering tobacco where other members of the Solanaceae have grown if there were disease problems of any kind.

▶ In warm regions, flowering tobacco is considered a short-lived perennial.

The tiny, dustlike seeds of flowering tobacco are carried in a small capsule. Seed is ready to harvest when pods are dry.

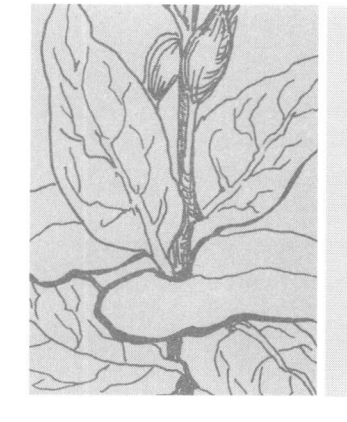

Light requirements for germination: Seeds need light for germination.

Optimum soil temperature for germination: 70° to 85°F

Germination time at optimum soil temperature: 7 to 21 days

Spacing/thinning: Space small varieties 12 inches apart, large varieties 18 to 24 inches apart.

Planting depth: Press lightly into the soil surface; do not cover.

Seed storage requirements: Cool, dark, and dry

Harvesting the Seed

When the seed capsule is dry, cut it off before it can shatter and shake the seeds out on a clean, white sheet of paper. Allow the seeds to dry for about a week before storing.

Indoor Sowing

1 Sow flowering tobacco seeds indoors six to eight weeks before the last spring frost. Because seeds are so tiny, seedlings will grow thickly. Thin by cutting away unwanted seedlings with scissors.

2 Set the plants out (after hardening off) when all danger of frost is past.

Outdoor Sowing

1 You can also sow the seeds directly outdoors after the last frost. The seeds are very tiny; some experts recommend mixing them with fine, dry sand to separate them and make sowing easier. Prepare the bed thoroughly, raking it smooth. Broadcast the seed-sand mixture over the bed.

2 Thin the seedlings as they grow.

Zinnia
Zinnia elegans

Because zinnias are cross-pollinated by insects, you should grow only one variety at a time if you wish to preserve the purity of a certain strain for seed saving. Many varieties are hybrids, and seeds from these will produce plants that vary in quality and color.

MASTER GARDENING TIPS

▶ Zinnia blight is a seed-borne disease that affects zinnias.

▶ Transplanting can cause double-flowered zinnias to revert to the single-flowered form.

▶ Don't grow zinnias where other zinnias have grown if there were problems with alternaria blight; the disease will infect new plants grown in the same spot.

seeds

Zinnia seeds are found at the center of the flower head. When the flower turns dry and brown, the seed is mature and ready to be harvested.

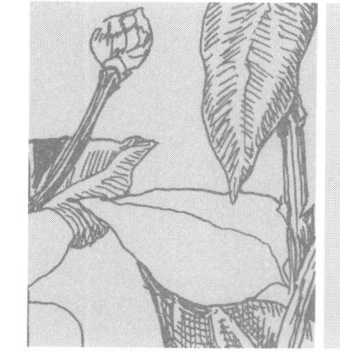

Optimum soil temperature for germination: 70° to 80°F

Germination time at optimum soil temperature: 2 to 7 days

Spacing/thinning: Space dwarf varieties 6 to 9 inches apart, medium varieties 10 to 12 inches apart, and tall varieties 15 to 18 inches apart.

Planting depth: ¼ inch

Seed storage requirements: Cool, dark, and dry

Harvesting the Seed

Pull out the seeds by hand and spread them out to dry for a week or so before storing.

Outdoor Sowing

Zinnias do best when direct-seeded outdoors after the last frost, when the soil is warm.

Indoor Sowing

1 You can start zinnia seeds indoors four to six weeks before the last frost date. They don't like being transplanted, so sow the seeds in peat pots to avoid disturbing the roots. Sow them thinly; seedlings growing too close together will be leggy and weak. The seedlings are susceptible to damping-off, so water the pots from the bottom and provide good air circulation.

2 Transplant the seedlings to the garden (weather permitting) as soon as they can be handled.

Coreopsis, page 172

Bellflower, page 158

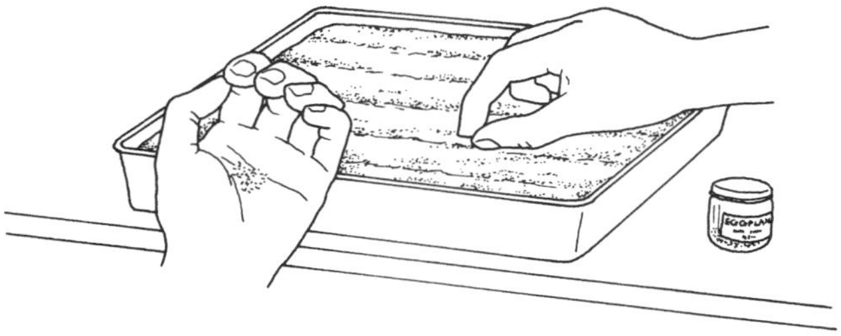

Sowing astilbe, page 153

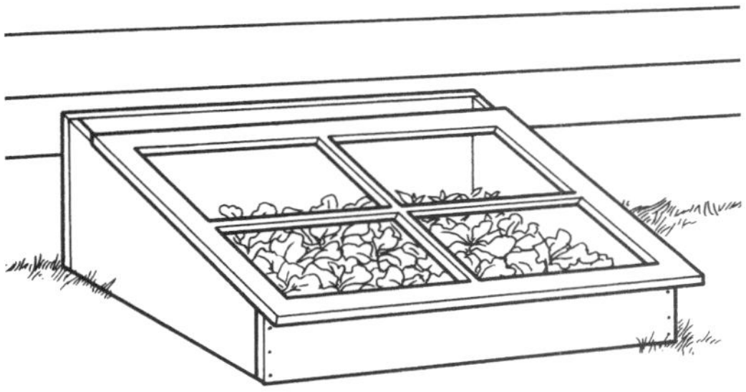

Sowing hollyhocks, page 179

Biennial and Perennial Flowers

When you sow seeds for biennials, you will have plants the first year and flowers and seeds the next. Once the plant has bloomed and set seed, its life cycle is complete. Many biennials reseed themselves freely to produce a new generation in the same spot the following year, and this dependability causes many people to think the plant is a perennial. Because they self-seed, you may find them popping up all over your garden. It's a good idea to move young plants to a single location for a better show! It is easy to collect seed from such plants, as long as you have the patience to wait until the second year, and as long as you can capture the seeds before they disperse. When you collect the seed, you then can control where your plant will grow in your garden. Biennials in this chapter include canterbury bells, foxglove, and lupine.

A perennial, on the other hand, develops a hardy root system that allows the plant to return year after year. There are limitations; some perennials will survive for decades, spreading and multiplying from the roots or crown. Others live only a few years, declining a little more each year until they simply fade away. It is not difficult to collect seed from perennials at the end of each season, but the seeds almost always require special treatment (chilling, for example) before they will germinate, and the seedlings are often slow-growing. For this reason, perennial seed should be sown either outdoors in fall, to germinate in spring after being chilled through the winter, or indoors in late winter, after being chilled in the refrigerator. Simply sowing perennial seed outdoors in spring is risky; the plants may not be well established enough to make it through the following winter.

In This Chapter

- Aster
- Astilbe
- Balloon Flower
- Bee Balm
- Bellflower
- Black-Eyed Susan
- Blazing Star, Gayfeather
- Canterbury Bells
- Clematis
- Columbine
- Coneflower, Purple
- Coreopsis
- Delphinium
- Foxglove
- Hollyhock
- Lupine
- Pinks
- Primrose

Aster

Aster spp.

Asters are cross-pollinated by insects, so grow only one variety at a time if you wish to preserve the purity of a certain strain for seed saving. Aster species can be grown from collected seed (although seedlings may be variable), but Hybrid varieties and some cultivars will not come true. The flowers bloom in shades of purple, lavender, pink, and sometimes white. If you're going to save seed, select plants that are resistant to powdery mildew. The plants often self-sow.

MASTER GARDENING TIPS

▶ The seeds of many asters frequently contain undeveloped embryos; for best results, sow thickly.

▶ Aster seed germinates best when sown fresh in fall.

flower head

seeds

The seeds are carried at the center of the flower head. Harvest them when they are dry and loose, a few weeks after the first fall frost.

Optimum soil temperature for germination: 70° to 75°F
Germination time at optimum soil temperature: 15 to 20 days
Spacing/thinning: Space small varieties 9 to 12 inches apart, tall varieties 24 inches apart.
Planting depth: ⅛ inch
Seed storage requirements: Cool, dark, and dry

Harvesting the Seed

1 Shake off the seeds into a bag, or pull them off by hand. Allow the seeds to dry before storing.

2 If planting in spring, store the dry seeds in the refrigerator.

Outdoor Sowing

Sow fresh aster seeds outdoors soon after harvesting in late fall. In cold regions, sow them in a cold frame. Set the seedlings out in spring after the last frost.

MASTER GARDENING TIPS

▶ Prune plants to 6 or 7 shoots in order to get larger blooms.

▶ Plan to stake tall species.

Indoor Sowing

1 Start aster seeds indoors 8 to 10 weeks before the last spring frost. The stored seeds must be stratified in order to germinate well. To stratify, sow seeds in flats or pots of moistened medium, cover with plastic wrap to retain moisture, and refrigerate for two weeks.

2 After removing them from the refrigerator, set them in a sunny place to germinate.

3 When the seedlings have three or four true leaves, transplant them into individual containers. Seedlings can be transplanted outdoors after the last spring frost.

Astilbe
Astilbe spp.

Astilbes are cross-pollinated by insects, so if you wish to preserve the purity of a certain strain for seed saving, grow only one variety at a time. The species can be grown from collected seed (be aware that seedlings may be variable), but hybrids and other cultivars will not come true.

MASTER GARDENING TIPS

▶ The seed heads of astilbes provide winter interest in the garden when left to dry on the plants.

▶ Plants grown from seed may not flower for two or three years after sowing.

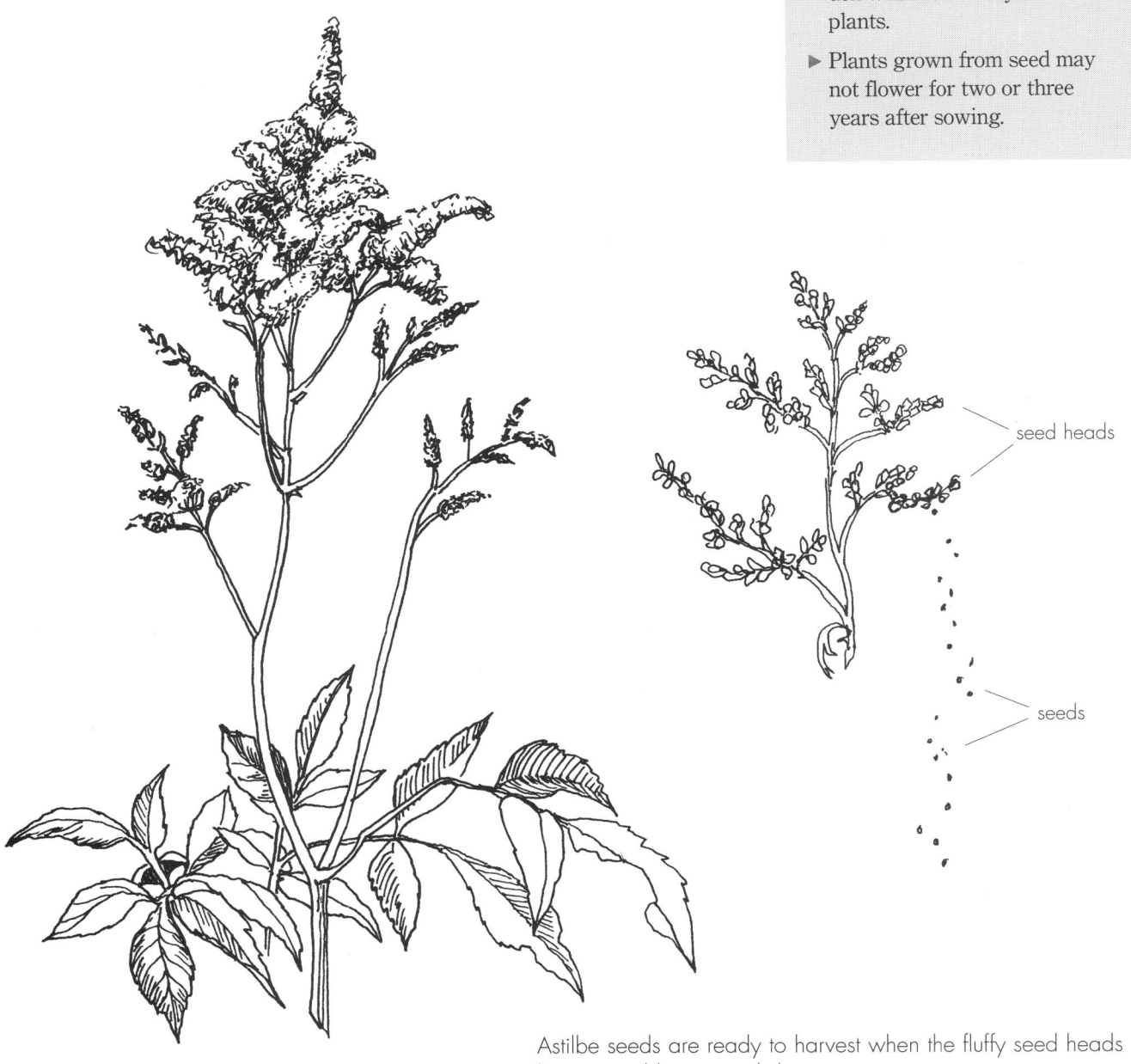

seed heads

seeds

Astilbe seeds are ready to harvest when the fluffy seed heads have turned brown and dry.

Light requirements for germination: Seeds need light for germination.

Optimum soil temperature for germination: 65°F

Germination time at optimum soil temperature: 14 to 21 days

Spacing/thinning: Space small varieties 12 inches apart, large varieties 20 to 30 inches apart.

Planting depth: Press lightly into the soil surface; do not cover.

Seed storage requirements: Cool, dark, and dry

Harvesting the Seed

Cut the seed heads from the plants and rub them between your hands over a bag or large sheet of paper. Winnow out the chaff, then allow the seeds to dry for a week or so before storing.

HINT FOR SUCCESS

If you don't want to sow seeds indoors, you can start seeds in a cold frame in late winter, and set the seedlings in the garden in spring after the last frost.

Outdoor Sowing

Sow fresh astilbe seeds outdoors soon after harvesting in late fall, or start stored seeds outdoors in early spring, before the last frost.

Indoor Sowing

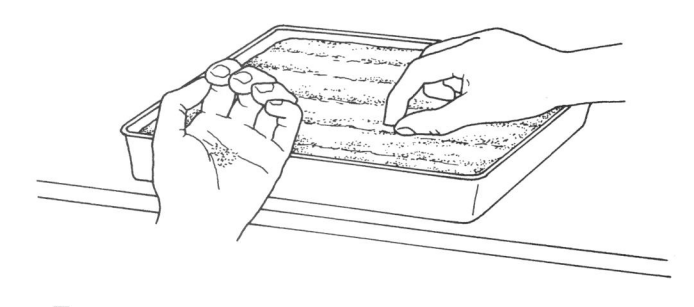

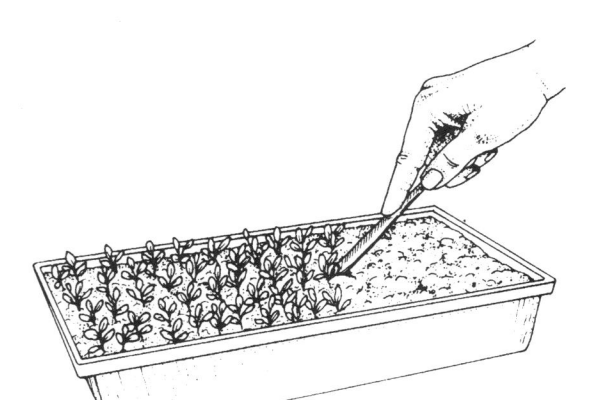

1 Astilbes can be started indoors six to eight weeks before transplanting outdoors. The seeds need light and humidity to germinate; cover the flat with clear plastic until you see the seedlings. The seedlings are susceptible to damping-off, so water the pots from the bottom and provide good air circulation. Do not allow the soil to dry out.

2 When the seedlings have three or four true leaves, transplant them into individual containers. Set seedlings out after the last spring frost.

Balloon Flower
Platycodon grandiflorus

Balloon flowers are cross-pollinated by insects, so grow only one variety at a time if you wish to preserve purity for seed-saving purposes. The balloon flower can be grown from collected seed, but hybrids and other cultivars will not come true. An exception is the cultivar 'Mariesii', which will come true from seed.

MASTER GARDENING TIP

Deadhead to extend blooming season, but be sure to let the strongest plants mature so that you can collect their seed.

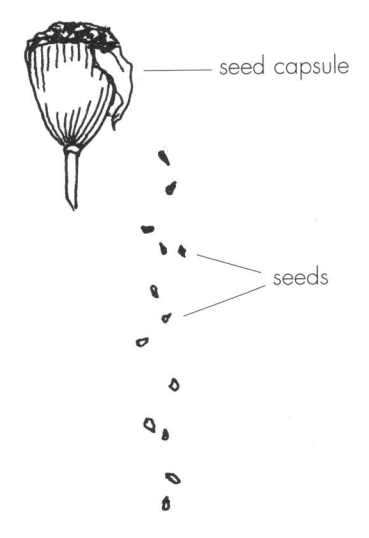

seed capsule

seeds

Balloon flower seeds are carried in capsules atop the flower stalks. Harvest the seed when the capsules are brown and dry.

Light requirements for germination: Seeds need light for germination.

Optimum soil temperature for germination: 70°F

Germination time at optimum soil temperature: 10 to 15 days

Spacing/thinning: Space small varieties 9 to 12 inches apart, large varieties 12 to 18 inches apart.

Planting depth: Press lightly into the soil surface; do not cover.

Seed storage requirements: Cool, dark, and dry

Harvesting the Seed

Split open the seed capsules and remove the seed by hand. Spread out the seeds to dry for a week or so before storing.

Indoor Sowing

1 Balloon flower doesn't like to be transplanted, so if starting seed indoors, sow in individual peat pots to avoid disturbing the roots when you set them in the garden. Indoor sowing can be done six to eight weeks before planting out in late spring.

2 Harden off plants and transplant them outdoors as soon as possible. The seedlings are fragile; handle with care.

Outdoor Sowing

It's best to sow balloon flower directly outdoors after the last spring frost, or in summer, since the plants develop a taproot and don't like to be transplanted.

Bee Balm

***Monarda* spp.**

Bee balm is cross-pollinated by (you guessed it!) bees, so grow only one variety at a time if you wish to preserve its purity for seed saving. The species can be grown from collected seed, but hybrids and other cultivars will not come true. Most seed strains bloom in pale shades of lilac and pink. If you're going to save seed, select plants that are most resistant to powdery mildew. The bright flowers attract not only bees but hummingbirds to your yard.

MASTER GARDENING TIPS

▶ After transplanting the seedlings to individual containers, pinch them back regularly to encourage bushy growth.

▶ Bee balm seedlings grow slowly.

▶ To give plants an early start without sowing indoors, sow seeds in late fall in a cold frame. Set the seedlings out in spring after the last frost.

seed head

seed head

The seeds ripen in late summer, one to three weeks after the plants stop blooming. Seeds are held in a round cluster; test them for ripeness by shaking the seed head. If the seeds fall off readily, it's time to harvest them.

Optimum soil temperature for germination: 60° to 70°F
Germination time at optimum soil temperature: 7 to 14 days
Spacing/thinning: 18 to 24 inches
Planting depth: ⅛ inch
Seed storage requirements: Cool, dark, and dry

Harvesting the Seed

1 Cut the seed heads from the plant and lay them out to dry for a few days.

2 When thoroughly dry, place the seed heads in a paper bag and shake until the seeds fall off. Winnow out the chaff and store the dry seeds.

3 If planting in the spring, store the dry seeds in the refrigerator.

Outdoor Sowing

Sow fresh seeds outdoors soon after harvesting in the fall.

Indoor Sowing

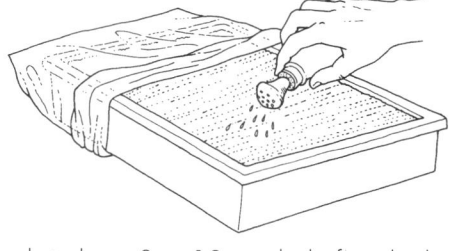

1 Start seeds indoors 8 to 10 weeks before the last spring frost. The stored seeds must be stratified in order to germinate well: Sow seeds in flats of moistened growing medium, cover with plastic wrap, and refrigerate for 2 weeks.

2 Remove from the refrigerator and set them in a sunny place to grow.

3 Transplant the seedlings to individual containers six or seven weeks after they have emerged.

4 Seedlings can be transplanted outdoors after the last spring frost, but only if the roots are well developed.

Bellflower
Campanula spp.

Bellflowers are cross-pollinated by insects, so grow only one variety at a time if you wish to preserve the purity of a certain strain for seed saving. The species can be grown from collected seed, but hybrids and other cultivars will not come true. Some varieties self-sow.

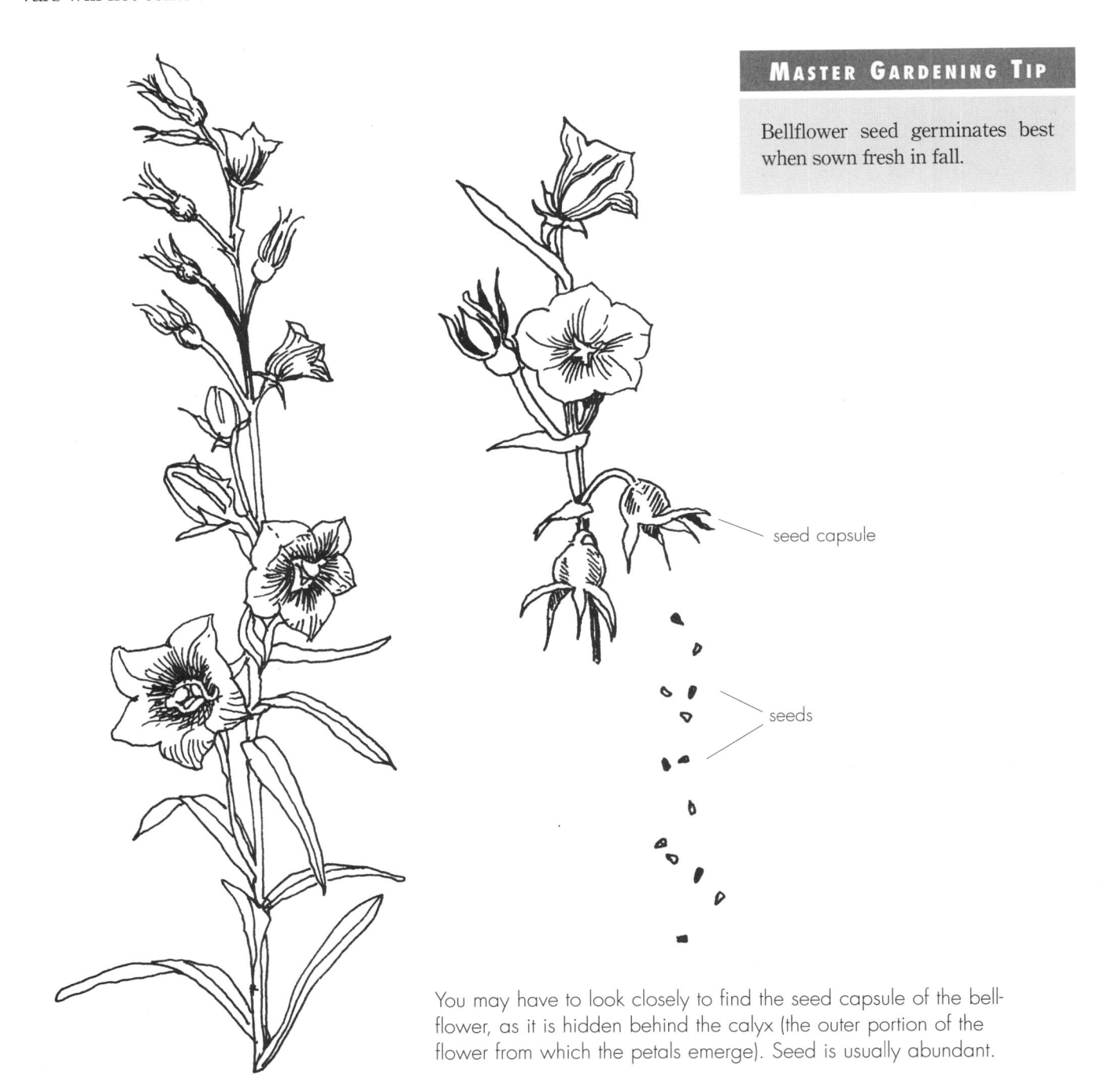

MASTER GARDENING TIP

Bellflower seed germinates best when sown fresh in fall.

seed capsule

seeds

You may have to look closely to find the seed capsule of the bell-flower, as it is hidden behind the calyx (the outer portion of the flower from which the petals emerge). Seed is usually abundant.

Light requirements for germination: Seeds need light for germination.

Optimum soil temperature for germination: 70° to 80°F

Germination time at optimum soil temperature: 6 to 14 days

Spacing/thinning: Space small varieties 5 to 10 inches apart, tall varieties 15 to 20 inches apart.

Planting depth: Press lightly into the soil surface; do not cover.

Seed storage requirements: Cool, dark, and dry

Harvesting the Seed

1 When the flowers fade, cut off the seed heads before they can shatter, and place them in a bag to continue ripening.

2 After a few weeks, you should be able to remove the seeds. Allow the seeds to dry thoroughly before storing.

3 If planting in spring, store the dry seeds in the refrigerators.

Outdoor Sowing

Sow fresh bellflower seeds outdoors soon after harvesting in late fall. Even in cold regions you can give these plants a head start by sowing seeds in a cold frame in late fall. Set seedlings out in spring after the last expected frost.

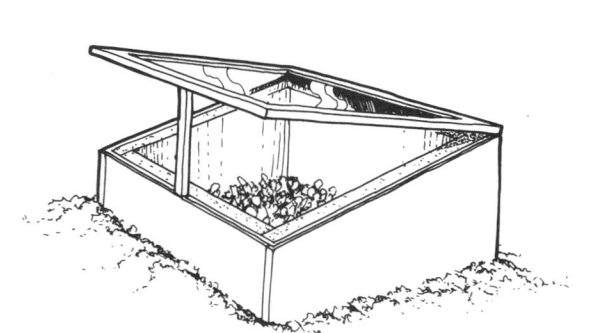

Indoor Sowing

1 Start seeds indoors 8 to 10 weeks before the last spring frost. Stored seeds must be stratified: Sow them in flats or pots of moistened medium, cover with plastic wrap to retain moisture, and refrigerate for three weeks.

2 After removing them from the refrigerator, set them in a sunny place to grow until it is time to transplant them outdoors after the last frost.

Black-Eyed Susan
Rudbeckia hirta

Black-eyed Susans are cross-pollinated by insects, so if you wish to preserve the purity of a certain strain for seed saving, grow only one variety at a time. If the species is grown from collected seed, hybrids and other cultivars will not come true. The plants may self-sow.

seed-bearing cone

seeds

MASTER GARDENING TIPS

▶ Annual species of *Rudbeckia* can also be grown from seed.

▶ The plants will usually flower the first year if sown in spring.

▶ Black-eyed Susans produce a high percentage of viable seed.

▶ The seed germinates best when sown fresh in fall.

The seeds are carried in a cone in the center of the flower head. Seed is mature when these cone-shaped seed heads turn gray and seeds loosen, about five or six weeks after the flowers have faded.

Light requirements for germination: Seeds need light for germination.

Optimum soil temperature for germination: 70° to 75°F

Germination time at optimum soil temperature: 7 to 14 days

Spacing/thinning: Space small varieties 12 to 18 inches apart, tall varieties 24 to 36 inches apart.

Planting depth: Press lightly into the soil surface; do not cover.

Seed storage requirements: Cool, dark, and dry

Harvesting the Seed

In fall, when the cones turn gray and the seeds have loosened, pull out the seeds by hand. Lay them out to dry for a week or two before storing.

Outdoor Sowing

Sow fresh seeds outdoors in late fall soon after harvesting. In cold regions, sow seeds in a cold frame in late fall. Set seedlings in the garden the following spring after the last expected frost.

Indoor Sowing

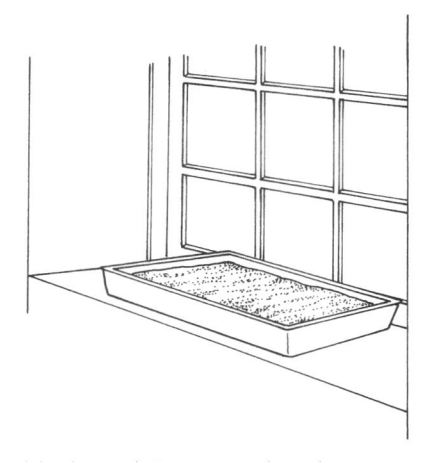

1 Start black-eyed Susan seeds indoors six to eight weeks before the last spring frost. Stored seeds must be stratified to germinate. Stratify seeds by sowing them in flats or pots of moistened medium, covering with plastic wrap to retain moisture. Refrigerate for two to three weeks. Remove them from the refrigerator and set them in a sunny place to grow.

2 Transplant to individual containers when three to four true leaves develop. Water regularly until they recover from transplanting, then let the soil dry out between waterings.

3 Transplant outdoors after the last frost.

Blazing Star, Gayfeather
***Liatris* spp.**

Blazing star is cross-pollinated by insects, so if you wish to preserve its purity for seed saving, grow only one variety at a time. Hybrids and other cultivars will not come true if species are grown from collected seed.

MASTER GARDENING TIPS

▶ Blazing star tends to produce a large percentage of empty or undeveloped seeds. Viable seeds will be plumper and larger than inviable seeds, which are usually thin, flat, and lightweight.

▶ The seedlings are slow-growing, but the plants will grow quickly once transplanted outdoors.

▶ The seed germinates best when sown fresh in fall.

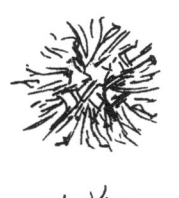

seed head

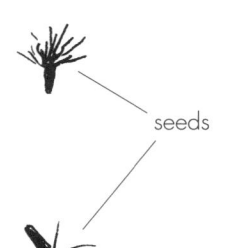

seeds

When all the flowers on the stalk fade and turn to fluffy seed heads (usually sometime in October), it is time to harvest seed.

SEED FACTS

Optimum soil temperature for germination: 65° to 75°F

Germination time at optimum soil temperature: 14 to 21 days

Spacing/thinning: 12 to 15 inches

Planting depth: ⅛ inch

Seed storage requirements: Cool, dark, and dry

Harvesting the Seed

Cut down the stalks, place them in a paper bag, and allow them to dry for a few days indoors. When the seed heads are well dried, they will expand, and you can then easily brush, shake, or pick out the seeds.

Outdoor Sowing

Sow fresh seeds outdoors soon after harvesting in the fall. In his book *Growing and Propagating Wild Flowers,* Harry R. Phillips suggests cutting the flowering stalk and laying it in an outdoor seedbed or cold frame and covering it with a half inch or so of soil. Seedlings, which look like slender blades of grass, appear the following spring.

Indoor Sowing

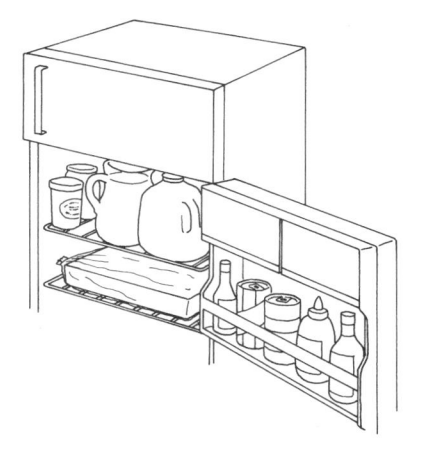

1 Start blazing star seeds indoors six to eight weeks before the last spring frost. Stored seeds must be stratified to germinate well. Stratify seeds by sowing them in flats or pots of moistened medium, and covering the flats with plastic wrap to retain moisture. Refrigerate for two or three weeks.

2 Remove flats from the refrigerator and set them in a sunny place to grow.

3 Transplant seedlings to individual containers (or into the garden, if weather permits) when they have developed good roots, usually 8 to 10 weeks after sowing.

Canterbury Bells
Campanula medium

Canterbury bells are cross-pollinated by insects, so grow only one variety at a time if you wish to preserve the purity of a certain strain for seed saving. If a cross should occur, darker colors will be genetically dominant over lighter ones. In addition to the normal bell-shaped flower, there are two unusual flower forms: the cup-and-saucer (a bell within a flared set of "petals") and the hose-in-hose (a bell within a bell). Both of these forms are partly dominant over the bellflower form. Double-flowered forms will not come true from seed.

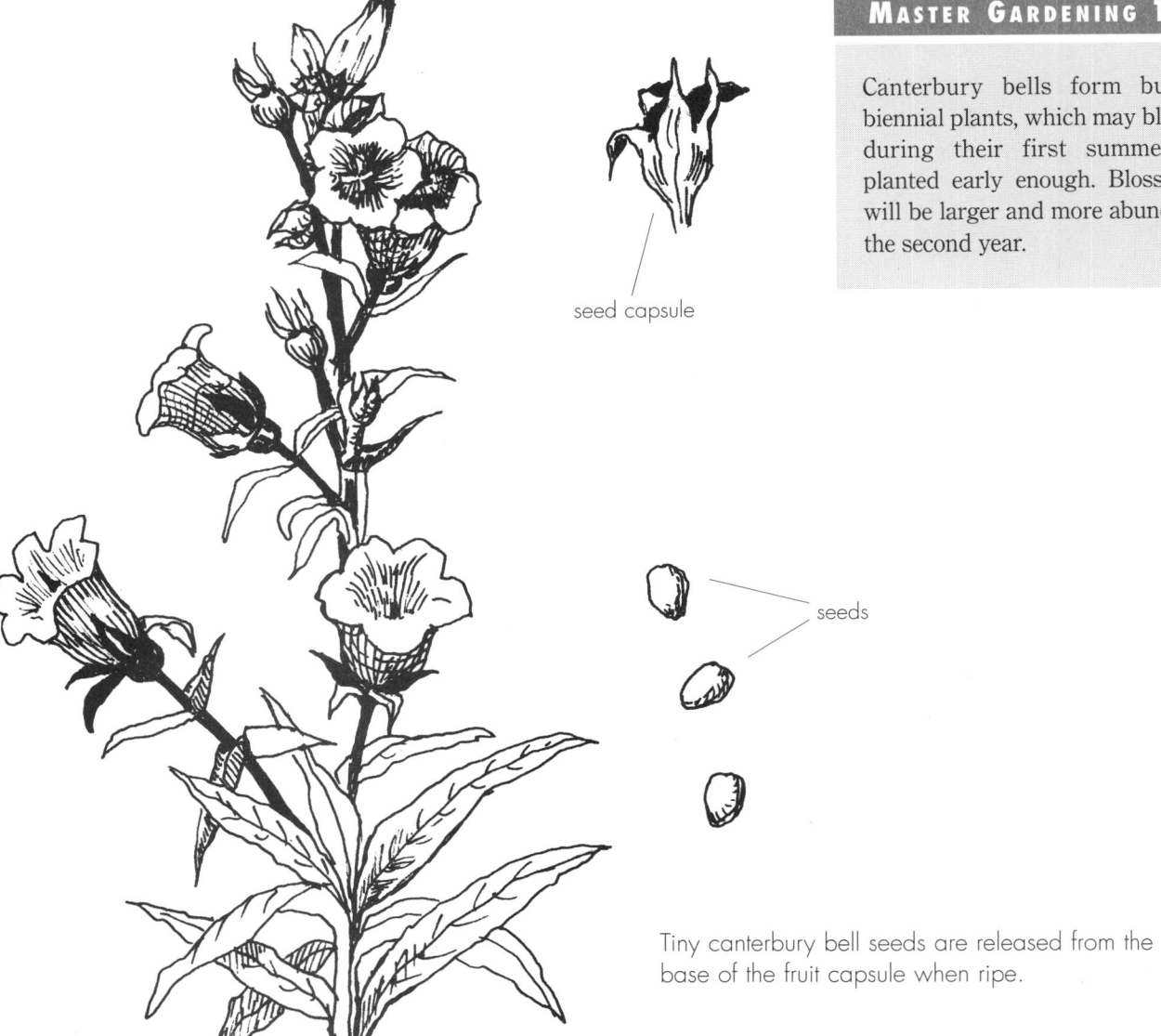

seed capsule

seeds

Tiny canterbury bell seeds are released from the base of the fruit capsule when ripe.

MASTER GARDENING TIP

Canterbury bells form bushy biennial plants, which may bloom during their first summer if planted early enough. Blossoms will be larger and more abundant the second year.

Light requirements for germination: Seeds need light for germination.

Optimum soil temperature for germination: 60° to 70°F

Germination time at optimum soil temperature: 6 to 12 days

Spacing/thinning: Space small varieties 5 to 10 inches apart, tall varieties 15 to 20 inches apart.

Planting depth: Press lightly into the soil surface; do not cover.

Seed storage requirements: Cool, dark, and dry

Harvesting the Seed

Collect the tiny seeds before they are released from the base of the fruit capsule, and spread them out to dry for a week or so before storing.

Indoor Sowing

1 Canterbury bells are easy to grow from seed. Start the seeds indoors in seed flat 8 to 10 weeks before transplanting outdoors.

2 When seedlings have two or more true leaves, remove them from the flat and set them in pots.

3 Harden off and plant seedlings in the garden after danger of frost is past. The plants will die down in the fall but return again the following spring and bloom that summer.

HINT FOR SUCCESS

Once you have raised Canterbury bells, you will recognize young plants that have self-sown. Move them together during their first season, so that when they bloom the following summer, their show will be more impressive.

Outdoor Sowing

Canterbury bells can be direct-sown outdoors in late spring or early summer. Prepare the bed carefully. Because the seed is so small, you may want to mix it with sand to facilitate dispersal.

Clematis
Clematis spp.

Clematis is cross-pollinated by insects, so grow only one variety at a time if you wish to preserve the purity of a certain strain for seed saving. Clematis species can be grown from collected seed, but hybrids and other cultivars will not come true. If you're going to save seed, select flower size, color, and abundance, and strong stems.

MASTER GARDENING TIPS

▶ The seed heads of clematis are very ornamental and provide winter interest in the garden when left to dry on the plants.

▶ The seed germinates best when sown fresh in fall.

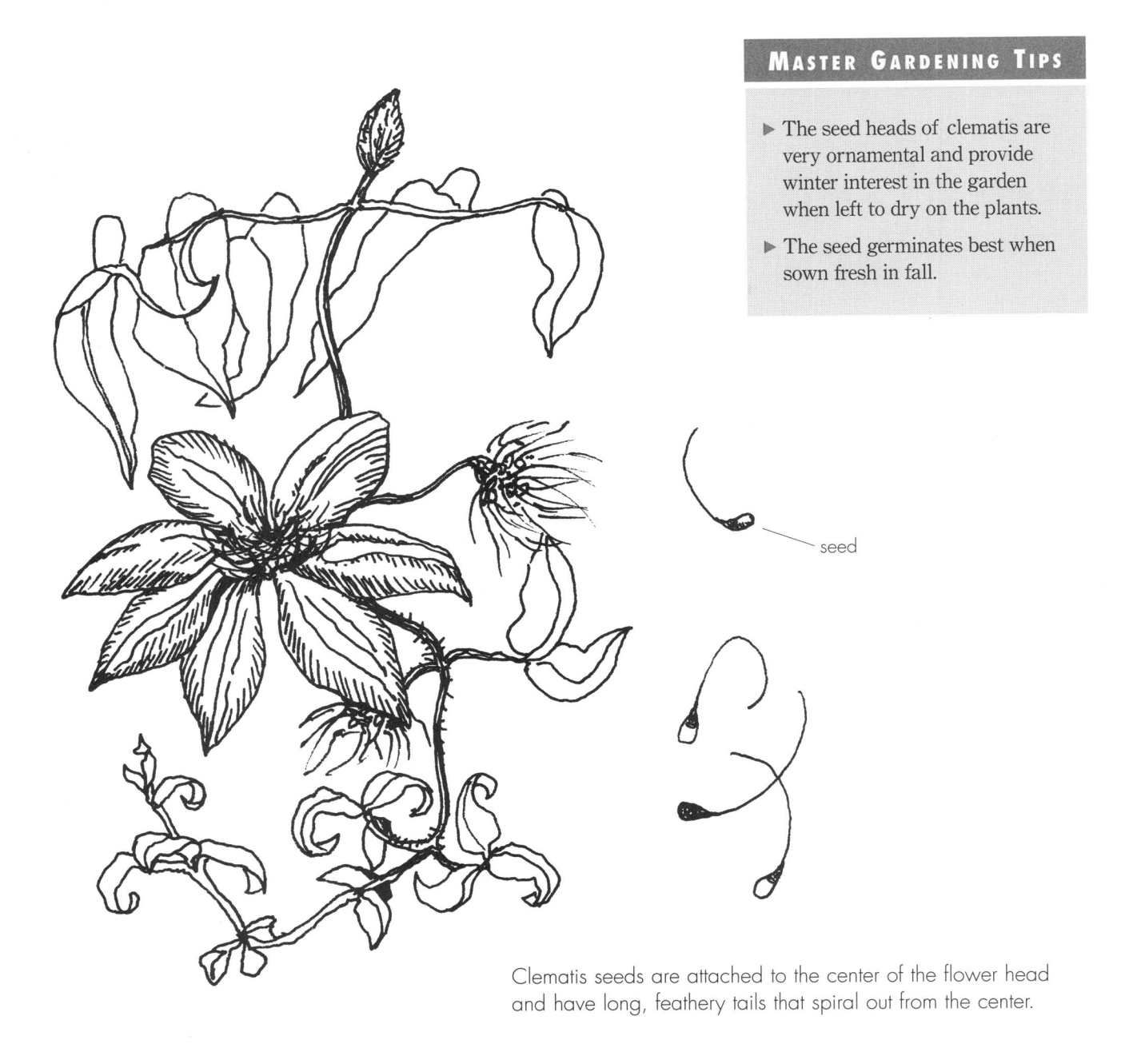

seed

Clematis seeds are attached to the center of the flower head and have long, feathery tails that spiral out from the center.

Optimum soil temperature for germination: 70° to 75°F

Germination time at optimum soil temperature: 1 to 9 months

Spacing/thinning: 24 to 36 inches

Planting depth: ⅛ inch

Seed storage requirements: Cool, dark, dry

Harvesting the Seed

1 Allow the seed heads to dry thoroughly on the plant, and then pull out the seeds by hand. Dry the seeds indoors for another week or so before storing.

2 If you plan to in spring, store the dry seeds in the refrigerator.

Outdoor Sowing

Sow fresh seeds outdoors in flats soon after harvesting. Protect the seeds by covering the flats with glass. Keep flats moist. Transplant the seedlings to their permanent location in spring.

Indoor Sowing

MASTER GARDENING TIPS

▶ Clematis is a climbing vine, so provide wire or string for it to twine around.

▶ The base of the stem is fragile and so should not be roughly handled. Although clematis thrives in sun, it's important to keep its roots cool and shaded.

1 Start seeds indoors 6 to 8 weeks before the last spring frost. Stored seeds must be stratified. To do this, sow seeds in flats or pots of moistened medium, cover with plastic wrap to retain moisture, and refrigerate for 4 to 12 weeks.

2 Remove from the refrigerator and set in a sunny place to germinate.

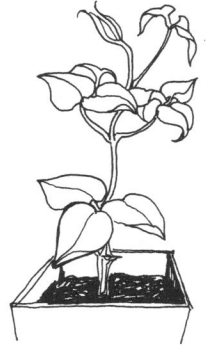

3 Transplant seedlings to the garden when they are big enough to handle, weather permitting.

Columbine

Aquilegia spp.

Columbine is cross-pollinated by insects, so if you wish to preserve its purity for seed saving, grow only one variety at a time. Many varieties are hybrids and will not come true from collected seed; check what kind you are growing before planning to harvest seed. Species will self-sow.

MASTER GARDENING TIPS

▶ Some cultivars will come true if isolated from other varieties. Be sure to pull out any self-sown rogue seedlings that appear.

▶ Columbine is easy to grow from seed. The seeds germinate best if sown fresh in fall.

▶ The seeds germinate quickly, but the seedlings are slow-growing.

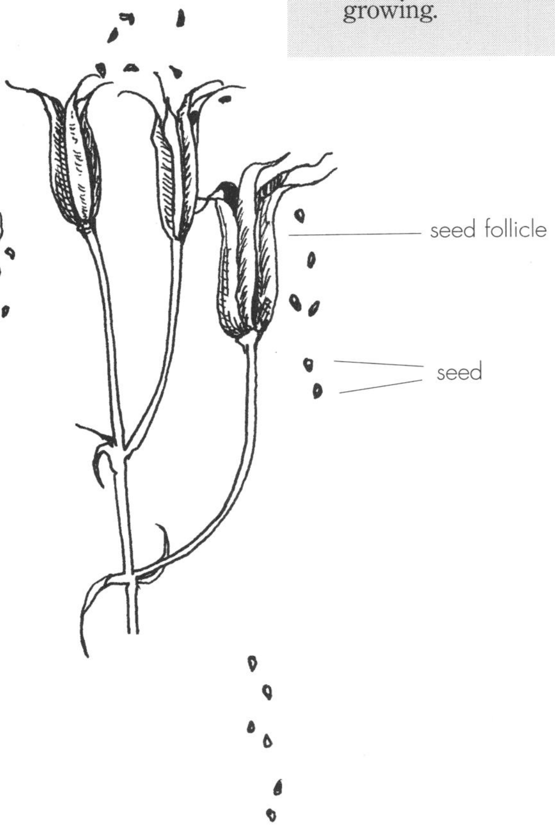

seed follicle

seed

The seed is easy to collect but requires good timing. When the flowers fade, the seeds begin to ripen inside a five-sectioned follicle that looks like a cluster of parchment rolls. The seeds ripen quickly to a shiny black, and the follicles expand and disperse the seeds only a few days later. Begin checking the follicles before they turn brown. When the seeds are dark green and almost black, they are ready to harvest.

Light requirements for germination: Seeds need light for germination.

Optimum soil temperature for germination: 70° to 75°F

Germination time at optimum soil temperature: 7 to 14 days

Spacing/thinning: Space small varieties 6 to 12 inches apart, tall varieties 15 to 20 inches apart.

Planting depth: Press lightly into the soil surface; do not cover.

Seed storage requirements: Cool, dark, and dry

Harvesting the Seed

1 Collect seeds by cutting the stalks and placing them in a paper bag. In a few days, the seeds will have finished ripening and can be easily shaken out of the follicles. Allow them to dry for another week before storing.

2 If you are planting columbine in spring, store the dry seeds in the refrigerator.

Outdoor Sowing

Sow fresh seeds outdoors in fall soon after harvesting.

Indoor Sowing

1 Start seeds indoors six to eight weeks before the last spring frost. The stored seeds must be stratified in order to germinate well. To stratify, sow seeds thinly in flats of moistened medium, pressing them gently into the soil. The seeds should be visible.

2 Cover with plastic and refrigerate for two weeks. Remove flats from the refrigerator and set them in a sunny place to germinate. Columbine seedlings are very fragile. Keep them out of strong sunlight, and make sure the soil is consistently moist. Do not fertilize.

3 Transplant the seedlings to individual containers when they have developed three or four true leaves.

4 Move them outdoors and harden them off after the last spring frost. Transplant columbines into their permanent location when young, after they have developed a good root system, but before they have grown a taproot.

Coneflower, Purple
Echinacea purpurea

Coneflowers are cross-pollinated by insects, so grow only one variety at a time if you wish to preserve the purity of a certain strain for seed saving. The species can be grown from collected seed, but hybrids and other cultivars will not come true. If you're going to save seed, select plants that are most resistant to powdery mildew. The plants may self-sow.

MASTER GARDENING TIPS

▶ If you have a lot of finches in your area, you might want to place bags over some of the ripening seed heads until harvest time so that you don't lose all your seeds to greedy birds.

▶ Coneflowers tend to produce a large percentage of empty or undeveloped seeds, and those that are viable don't stay viable for very long; the seed germinates best when sown fresh in fall.

seed-bearing cone

seeds

The seeds are carried in a cone in the center of the flower head. Five or six weeks after the flowers fade, the cones turn gray, signaling seed maturation.

Optimum soil temperature for germination: 70° to 75°F

Germination time at optimum soil temperature: 7 to 14 days

Spacing/thinning: Space small varieties 12 to 15 inches apart, tall varieties 18 to 24 inches apart.

Planting depth: ⅛ inch

Seed storage requirements: Cool, dark, and dry

Harvesting the Seed

1 In fall, when the cones turn gray and the seeds have loosened, pull out the seeds by hand and lay them out to dry for a week or two.

2 Pick out any lightweight or shriveled seeds before storing.

3 If planting in spring, store dried seeds in the refrigerator.

Outdoor Sowing

Sow fresh seeds outdoors soon after harvesting in fall.

Indoor Sowing

1 Sow seeds indoors six to eight weeks before the last spring frost. The stored seeds must be stratified: Sow seeds in flats or pots of moistened medium, cover with plastic wrap, and refrigerate for at least four weeks.

2 After removing them from the refrigerator, set them in a sunny place to grow.

3 Transplant the seedlings to larger individual containers when they have developed two to three true leaves.

4 Move them outdoors when they have developed a strong root system, usually three to four weeks after transplanting.

Coreopsis
Coreopsis grandiflora

Coreopsis is cross-pollinated by insects, so if you wish to preserve the purity of a certain strain for seed saving, be sure to grow just one variety at a time. The species can be grown from collected seed, but hybrids and other cultivars will not come true and are often inferior.

MASTER GARDENING TIP

The seed germinates best when sown fresh in fall.

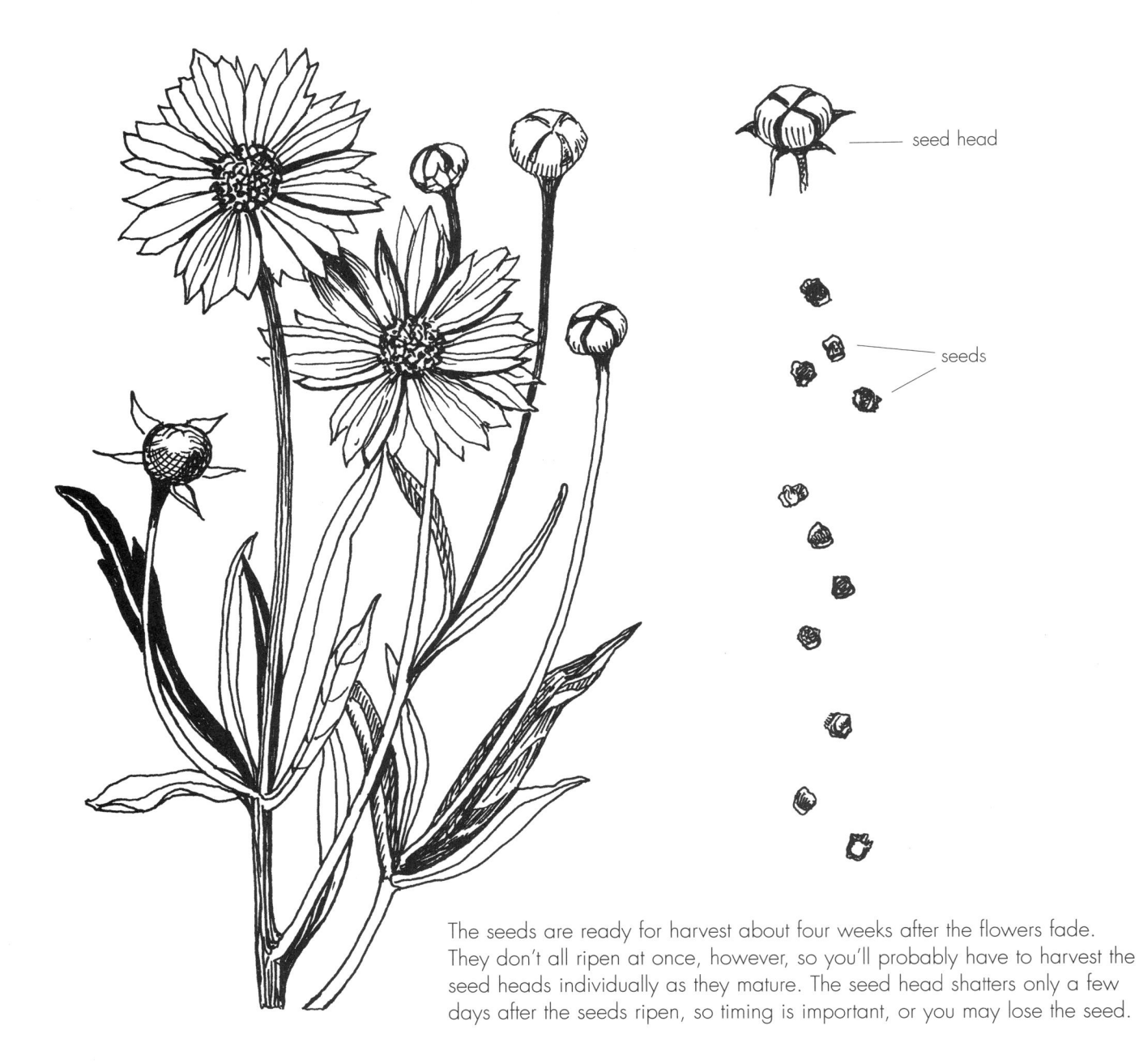

seed head

seeds

The seeds are ready for harvest about four weeks after the flowers fade. They don't all ripen at once, however, so you'll probably have to harvest the seed heads individually as they mature. The seed head shatters only a few days after the seeds ripen, so timing is important, or you may lose the seed.

Light requirements for germination: Seeds need light for germination.

Optimum soil temperature for germination: 55° to 70°F

Germination time at optimum soil temperature: 7 to 14 days

Spacing/thinning: Space dwarfs 6 to 10 inches apart, tall varieties 12 to 18 inches apart.

Planting depth: Press lightly into the soil surface; do not cover.

Seed storage requirements: Cool, dark, and dry

Seed viability: At least 3 years

Harvesting the Seed

1 Cut the stalks and remove the seeds from the seed heads by hand. Winnow out the chaff (there will be plenty), and let the seeds dry for a week or so before storing.

2 If planting in spring, store dry seeds in the refrigerator.

Outdoor Sowing

Sow fresh seeds outdoors in fall soon after harvesting.

Indoor Sowing

1 Start coreopsis seeds indoors 8 to 10 weeks before the last spring frost. Stored seeds must be stratified in order to germinate well. To stratify, sow seeds in flats or pots of moistened medium. Cover with plastic wrap, and refrigerate 3 to 4 weeks.

2 After removing flats from the refrigerator, set them in a sunny place to grow.

3 Transplant the seedlings to larger individual containers when they have developed two to three true leaves. Coreopsis seedlings grow quickly, and you may be able to transplant them three weeks after sowing. When transplanting, don't let the leaves rest on wet soil; this could be fatal.

4 Move the young plants outdoors when their roots are filling the pots after the last frost in spring.

Delphinium

Delphinium elatum

Delphiniums are cross-pollinated by insects, so grow only one variety at a time if you wish to preserve the purity of a certain strain for seed saving. The species can be grown from collected seed, but hybrids and other cultivars will not come true. Darker colors are genetically dominant over lighter colors. The plants may self-sow.

MASTER GARDENING TIPS

▶ Dark blue varieties often take longer to germinate than light-colored varieties.

▶ Delphinium seed is poisonous; keep out of reach of children.

▶ The seeds lose viability quickly, and germinate best when sown fresh in fall.

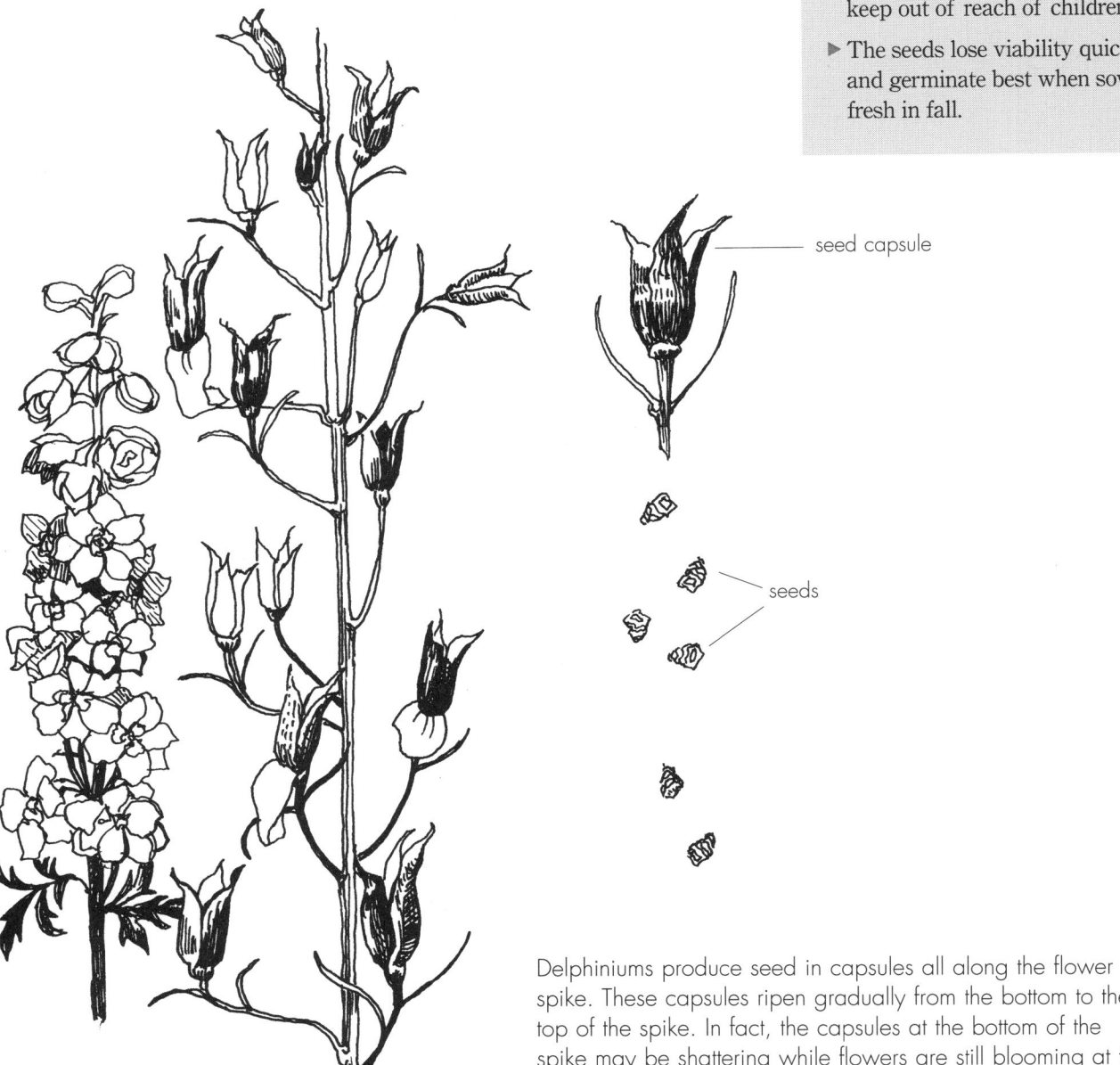

seed capsule

seeds

Delphiniums produce seed in capsules all along the flower spike. These capsules ripen gradually from the bottom to the top of the spike. In fact, the capsules at the bottom of the spike may be shattering while flowers are still blooming at the top of the spike.

Optimum soil temperature for germination: 60° to 75°F

Germination time at optimum soil temperature: 8 to 15 days

Spacing/thinning: Space small varieties 12 to 18 inches apart, tall varieties 24 to 36 inches apart.

Planting depth: ⅛ to ¼ inch

Seed storage requirements: Sealed container in refrigerator

Harvesting the Seed

1 Begin to collect the seed when you see the bottom capsules start to open. Cut off the capsule, and shake the seed out of the end into a bag. Make sure the seeds are completely dry before storing.

2 If planting in spring, store dry seeds in the refrigerator.

Outdoor Sowing

Sow fresh seeds outdoors soon after harvesting in fall.

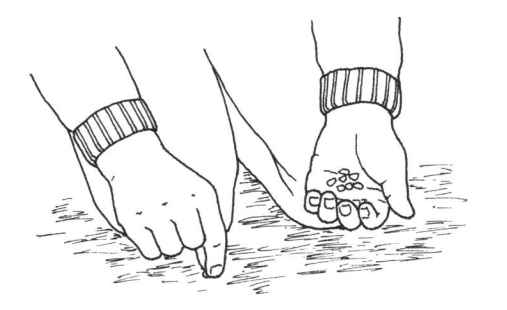

Indoor Sowing

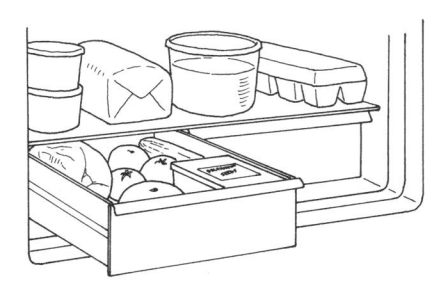

1 Start seeds indoors 8 to 10 weeks before the last spring frost. Stored seeds must be stratified: Sow seeds in flats or pots of moistened medium, cover with plastic wrap to retain moisture, and refrigerate for 2 weeks.

3 When the seedlings emerge, try not to disturb them until it is time to transplant them outdoors in early spring, around the time of the last frost.

2 After removing them from the refrigerator, set them in a sunny place to grow. Keep the soil temperature between 60° and 68°F — a higher temperature may cause the seeds to return to dormancy.

Foxglove
Digitalis purpurea

Foxglove is cross-pollinated by insects, so grow only one variety at a time if you wish to preserve the purity of a certain strain for seed saving. The purple-flowered form is genetically dominant; if you want white flowers, you must rogue out purple-flowering plants regularly for a few years. Purple-flowering plants can be identified as such before they bloom by their purple-streaked stems. If you're going to save seed, select early-blooming plants that are resistant to crown rot. The plants often self-sow.

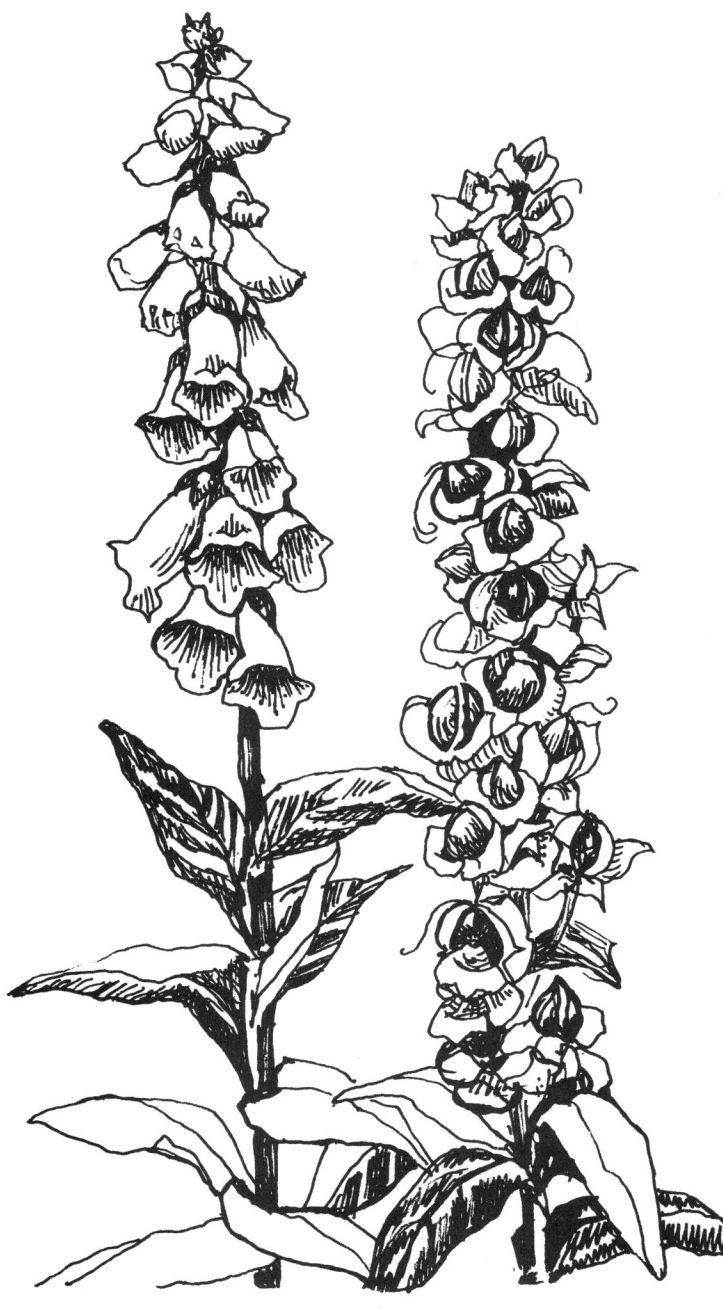

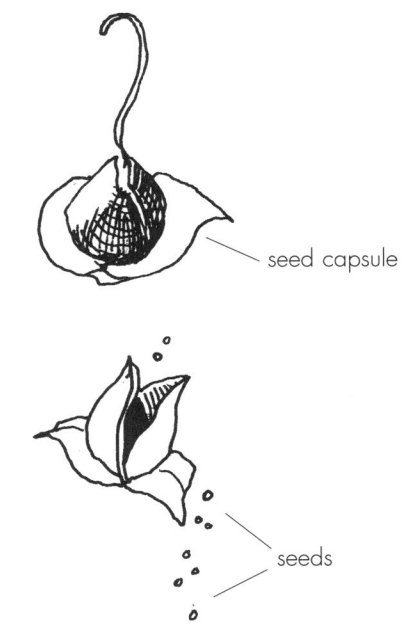

seed capsule

seeds

> **MASTER GARDENING TIP**
>
> Cross breeding *Digitalis purpurea* and *D. lutea* produces sterile plants. The hybrid *D.* x *mertonensis* will come true from seed.

Foxgloves produce abundant seed in capsules all along the flower spike. These capsules shatter suddenly, but not all at the same time. In fact, the capsules at the bottom of the spike may be shattering while flowers are still blooming at the top of the spike.

Light requirements for germination: Seeds need light for germination.

Optimum soil temperature for germination: 60° to 70°F

Germination time at optimum soil temperature: 15 to 20 days

Spacing/thinning: 18 to 24 inches

Seed planting depth: Press lightly into the soil surface; do not cover.

Seed storage requirements: Cool, dark, and dry

Harvesting the Seed

Begin to collect the seed when you see the bottom capsules start to open. Make sure the seeds are completely dry before storing.

Outdoor Sowing

Foxgloves are easy to grow from seed: Simply scatter a handful of seeds on the ground after the last spring frost. You can also start them in a cold frame in late fall and transplant them to the garden in summer.

Indoor Sowing

For an early start, sow seeds indoors 8 to 10 weeks before transplanting outdoors. Plant the seedlings out 2 to 3 weeks before the last spring frost.

MASTER GARDENING TIPS

▶ In warm regions, plant seeds outdoors in late summer or early fall.

▶ Foxgloves are often short-lived, so plan to save seed so that you can start new plants and be assured of a continuous supply.

Hollyhock
Alcea rosea

Hollyhocks are cross-pollinated by insects, so grow only one variety at a time if you wish to preserve the purity of a certain strain for seed saving. Unless you are growing the plants from commercially produced seed, the seedlings will be variable. Double-flowered forms are most likely to come true from seed. Double forms are incompletely dominant over singles; if the two forms are cross-bred, the F_1 generation will have semidouble flowers, and the F_2 generation will be a combination of double, semidouble, and single flowers. If you're going to save seed, select plants that are most resistant to powdery mildew, rust, and leaf spot, and rogue out the rest. The plants often self-sow.

MASTER GARDENING TIP

Be sure to put hollyhocks in their permanent spot in the garden before they develop a taproot.

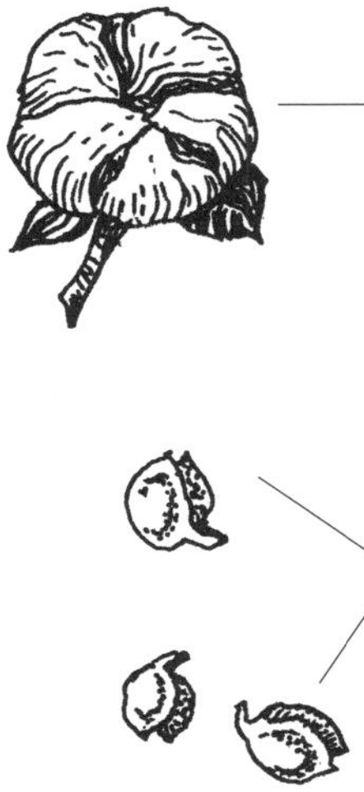

seed-bearing fruit capsule

seeds

The abundant seeds are packed tightly in a disk-shaped fruit capsule.

Light requirements for germination: Seeds need light for germination.

Optimum soil temperature for germination: 60° to 70°F

Germination time at optimum soil temperature: 10 to 14 days

Spacing/thinning: 2 to 3 feet

Seed planting depth: Press lightly into the soil surface; do not cover.

Seed storage requirements: Cool, dark, and dry

Harvesting the Seed

1 Cut off the capsules two or three weeks after the plant has flowered and dry them thoroughly.

2 Separate the seeds by hand and winnow out the chaff.

3 Allow the seeds to dry for another week before storing.

Outdoor Sowing

Hollyhocks are easy to grow from seed. Sow the seeds outdoors in early fall or late spring. Alternatively, you can start them in a cold frame in late summer and transplant the seedlings out early the following spring.

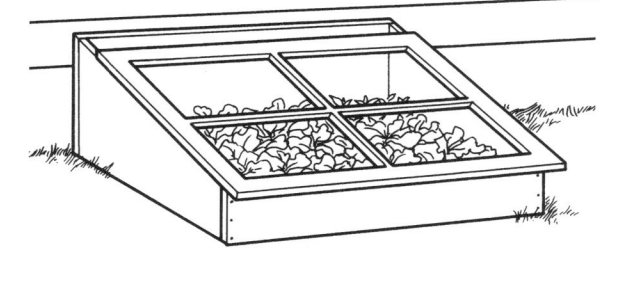

Indoor Sowing

1 Hollyhocks can also be started indoors six to eight weeks before transplanting outdoors. They don't like being transplanted, however, so sow the seeds in peat pots to avoid disturbing the roots.

2 Set them out in early fall for flowers the following spring. If they have been growing in peat pots, be sure to set the entire pot in the hole so that the top edges are below ground level. Exposed material can cause moisture to wick away from the plant's roots.

Lupine

Lupinus spp.

Lupines are self-pollinated, so different varieties usually do not cross. All lupines will come reasonably true from collected seed, although hybrids are best propagated by division or cuttings. The plants often self-sow, but over time these populations generally revert to a drab purple color. Be careful about roguing or thinning plants; the weakest-looking lupine seedlings often produce the best flower colors.

seeds

seed pod

MASTER GARDENING TIPS

▶ For best results, grow lupines as biennials.

▶ The species *Lupinus arboreus* needs no pretreatment.

▶ With lupines, hybrids often grow more easily from seeds than the species.

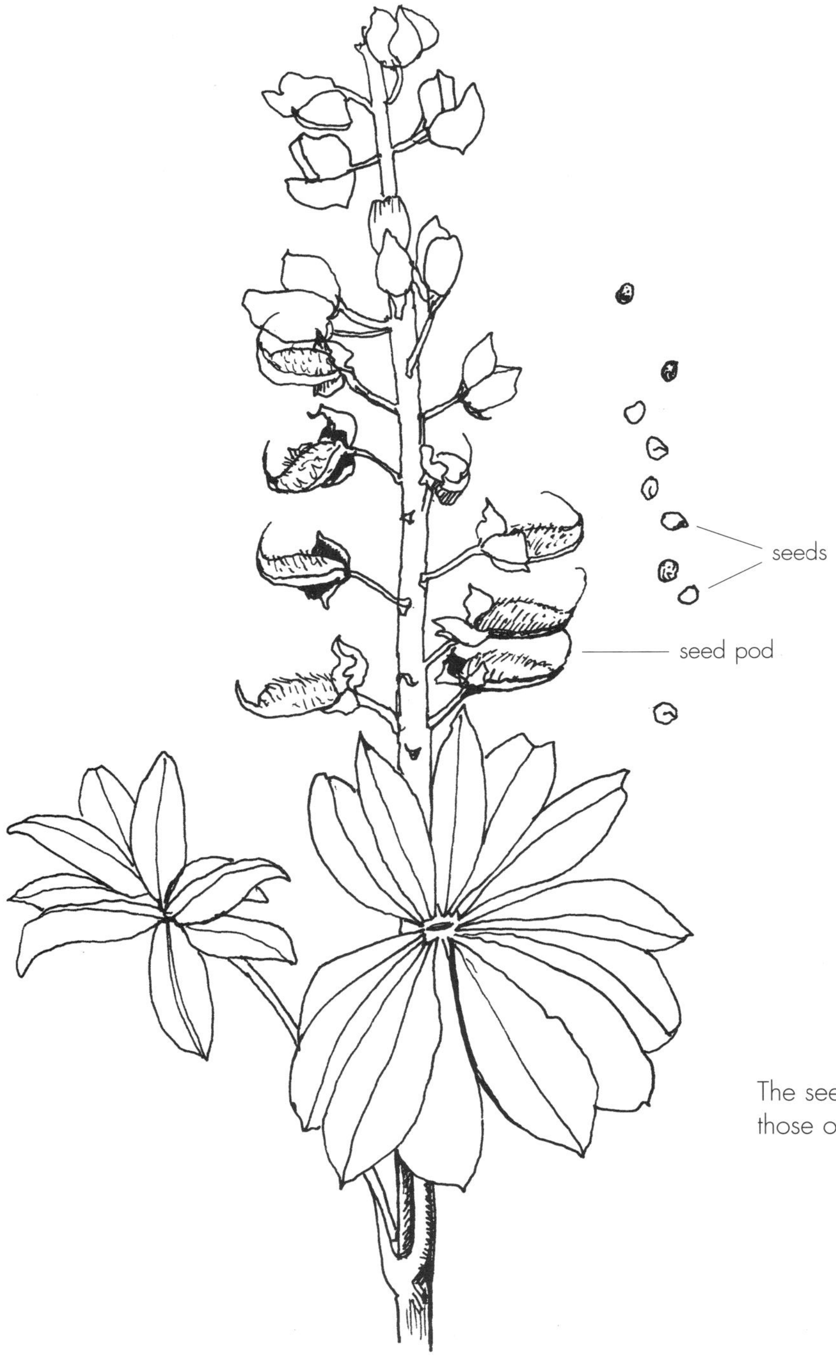

The seeds are carried in small pods, similar to those of garden peas.

Optimum soil temperature for germination: 55° to 65°F

Germination time at optimum soil temperature: 14 to 21 days

Spacing/thinning: Space small varieties 12 to 18 inches apart, tall varieties 24 to 36 inches apart.

Planting depth: ⅛ inch

Seed storage requirements: Cool, dark, and dry

Harvesting the Seed

The seeds are carried in small pods, like those of garden peas. Let the pods remain on the plants until they turn brown, then remove the seeds by hand and spread them out to dry for a few weeks before storing.

Outdoor Sowing

1 Lupines have very hard seed coats. To help the seeds germinate more quickly, nick the seed coats with a file.

MASTER GARDENING TIPS

▶ If you are sowing seed outdoors in fall, nick the seed coat, but do not soak the seed in water before planting.

▶ In warm regions, lupine can be grown as annuals. Sow seed in late fall for spring flowers.

2 Sow fresh seed directly outdoors in falll; it will germinate in spring. Lupines can also be sown outdoors in early spring just before the last frost.

Indoor Sowing

1 Because lupines develop a long taproot, they dislike being transplanted, and it's best to sow them directly outdoors. However, you can start them indoors in peat pots six to eight weeks before the last spring frost. Pretreat seeds by nicking the hard seed coat with a file, then soaking overnight in warm water.

2 In the spring, transplant seedlings outdoors after the last frost. Be sure to set peat pots deeply so that top edges of pot aren't exposed to the air.

Pinks

***Dianthus* spp.**

Pinks are cross-pollinated by insects, so if you are trying to preserve the purity of a strain for seed-saving purposes, it is best to grow only one variety at a time. It is possible to grow the species from collected seed, but hybrids and other cultivars will not come true. The plants often self-sow; to preserve the quality of your plants, rogue out all inferior seedlings.

MASTER GARDENING TIP

Pinks have a high rate of germination, so sow the seed thinly.

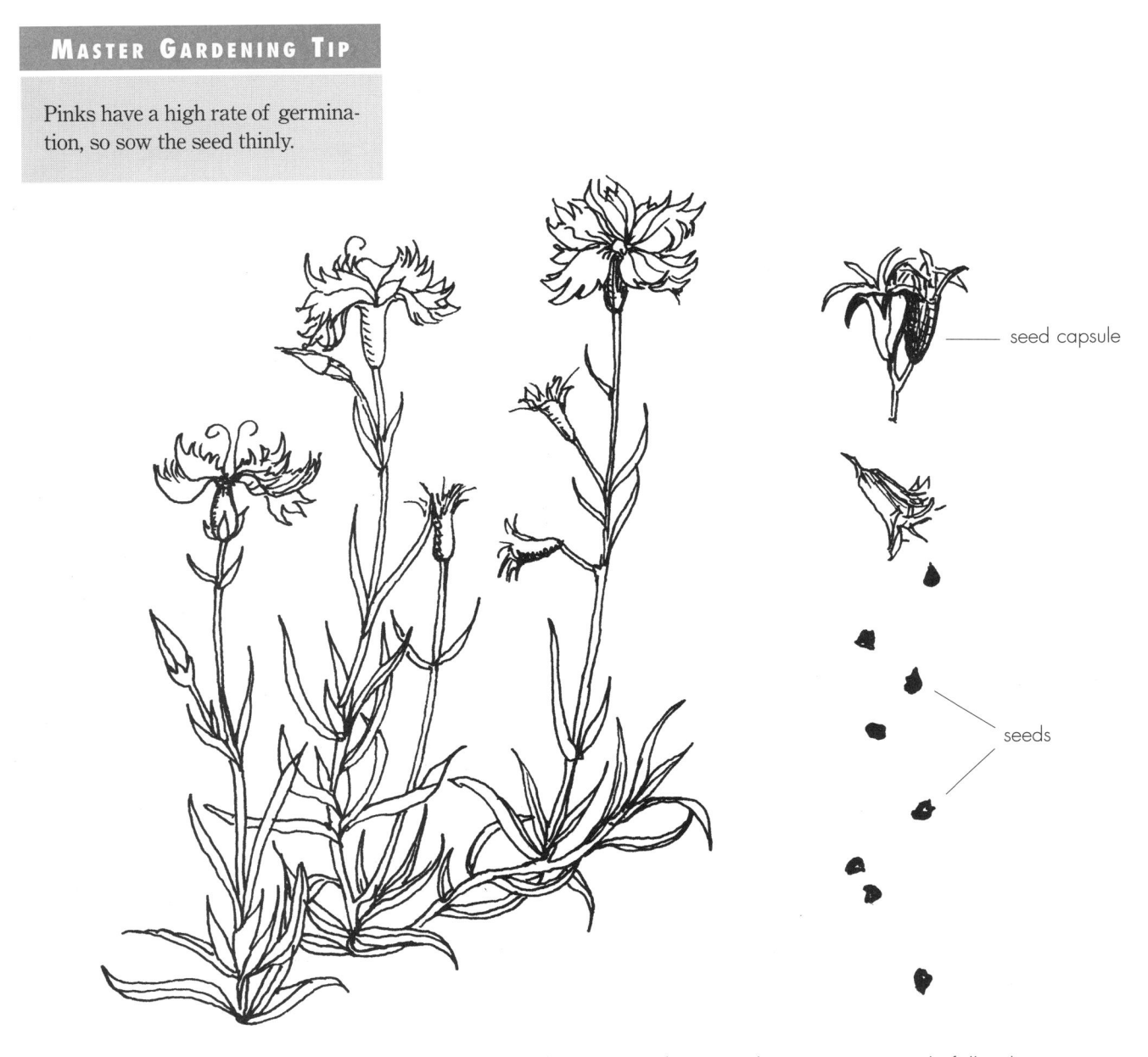

seed capsule

seeds

The seeds are carried in capsules. Harvest in early fall, when the capsules turn hard and brown.

Optimum soil temperature for germination: 60° to 70°F

Germination time at optimum soil temperature: 14 to 21 days

Spacing/thinning: Space small varieties 6 inches apart, tall varieties 9 inches apart.

Planting depth: ⅛ inch

Seed storage requirements: Cool, dry place

Harvesting the Seed

Because the capsules shatter to disperse the seed, watch plants closely and harvest seed before this happens. Cut the capsules from the plant, place them in a paper bag, and allow them to dry indoors for at least two weeks. During this time, they will open and release the seeds, which will fall to the bottom of the bag. Make sure the seeds are completely dry before storing.

Outdoor Sowing

Pinks are easy to grow from seed. Scatter fresh seed in the fall on a well-prepared seed bed. Seed may also be stored over winter and sowed in early spring.

Indoor Sowing

1 Start seeds indoors 8 to 10 weeks before the last spring frost.

2 Keep seed flats evenly moist until plants germinate.

3 Near the time of the last expected frost, harden off plants and then transplant seedlings into the garden.

Primrose

Primula spp.

Primroses are cross-pollinated by insects and hybridize freely, so grow only one variety at a time if you wish to preserve the purity of a certain strain for seed saving. The species can be grown from collected seed, but hybrids and other cultivars will not come true unless the plants are isolated. Some types will self-sow.

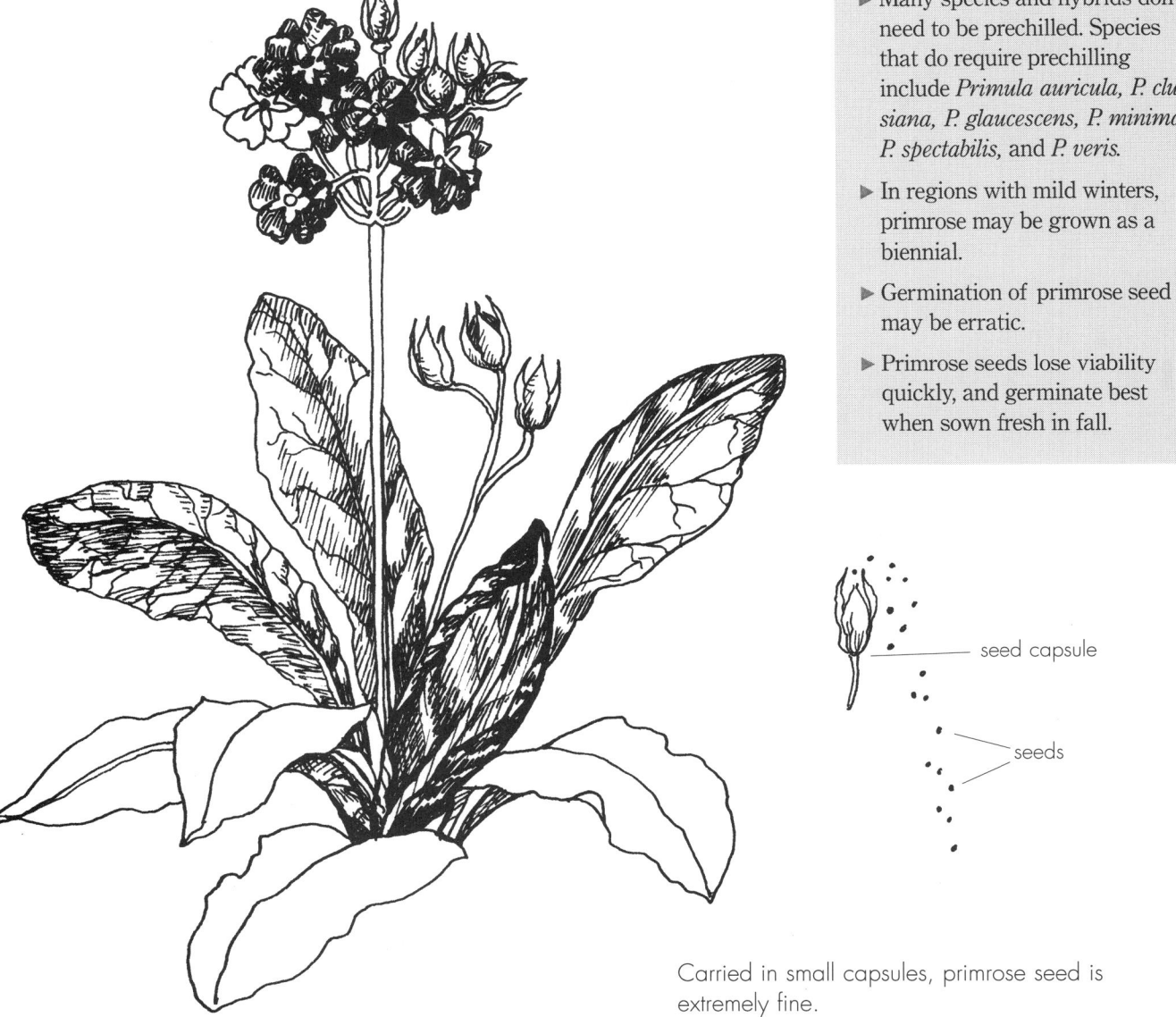

Carried in small capsules, primrose seed is extremely fine.

MASTER GARDENING TIPS

▶ Many species and hybrids don't need to be prechilled. Species that do require prechilling include *Primula auricula, P. clusiana, P. glaucescens, P. minima, P. spectabilis,* and *P. veris.*

▶ In regions with mild winters, primrose may be grown as a biennial.

▶ Germination of primrose seed may be erratic.

▶ Primrose seeds lose viability quickly, and germinate best when sown fresh in fall.

seed capsule

seeds

Light requirements for germination: Seeds need light for germination.

Optimum soil temperature for germination: 60° to 68°F

Germination time at optimum soil temperature: 14 to 70 days

Spacing/thinning: Space small varieties 6 to 8 inches apart, large varieties 12 to 18 inches apart.

Planting depth: Press lightly into the soil surface; do not cover.

Seed storage requirements: Cool, dark, and dry

Harvesting the Seed

1 Carefully watch the small capsules that carry primrose seed, so that you can harvest the fine seed as soon as the capsules begin to open. Allow the seed to dry before storing.

2 If sowing in spring, store dry seeds in the refrigerator.

Outdoor Sowing

Sow fresh primrose seeds in late summer, as soon as it has been harvested.

Indoor Sowing

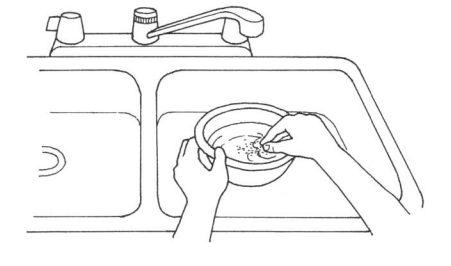

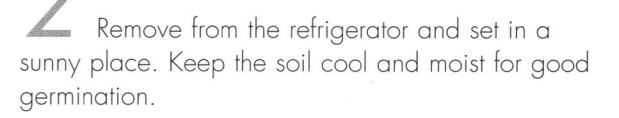

1 Sow seeds indoors 8 to 10 weeks before the last spring frost. Some primrose varieties germinate very slowly because of a growth-inhibiting compound on the seed coat. You can dissolve this compound by washing the seeds in warm water just before sowing. Stored seeds must be stratified to germinate well. Sow seeds in pots filled with moistened medium, cover with plastic wrap, and refrigerate for 3 weeks.

2 Remove from the refrigerator and set in a sunny place. Keep the soil cool and moist for good germination.

3 Transplant the seedlings to the garden after the last frost; the soil should be deep, acidic, and moist.

Appendices

OPTIMAL GERMINATION TEMPERATURES FOR SEEDS		
Crop	**Ideal Temperature (Degrees F)**	**Acceptable Range (Degrees F)**
Asparagus	75	60–85
Basil	70	75–86
Beans	80	65–85
Beets	85	50–85
Broccoli	80	50–85
Cabbage	85	45–95
Carrots	80	45–85
Cauliflower	80	45–85
Celery*	70	60–70
Chervil	55	50–60
Chives	70	60–70
Corn	75	65–95
Cucumber	95	65–95**
Dill	70	50–70
Eggplant	85	75–90**
Fennel	70	60–80
Leek	80	50–95
Lettuce	75	40–80

Crop	Ideal Temperature (Degrees F)	Acceptable Range (Degrees F)
Lovage	65	60–70
Muskmelon	90	75–95
Okra	95	70–95
Onions	75	50–95**
Oregano, Greek	60	60–75
Parsley	75	70–80
Parsnip	65	45–85
Peas	75	40–75
Pepper	85	65–95
Pumpkin	95	70–95
Radish	85	45–90
Sage	70	60–70
Sorrel	70	55–70
Spinach	70	45–75
Squash	95	70–95
Summer savory	70	60–70
Swiss chard	85	50–85
Tomato	85	60–85
Turnip	85	45–85**
Watermelon	95	75–95**

* Best with a 10-degree F drop at night
** Germinates at over 100°F

Sources: Adapted from *The Harvest Gardener* by Susan McClure (Garden Way Publishing, 1993) and *The Organic Gardener's Home Reference* by Tanya Denckla (Garden Way Publishing, 1994)

CHARACTERISTICS OF COMMON VEGETABLES SAVED FOR SEED

Crop	Plant Type	Seed Viability* (Years)	How Pollinated	Need Isolation If You Are Collecting & Saving Seed
Asparagus	Perennial	3	Insects	Yes
Beans	Annual	3	Self	Limited
Beets	Biennial	4	Wind	Yes
Broccoli	Annual	5	Insects	Yes
Brussels sprouts	Biennial	5	Insects	Yes
Cabbage	Biennial	5	Insects	Yes
Carrots	Biennial	3	Insects	Yes
Cauliflower	Biennial	5	Insects	Yes
Celeriac	Biennial	5	Insects	Yes
Celery	Biennial	5	Insects	Yes
Chinese cabbage	Annual	5	Insects	Yes
Chives	Perennial	2	Insects	Yes
Corn, Sweet	Annual	2	Wind	Yes
Cowpea	Annual	3	Self	Limited
Cucumber	Annual	5	Insects	Yes
Eggplant	Annual	5	Self	Limited
Jerusalem artichoke	Perennial	NA	NA	No
Kale	Biennial	5	Insects	Yes
Kohlrabi	Biennial	5	Insects	Yes
Leek	Biennial	3	Insects	Yes
Lettuce	Annual	5	Self	Limited
Lima beans	Annual	3	Self	Limited
Muskmelon	Annual	5	Insects	Yes
New Zealand spinach	Annual	5	Wind	Yes
Okra	Annual	2	Self	Limited
Onions	Biennial	1–2	Insects	Yes
Parsley	Biennial	1–2	Insects	Yes
Parsnip	Biennial	1–2	Insects	Yes
Peas	Annual	3	Self	Limited
Peanut	Annual	1–2	Self	Limited
Pepper	Annual	2	Self	Limited

Crop	Plant Type	Seed Viability* (Years)	How Pollinated	Need Isolation If You Are Collecting & Saving Seed
Popcorn	Annual	1–2	Wind	Yes
Potato	Annual	NA	Self	No
Pumpkin	Annual	5	Insects	Yes
Radish	Annual	5	Insects	Yes
Rutabaga	Biennial	5	Insects	Yes
Salsify	Biennial	2	Self	No
Soybeans	Annual	3	Self	Limited
Spinach	Annual	5	Wind	Yes
Squash, Summer	Annual	4	Insects	Yes
Squash, Winter	Annual	4	Insects	Yes
Swiss chard	Biennial	4	Wind	Yes
Tomato	Annual	4	Self	Limited
Turnip	Annual	5	Insects	Yes
Watermelon	Annual	5	Insects	Yes

*As reported by various authorities. Ideal storage techniques can significantly prolong seed viability.

Source: *Saving Seeds* by Marc Rogers (Garden Way Publishing, 1990)

SEEDS THAT REQUIRE SPECIAL TREATMENT

Common Name	Botanical Name	Treatment
African daisy	*Arctotis* species/hybrids	Sow early
Angelica	*Angelica archangelica*	Stratify ASAP
Anise	*Pimpinella anisum*	Resents transplant
Annual phlox	*Phlox drummondii*	Cool/resents transplant/sow early
Asparagus	*Asparagus officinalis*	Soak
Baby-blue-eyes	*Nemophila menziesii*	Sow early/cool
Baby's-breath	*Gypsophila* species	Sow early
Bachelor's-button, cornflower	*Centaurea cyanus*	Sow early/dark
Balloon flower	*Platycodon grandiflorus*	Light
Basket-of-gold	*Alyssum montanum*	Light
Beard-tongue	*Penstesmon* hybrids	Cool
Beet, Swiss chard	*Beta vulgaris*	Sow early
Begonia	*Begonia* species	Light
Bellflower	*Campanula* species	Light
Bells-of-Ireland	*Moluccella laevis*	Sow early/light/cool
Blanket flower	*Gaillardia* × *grandiflora*	Light
Blazing star	*Mentzelia lindleyi*	Sow early
Bleeding-heart	*Dicentra spectabilis*	Stratify
Blue lace flower	*Trachymene coerulea*	Resents transplant
Borage	*Borago officinalis*	Dark/resents transplant/sow early
Broccoli, Brussels sprouts, cabbage, cauliflower, Chinese cabbage, collards, kale, kohlrabi, mustard, turnip	*Brassica* species	Sow early
Browallia	*Browallia speciosa*	Light
Burning bush	*Kochia scoparia*	ASAP
Butterfly flower, poor-man's orchid	*Schizanthus* × *wisetonensis*	Dark

Key: Light   = Needs light to germinate
      Dark   = Needs darkness to germinate
      Soak   = Requires soaking before sowing
      Stratify = Requires stratification (cold treatment) before sowing
      Scarify = Requires scarification (nicking or filing) before sowing
      Cool   = Needs cool temperature (55°F) to germinate
      ASAP   = Seeds are not long-lived and should be sown as soon as soil can be worked

Common Name	Botanical Name	Treatment
California poppy	*Eschscholzia californica*	Sow early/cool/resents transplant
Candytuft	*Iberis sempervirens*	Cool
Cape marigold	*Dimorphotheca sinuata*	Plant ASAP
Caraway	*Carum carvi*	Resents transplant
Carrot	*Daucus carota*	Resents transplant
Carrot	*Daucus carota* var. *sativus*	Sow early
Chamomile	*Matricaria recutita*	Cool/sow early
Chervil	*Anthriscus cerefolium*	Resents transplant/sow early
Chinese primrose	*Primula sinensis*	Dark
Christmas rose	*Helleborus niger*	Stratify
Coleus	*Coleus × hybridus*	Light
Columbine	*Aguilegia* species/hybrids	Light/stratify
Coralbells	*Heuchera sanguinea*	Cool
Coriander	*Coriandrum sativum*	Sow early/resents transplant/dark
Corn	*Zea mays*	Resents transplant
Cranesbill	*Geranium sanguineum*	Plant ASAP
Creeping zinnia	*Sanvitalia procumbens*	Resents transplant/light
Daylily	*Hemerocallis* hybrids	Stratify
Delphinium	*Delphinium* species	Plant ASAP/dark
Dill	*Anethum graveolens*	Sow early/resents transplant/light
False rock cress, purple rock cress	*Aubrieta deltoidea*	Cool
Fennel	*Foeniculum* species	Resents transplant/dark
Flax	*Linum* species	Resents transplant
Flossflower	*Ageratum houstonianum*	Light
Flowering tobacco	*Nicotiana alata*	Light
Forget-me-not	*Myosotis* species	Dark
Garden cress	*Lepidium sativum*	Sow early
Gas plant	*Dictamnus albus*	Stratify/cool
Globeflower	*Trollius europaeus*	Stratify
Impatiens	*Impatiens wallerana*	Light
Larkspur	*Consolida ambigua*	Dark/sow early
Lavender	*Lavandula angustifolia*	Stratify
Leek	*Allium ampeloprasum*	Sow early
Leopard's-bane	*Doronicum cordatum*	Light

Common Name	Botanical Name	Treatment
Lettuce	*Lactuca sativa*	Light/sow early
Lilyturf	*Liriope muscari*	Soak
Love-in-a-mist	*Nigella damascena*	Resents transplant
Lupine	*Lupinus* species	Resents transplant/soak/scarify
Mallow	*Hibiscus* species	Scarify/soak
Maltese-cross	*Lychnis chalcedonica*	Light
Marjoram	*Origanum majorana*	Sow early
Matricaria, feverfew	*Chrysanthemum parthenium*	Light
Mexican sunflower	*Tithonia rotundifloia*	Light
Midsummer aster, fleabane	*Erigeron* species	Cool
Mignonette	*Reseda odorata*	Light/sow early/resents transplant
Morning glory and other closely related plants	*Ipomoea* species	Soak/scarify
Mustard, rutabaga, turnip	*Brassica* species	Resents transplant
Nasturtium	*Tropaeolum majur*	Resents transplant/dark
Nemesia	*Nemesia strumosa*	Dark
Okra	*Abelmoschus esculentus*	Soak
Onion	*Allium cepa*	Sow early
Oriental poppy	*Papaver orientale*	Light
Ornamental cabbage	*Brassica oleracea* 'Acephala'	Stratify/light
Ornamental pepper	*Capsicum annuum*	Light
Painted-tongue	*Salpiglossis sinuata*	Dark
Parsley	*Petroselinum crispum*	Sow early/soak/resents transplant
Parsnip	*Pastinaca sativa*	Resents transplant/soak/sow early
Pea	*Pisum sativum*	Sow early/resents transplant
Perennial and sweet pea	*Lathyrus* species	Scarify
Perennial pea	*Lathyrus latifolius*	Soak/cool
Periwinkle	*Catharanthus roseus*	Dark
Petunia	*Petunia* × *hybrida*	Light
Phlox	*Phlox paniculata*	Stratify
Phlox	*Phlox* species	Dark
Poppy	*Papaver* species	Resents transplant/cool/dark — except *P. orientale*
Pot marigold	*Calendula officinalis*	Dark
Primrose	*Primula* species	Stratify/light — except *P. sinensis*

Common Name	Botanical Name	Treatment
Pyrethrum, painted daisy	*Chrysanthemum coccineum*	ASAP
Radish	*Raphanus sativus*	Resents transplant/sow early
Rock cress, wall cress	*Arabis* species	Light
Rocket	*Eruca vesicaria*	Sow early/resents transplant
Rosemary	*Rosmarinus officinalis*	Cool
Salvia (red-flowered varieties)	*Salvia* species	Light
Savory	*Satureja* species	Light
Scarlet sage	*Salvia splendens*	Plant ASAP
Sesame	*Sesamum indicum*	Resents transplant
Shasta daisy	*Chrysanthemum* × *superbum*	Light
Snapdragon	*Antirrhinum majus*	Light
Spinach	*Spinacia oleraea*	Resents transplant/sow early
Stock	*Matthiola* species	Light
Strawflower	*Helichrysum bracteatum*	Light
Sweet alyssum	*Lobularia maritima*	Sow early/light
Sweet pea	*Lathyrus odoratus*	Cool/soak/dark
Swiss chard, beet	*Beta vulgaris*	Resents transplant
Tahoka daisy	*Machaeranthera tanacetifolia*	Sow early/stratify
Thrift, sea pink	*Armeria maritima*	Soak
Thyme, mother-of-thyme	*Thymus* species	Cool
Tickseed	*Coreopsis grandiflora*	Light
Transvaal daisy	*Gerbera jamesonii* hybrids	Light/plant ASAP
Treasure flower	*Gazania rigens*	Dark
Tree mallow	*Lavatera* hybrids	Resents transplant
Verbena	*Verbena* species	Dark
Viola, violet, pansy	*Viola* species	Stratify/dark
Wake-robin	*Trillium ovatum*	Stratify
Wallflower	*Cheiranthus cheiri*	Cool
Wild blue indigo, false indigo	*Baptisia australis*	Scarify
Yarrow	*Achillea* species	Light

Source: *Starting Seeds Indoors* by Ann Reilly (Garden Way Publishing, 1988)

OPEN-POLLINATED (STANDARD) VARIETIES

This chart includes only a selection of open-pollinated varieties. Consult seed catalogs for additional possibilities.

Vegetable	Name of Variety
Asparagus	'Martha Washington', 'Mary Washington', 'UC 72', 'Viking', 'Waltham'
Beans, snap bush	'Blue Lake Bush', 'Bountiful', 'Commodore', 'Contender', 'Derby', 'Earliserve', 'Greencrop', 'Harvester', 'Jumbo', 'Kentucky Wonder No. 125', 'Provider', 'Roma II', 'Royal Burgundy', 'Topcrop', 'White Half Runner'
Beans, snap pole	'Blue Lake Pole', 'Kentucky Wonder', 'McCaslan', 'Rattlesnake', 'Romano Pole'
Beans, wax bush	'Brittle Wax', 'Cherokee Wax', 'Golden Wax', 'Kinghorn Wax', 'Pencil Pod Black Wax'
Beans, wax pole	'Goldmarie', 'Kentucky Wonder Wax'
Beets	'Burpee's Golden', 'Chioggia', 'Crosby's Early Egyptian', 'Cylindra', 'Detroit Dark Red', 'Early Wonder', 'Lutz Green Leaf', 'Ruby Queen'
Broccoli	'Calabrese', 'De Cicco', 'Green Goliath', 'Italian Green Sprouting', 'Romanesco', 'Waltham 29'
Cabbage, green	'Charleston Wakefield', 'Copenhagen Market', 'Danish Ballhead', 'Dutch' (several varieties), 'Early Jersey Wakefield', 'Golden Acre', 'Wisconsin All Seasons'
Cabbage, red	'Lasso', 'Mammoth Red Rock', 'Red Acre'
Cabbage, savory	'Chieftain Savoy', 'Drumhead Savoy', 'January King'
Carrots	'Amsterdam Forcing', 'Imperator 58', 'Little Finger', 'Thumbelina', 'Touchon'
Cauliflower	'All-The-Year-Round', 'Alverda', 'Amazing', 'Andes', 'Burpeeana', 'Dominant', 'Self-Blanche', 'Snowball', 'Whiterock'
Chives	'Chinese', 'Curly Mauve', 'Forescate', 'Garlic'
Corn, sweet	'Ashworth', 'Black Aztec', 'Country Gentleman', 'Golden Bantam', 'Luther Hill', 'Stowell's Evergreen', 'Double Standard'
Cucumbers	'Ashley', 'Boston Pickling', 'Bush Pickle', 'Long Green Improved', 'Lemon', 'Marketmore', 'Poinsett', 'Straight Eight', 'White Wonder'
Eggplant	'Black Beauty', 'Florida Market', 'Long Purple'
Leeks	'American Flag', 'Elephant Garlic', 'Giant Musselburgh', 'King Richard', 'Varna'
Lettuce, head	'Anuenue', 'Bibb', 'Boston', 'Buttercrunch', 'Great Lakes', 'Iceberg', 'Ithaca', 'Merveille des Quatre Saisons', 'Sierra', 'Summertime', 'Tom Thumb'

Vegetable	Name of Variety
Lettuce, leaf	'Black-Seeded Simpson', 'Grand Rapids', 'Green Ice', 'Oakleaf', 'Prizehead', 'Red Sails', 'Salad Bowl', 'Simpson Elite', 'Slobolt'
Lettuce, romaine	'Cimmaron', 'Parris Island Cos', 'Romaine', 'Rouge d'Hiver', 'Valmaine'
Melons	'Armenian', 'Banana', 'Canary Yellow', Casaba 'Golden Beauty', 'Hale's Best Jumbo', 'Hearts of Gold', 'Honeydew', 'Iroquois', 'Rocky Ford'
Onions	'Burgundy', 'Crystal Wax', 'Early Yellow Globe', 'Evergreen White Bunching', 'He-Shi-Ko Bunching', 'New York Early', 'Red Creole', 'Red Wethersfield', 'Southport Red Globe', 'Southport White Globe', 'Walla Walla Sweet Yellow', 'White Sweet Spanish', 'Yellow Sweet Spanish'
Parsley	' Dark Green Italian', 'Forest Green', 'Hamburg', 'Italian Parsley', 'Moss Curled', 'Plain'
Peas	'Alaska', 'Alderman', 'Dwarf Gray Sugar', 'Early Frosty', 'Green Arrow', 'Knight', 'Lincoln', 'Little Marvel', 'Maestro', 'Mammoth Melting Sugar', 'Novella', 'Oregon Sugar Pod', 'Sugar Ann', 'Sugar Snap', 'Thomas Laxton', 'Wando'
Peppers, hot	'Anaheim', 'Ancho', 'Habanero', 'Hungarian Yellow Wax Hot', 'Early Jalapeño', 'Large Red Cherry', 'Paprika', 'Red Chili', 'Serrano', 'Thai Hot'
Peppers, sweet	'California Wonder', 'Emerald Giant', 'Jupiter', 'Italia', 'Keystone Resistant Giant', 'Lipstick', 'Purple Beauty', 'Sweet Banana', 'Sweet Chocolate', 'Yolo Wonder'
Radishes	'Black Spanish', 'Champion', 'Cherry Belle', 'China Rose', 'Crimson Giant', 'Early Scarlet Globe', 'French Breakfast', 'Sparkler', 'White Icicle'
Spinach	'America', 'Bloomsdale Long Standing', 'Giant Nobel', 'King of Denmark', 'Viroflay'
Squash	'Atlantic Giant', 'Big Max', 'Black Beauty Zucchini', 'Connecticut', 'Delicata,' 'Early White Bush Scallop', 'Gold Nugget', 'Jack Be Little', 'Jack-O'-Lantern', 'Lumina', 'Pink Jumbo Banana', 'Small Sugar', 'Sweet Meat', 'Tahitian Melon', 'Turk's Turban', 'Vegetable Spaghetti'
Tomatoes	'Bonny Best', 'Brandywine', 'Burpee's Long-Keeper', 'Campbell 1327', 'Delicious', 'Floradade', 'Glamour', 'Gold Nugget', 'Jubilee', 'Marglobe', 'Oregon Spring', 'Oxheart', 'Ponderosa Scarlet', 'Red Pear', 'Red Plum', 'Roma VF', 'Rutgers', 'Sweetie', 'Tiny Tim', 'Yellow Currant', 'Yellow Pear', 'Yellow Plum'

Zone Map

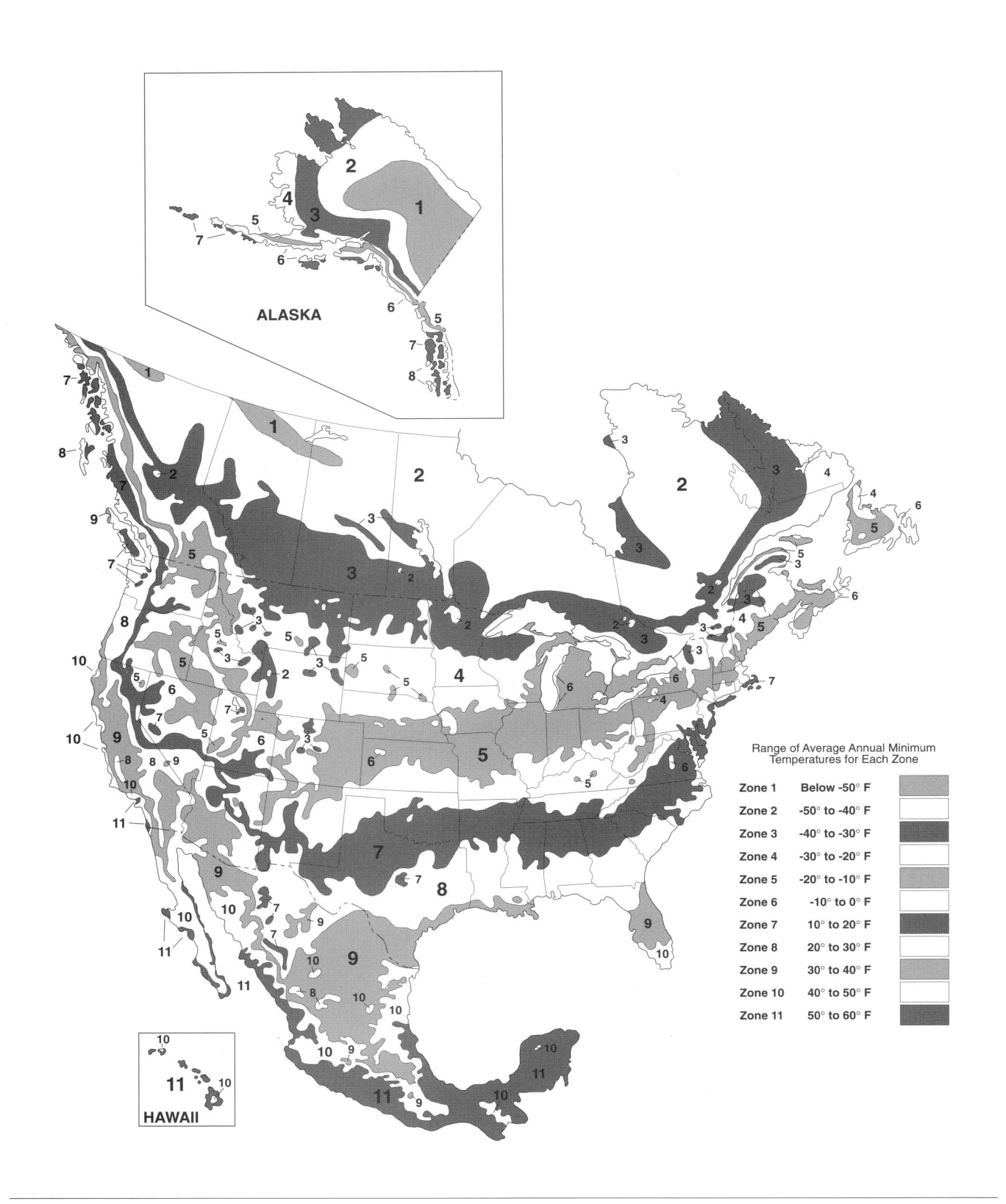

ALASKA

HAWAII

Range of Average Annual Minimum
Temperatures for Each Zone

Zone 1	Below -50° F
Zone 2	-50° to -40° F
Zone 3	-40° to -30° F
Zone 4	-30° to -20° F
Zone 5	-20° to -10° F
Zone 6	-10° to 0° F
Zone 7	10° to 20° F
Zone 8	20° to 30° F
Zone 9	30° to 40° F
Zone 10	40° to 50° F
Zone 11	50° to 60° F

Mail-Order Sources

Seed Companies

W. R. Aimers Limited
81 Temperance Street
Aurora, Ontario
Canada L4G 2R1
905-841-6226

Alberta Nurseries & Seeds, Ltd.
P.O. Box 20
Bowden, Alberta
Canada T0M 0K0
800-733-3566
Fax: 403-224-2455
$2 for catalog requests out of Canada. Wide variety of seeds.

Apothecary Rose Shed
P.O. Box 194
Route 160
Pattersonville, NY 12137
518-887-2035

Applewood Seed Company
5380 Vivian Street
Arvada, CO 80002
303-431-6283

Arrowhead Alpines
P.O. Box 857
Fowlerville, MI 48836
517-223-3581
Fax: 517-223-8750
e-mail: stuart@livingonline.com
Catalog $2. Wide variety of seeds.

The Banana Tree
715 Northhampton Street
Easton, PA 18042
610-253-9589
e-mail: faben@enter.net
Web site: www.banana/tree.com
Catalog $3. Specializes in tropical seeds.

Becker's Seed Potatoes
RR #1
Trout Creek, Ontario
Canada P0H 2L0
705-724-2305

Bluestem Prairie Nursery
Route 2, Box 106
Hillsboro, IL 62049
217-532-6344
Free catalog.

Boothe Hill Wildflower Seeds
921 Boothe Hill
Chapel Hill, NC 27514
919-967-4091
Catalog $1.

Bowman's Hill Wildflower
Preserve Association, Inc.
Washington Crossing Historic Park
P.O. Box 103
Washington Crossing, PA 18977
215-862-2924
Fax: 215-862-1846
Catalog $1. Specializes in Pennsylvania native plants.

Burgess Seed and Plant Co.
905 Four Seasons Road
Bloomington, IL 61701
309-674-4900

W. Atlee Burpee Seed Co.
300 Park Avenue
Warminster, PA 18974
800-888-1447

D.V. Burrell Seed Growers Co.
P.O. Box 150
Rocky Ford, CO 81067
719-254-3318
Fax: 719-254-3319
Free catalog.

Caprilands Herb Farm
534 Silver Street
Coventry, CT 06238
860-742-7244
Free catalog. Variety of plants and herbs.

Catnip Acres Herb Farm
67 Christian Street
Oxford, CT 06483
203-888-5649
Free catalog.

Comstock, Ferre, and Co.
263 Main Street
Wethersfield, CT 06109
860-571-6590
Fax: 860-571-6595
Free catalog. Variety of seeds.

The Cook's Garden
P.O. Box 535
Londonderry, VT 05148
800-457-9703
Web site: www.cooksgarden.com

Cruickshank's Inc.
1015 Mount Pleasant Road
Toronto, Ontario
Canada M4P 2M1
416-488-8292

William Dam Seeds
P.O. Box 8400
279 Highway 8, West
Flamborough
Dundas, Ontario
Canada L9H 6M1
905-628-6641
416-628-6641
Fax: 905-627-1729
*$2 for catalog requests out of Canada. Wide
variety of untreated tree and herb seeds.*

DeGiorgi Seed Co., Inc.
6011 N Street
Omaha, NE 68117-1634
800-858-2580
Fax: 402-731-8475
Wide variety of seeds.

Desertland Nursery
P.O. Box 26126
11306 Gateway East
El Paso, TX 79926
915-858-1130
Fax: 915-858-1560
e-mail: smg.915@aol.com
*Catalog $1. Specializes in
Mexican seeds*

Desert Moon Nursery
P.O. Box 600
Veqiota, NM 87062
505-864-0614
*Catalog $1. Specializes in
native desert plants.*

Elixir Farm Botanicals, LLC
Brixey, MO 65618
417-261-2393
Fax: 417-261-2355
e-mail: efbechofoxbravo@aerostatle.net
Free catalog. Specializes in Chinese seeds.

Farmer Seed & Nursery Co.
P.O. Box 129
Faribault, MN 55021
507-334-1623
Free catalog.

Ferry-Morse Seeds
P.O. Box 488
Fulton, KY 42041-0488
800-283-3400
Fax: 800-283-2700
e-mail: advasee@atex.net
Free catalog. Wide variety of seeds.

Henry Field Seed & Nursery Co.
415 North Burnett
Shenandoah, IA 51602
605-665-9391

Flowery Branch Seed Company
P.O. Box 1330
Flowery Branch, GA 30542
770-536-8380
Catalog $4. Wide variety of seeds.

Four Seasons Nursery
1706 Morrissey Drive
Bloomington, IL 61701
309-663-9551
Free catalog. Wide variety of seeds.

Fox Hill Farm
444 W. Michigan Avenue
Parma, MI 49269
517-531-3179

Frosty Hollow Ecological Restoration
Box 53
Langley, WA 98260
360-579-2332
Fax: 360-579-6456
e-mail: hed@whidby.com
Wide variety of seeds.

Gardens North
34 Helena Street
Ottawa, Ontario
Canada K1Y 3M8
613-489-0065
e-mail: garnorth@Iftar.com

Girard Nurseries
P.O. Box 428
Geneva, OH 44041
216-466-2881
Fax: 216-466-3999
Free catalog. Wide variety of seeds.

Gleckers Seedsman
Metamora, OH 43540
419-923-5463

GreenLady Gardens
(formerly Anthony J. Skittone)
1415 Eucalyptus Dr.
San Francisco, CA 94132
800-348-7002
Fax: 800-841-1377
Free catalog. Sells bulb seeds only.

Gurney's Seed & Nursery Co.
110 Capital Street
Yankton, SD 57079
605-665-1671

Halcyon Gardens Herbs
P.O. Box 124-M
Gibsonia, PA 15044
Fax: 412-443-5544

Harris Seeds
60 Saginaw Drive
Box 22960
Rochester, NY 14624-2960
800-514-4441
Fax: 716-442-9386
*Free catalog. Specializes in
flower and vegetable seeds.*

The Charles C. Hart Seed Co.
304 Main Street
Wethersfield, CT 06109
800-326-4278
Fax: 860-563-7221
Free catalog. Wide variety of seeds.

Herb Gathering, Inc.
5742 Kenwood
Kansas City, MO 64110
816-523-2653

High Altitude Gardens
308 South River
P.O. Box 1048
Hailey, ID 83333
208-788-4363
e-mail: higarden@micron.net

Holland Wildflower Farm
290 O'Neal Lane
Elkins, AR 72727
501-643-2622
800-684-3734
Fax: 501-643-2249
e-mail: info@hwildflower.com
*Free catalog. Specializes in
perennial wildflowers.*

Horticultural Enterprises
P.O. Box 810082
Dallas, TX 75381
214-350-0216
Fax: 214-350-0889
Free catalog. Wide variety of seeds.

Johnny's Selected Seeds
299 Foss Hill Road
Albion, ME 04910-9731
207-437-9294
Web site: www.johnnyseeds.com

J.W. Jung Seed Co.
335 S. High Street
Randolph, WI 53957
800-247-5864

Kitazawa Seed Co.
1111 Chapman Street
San Jose, CA 95126
408-243-1330

Larner Seeds
P.O. Box 407
Bolinas, CA 94924
415-868-9407

Orol Ledden & Sons
P.O. Box 7
Sewell, NJ 08080-0007
609-468-1000
Fax: 609-468-9095
Free catalog. Wide variety of seeds.

Liberty Seed Co.
P.O. Box 806
128 1st Drive S.E.
New Philadelphia, OH 44663
330-364-1611
Fax: 330-364-6415
Free catalog.

Little Valley Farm
5693 Snead Creek Road
Spring Green, WI 53588
608-935-3324
Free catalog. Wide variety of seeds.

McLaughlin's Seeds
Buttercup's Acre
Mead, WA 99021-0550
509-466-0230

Meadowbrook Herb Garden
Rte. 138
Wyoming, RI 02898
401-539-7603
800-569-7603
Free catalog.

Mellinger's Nursery, Inc.
2310 W. South Range Road
North Lima, OH 44452
800-321-7444

Mesa Garden
P.O. Box 72
Belen, NM 87121
505-864-3131
Fax: 505-864-3124
e-mail: cactus@swcp.com
Free catalog. Wide variety of seeds.

Midwest Wildflowers
Box 64
Rockton, IL 61072
Catalog $1. Wide variety of wildflowers.

Missouri Wildflowers Nursery
9814 Pleasant Hill Road
Jefferson City, MO 65109
573-496-3492
Fax: 573-496-3003
e-mail: mowleflrf@socket.net
Catalog $1. Specializes in native wildflowers.

Moon Mountain Wildflowers
P.O. Box 725
Carpinteria, CA 93014
805-684-2565

Sandy Mush Herb Nursery
Rte. 2, Surrett Cove Road
Leicester, NC 28748
704-683-2014

Native American Seed
3400 Long Prairie Road
Flower Mound, TX 75028
214-539-0534

Native Gardens
Rte. 1, Box 494
5737 Fisher Lane
Greenback, TN 37742
423-856-0220

Native Seeds, Inc.
14590 Triadelphia Mill Road
Dayton, MD 21036
301-596-9818
Fax: 301-854-3195
Free catalog. Specializes in wildflower seeds.

Native Seeds/SEARCH
2509 North Campbell Avenue, Box 325
Tucson, AZ 85719
520-622-5561
Fax: 520-622-5591
e-mail: yhosofaz@aol.com
Catalog $1. Wide variety of seeds.

Native Sons
379 West El Campo Road
Arroyo Grande, CA 93420
805-481-5996
Fax: 805-489-8991
Web site: www.nativeson.com
Catalog $5. Wide variety of seeds.

The Natural Gardening Company
217 San Anselmo Avenue
San Anselmo, CA 94960
707-766-9303
Fax: 707-766-9747
Free catalog. Wide variety of seeds.

Nature's Way
R.R. 1, Box 62
Woodburn, IA 50275
515-342-6246
Free catalog. Wide variety of seeds.

Nichols Garden Nursery
1190 North Pacific Highway NE
Albany, OR 97321-4598
541-928-9280

Northplan/Mountain Seed
P.O. Box 9107
Moscow, ID 83843
208-882-8040
Fax: 208-882-7446
e-mail: norplan@moscow.com
Catalog $1. Wide variety of seeds.

Orchid Gardens
2232 139th Avenue NW
Andover, MN 55744
612-755-0205

Oregon Exotics Rare Fruit Nursery
1065 Messinger Road
Grants Pass, OR 97527
541-846-7578

Palms for Tropical Landscaping
6600 S.W. 45th Street
Miami, FL 33155
305-666-1457
Free catalog. Specializes in rare palms.

George W. Park Seed Co., Inc.
Cokesbury Road
Greenwood, SC 29647-0046
800-845-3369

Theodore Payne Foundation
10459 Tuxford Street
Sun Valley, CA 91352
818-768-1802
Fax: 818-768-5215

Peter Pauls Nurseries
4665 Chapin Road
Canandaigua, NY 14424
716-394-7397
Fax: 716-394-4122
e-mail: ppnurse@eznet.net
Web site: www.peterpauls.com
Free catalog. Specializes in plant seeds.

Pinetree Garden Seeds
Box 300
New Gloucester, ME 04260
207-926-3400
Fax: 888-527-3337
e-mail: superseeds@worldnet.ATT.net
Free catalog. Wide variety of seeds.

Plants of the Southwest
Agua Fria Route 6, Box 11A
Santa Fe, NM 87501
800-788-7333

Prairie Moon Nursery
Rte. 3, Box 163
Winona, MN 55987
507-452-1362
507-452-5231

Prairie Nursery
P.O. Box 306
Westfield, WI 53964
608-296-3679
Fax: 608-296-2741
Free catalog. Specializes in native wildflowers and grasses.

Prairie Ridge Nursery
CRM Ecosystems, Inc.
9738 Overland Road
Mount Horeb, WI 53572
608-437-5245
Fax: 608-437-8982
e-mail: crmprairie@aol.com
Specializes in native wildflowers and grasses.

Prairie Seed Source
P.O. Box 83
North Lake, WI 53064

Redwood City Seed Co.
P.O. Box 361
Redwood City, CA 94064
415-325-7333
Web site: www.batnet.com/rwc-seed

Richter's
357 Highway 47
Goodwood, Ontario
Canada L0C 1A0
905-640-6677
Fax: 905-640-6641
Free catalog. Wide variety of herbs.

Clyde Robin Seed Co.
P.O. Box 2366
Castro Valley, CA 94546
510-785-0425
510-785-6463
Specializes in wildflower seeds.

The Rosemary House
120 S. Market Street
Mechanicsburg, PA 17055
717-697-5111
Fax: 717-697-3227
e-mail: RosemaryHs@aol.com
Catalog $3. Specializes in herbs.

Roswell Seed Co.
P.O. Box 725
115-117 South Main Street
Roswell, NM 88202
505-622-7701
Fax: 505-623-2885
Free catalog. Wide variety of seeds.

F.W. Schumacher Co., Inc.
36 Spring Hill Road
Sandwich, MA 02563
508-888-0659
Fax: 508-833-0322
Free catalog. Wide variety of seeds.

Seeds Blüm
Idaho City Stage Box 2057
Boise, ID 83706
208-342-0858
800-528-3658
Fax: 208-338-5658

Seeds of Change
P.O. Box 15700
Santa Fe, NM 87506-5700
888-762-7333
Offers organically grown seeds.

Seeds of Distinction
P.O. Box 86
Station A
Toronto, Ontario
Canada M9C 4V2
416-255-3060

Seeds Trust
High Altitude Gardens
P.O. Box 1048
308 S. River
Hailey, ID 83333
208-788-4363

Select Seeds
180 Stickney Road
Union, CT 06076-4617
860-684-9310
Fax: 860-684-9224
e-mail: select@nec.com
Web site:
www.trine.com/GardenNet/SelectSeeds/
Catalog $1. Specializes in antique flowers.

Sharp Brothers Seed
396 SW Davis Street, Ladue
Clinton, MO 64735
800-451-3779
Fax: 816-885-8647
e-mail: Sharpbros@sprintmail.com
Free catalog. Specializes in native grasses.

Shepherd's Garden Seeds
30 Irene Street
Torrington, CT 06790
860-482-3638
e-mail: sghort@aol.com
Web site: www.shepherdseeds.com

R.H. Shumway Seedsman
P.O. Box 1
Graniteville, SC 29829
803-663-9771

Stock Seed Farms, Inc.
28008 Mill Road
Murdock, NE 68407
800-759-1520
Fax: 402-867-2442
e-mail: stockseed@navix.net
Web site: www.stockseed.com
Free catalog. Wide variety of seeds.

Stokes Seeds
P.O. Box 548
Buffalo, NY 14240
716-695-6980
Also in Canada:
Box 10
Street Catharines, Ontario
Canada L2R 6R6
416-688-4300

Sunrise Enterprises
P.O. Box 330058
West Hartford, CT 06133
860-666-8071

Territorial Seed Co.
P.O. Box 157
Cottage Grove, OR 97424
541-942-9547
Fax: 888-657-3131
Web site: www.territorial/seed.com
Free catalog.

Thompson & Morgan
P.O. Box 1308
Jackson, NJ 08527
800-274-7333

Tomato Growers Supply Co.
P.O. Box 2237
Fort Myers, FL 33902
941-768-1119
Fax: 941-768-3476
Free catalog. Specializes in tomato and pepper seeds.

Otis Twilley Seed Company
P.O. Box 65
Trevose, PA 19053
800-622-7333
Fax: 215-245-1949
Free catalog. Specializes in triploid watermelon and sweet corn.

Vermont Bean Seed Co.
Garden Lane
Fair Haven, VT 05743
802-273-3400

The Vermont Wildflower Farm
Route 7
Charlotte, VT 05445-0005
802-425-3931
Fax: 802-425-3504
Free catalog. Wide variety of seeds.

Vesey's Seeds Ltd.
York, Prince Edward Island
Canada C0A 1P0
800-363-7333
Fax: 902-566-1620
Free catalog. Wide variety of seeds.

Well-Sweep Herb Farm
205 Mt. Bethel Road
Port Murray, NJ 07865
908-852-5390

Wildseed Farms, Inc.
P.O. Box 308
1101 Campo Rosa Road
Eagle Lake, TX 77434
800-848-0078
Fax: 409-234-7407
Web site: www.wildseedfarm.com
Variety of wildflowers and herbs.

Wyatt-Quarles
Box 739
Garner, NC 27529
800-662-7591
Fax: 919-772-4278
Free catalog. Specializes in vegetable and garden seeds.

Yerba Buena Nursery
19500 Skyline Blvd.
Woodside, CA 94062
415-851-1668
Fax: 415-851-5565
Web site: www.yerbabuenanursery.com
Specializes in native plants.

Seed Exchanges

Alpine Garden Society
AGS Centre, Avon Bank
Pershore
Worcestershire WR10 3JP
England
01386 554790

American Horticultural Society
7931 East Boulevard Drive
Alexandria, VA 22308
800-777-7931
Fax: 703-768-8700
e-mail: gardenhas@aol.com
Catalog $3.95. Wide variety of seeds.

American Penstemon Society
1569 Holland Ct.
Lakewood, CO 80232
303-986-8096
e-mail: adartlll@aol.com

American Rhododendron Society
Deanna Daneri
11 Pine Crest Drive
Fortuna, CA 95540
707-725-3043
Fax: 707-725-1217
e-mail: Dedaneri@aol.com

American Rock Garden Society
15 Fairmead Road
Darien, CT 06820
203-655-2750

Hardy Plant Society
710 Hemlock Road
Media, PA 19063
215-566-0861

Herb Society of America
9019 Kirtland Chardon Road
Mentor, OH 44060
216-256-0514
Fax: 216-256-0541
Web site: www.herbsociety.com
Free catalog. Wide variety of seeds.

Mississippi Native Plant Society
P.O. Box 2151
Starkville, MS 39759
601-324-0430

National Gardening Association
180 Flynn Avenue
Burlington, VT 05401
800-538-4769
Fax: 802-863-5962
e-mail: nga@garden.org
Web site: www.garden.org

National Wildflower Research Center
4801 La Crosse Avenue
Austin, TX 78739
512-292-4200
Fax: 512-292-4627
e-mail: anwac@aor.com
Web site: www.wildflower.org
Free catalog. Wide variety of seeds.

Native Seeds/SEARCH
2509 North Campbell Avenue, Box 325
Tucson, AZ 85719
520-622-5561
Fax: 520-622-5591
e-mail: yhosofaz@aol.com
Catalog $1. Wide variety of seeds.

Northern Nut Grower's Association
9870 S. Palmer Road
New Carlisle, OH 45344
937-878-2610

Northwest Horticultural Society
Yoosun Park
V. Isaacson Hall
University of Washington, GF-15
Seattle, WA 98195
206-527-1794

Ohio Native Plant Society
6 Louise Drive
Chagrin Falls, OH 44022
216-338-6622

Passiflora Society International
3900 W. Sample Road
Coconut Creek, FL 33073
954-977-4434
Fax: 954-977-4501
Web site: www.fireflyworld.com

Royal Horticultural Society
80 Vincent Square
London SW1P 2PE
England
01733 898100

Rural Advancement Fund International
P.O. Box 1029
Pittsboro, NC 27312
888-800-9300
Fax: 919-734-6657
Free catalog.

Sedum Society
10502 North 135 W.
Sedgwick, KS 67135
316-796-0496
Free catalog.

Seed Savers Exchange
3076 North Winn Road
Decorah, IA 52101
319-382-5872

Southern Exposure Seed Exchange
P.O. Box 158
North Garden, VA 22959
804-973-4703
Fax: 804-973-8717
Web site: www.southernexposure.com
Catalog $2.

Seed-Starting Supplies

Charley's Greenhouse Supplies
1569 Memorial Highway
Mount Vernon, WA 98273
800-322-4707
Fax: 800-233-3017
e-mail: cgh@charleysergenhouse.com.
Web site: www.charleysergen
Catalog $2. Wide variety of seeds.

Gardener's Supply Co.
128 Intervale Road
Burlington, VT 05401
802-863-1700

Johnny's Selected Seeds
299 Foss Hill Road
Albion, ME 04910-9731
207-437-9294
Fax: 800-437-4290
Web site: www.johnnyseeds.com
Free catalog. Specializes in organic seeds.

A.M. Leonard, Inc.
241 Fox Drive
P.O. Box 816
Piqua, OH 45356
800-543-8955
Fax: 800-433-0633
Web site: www.amleo.com
Free catalog.

Mellinger's Nursery, Inc.
2310 W. South Range Road
North Lima, OH 44452
800-321-7444

Walt Nicke
36 McLeod Lane
P.O. Box 433
Topsfield, MA 01983
800-822-4114
Fax: 508-887-9853
Web site: www.gardentalk.com
Free catalog. Specializes in garden tools.

Further Reading

Abraham, Doc and Katy. **Growing Plants from Seed.** (Lyons & Burford, 1991)

Ashworth, Suzanne. **Seed to Seed.** (Seed Savers Exchange, 1995)

Bird, Richard. **The Propagation of Hardy Perennials.** (Trafalgar Square, 1993)

Bryant, Geoff. **Propagation Handbook: Basic Techniques for Gardeners.** (Stackpole Books, 1995)

Bubel, Nancy. **The New Seed Starters Handbook.** (Rodale Press, 1988)

Cook, Allen, ed. **Propagation for the Home Gardener.** (Brooklyn Botanic Garden, 1984)

Garden Way editors. **The Big Book of Gardening Skills.** (Garden Way Publishing, 1993)

Garden Way editors. **Just the Facts! Dozens of Garden Charts, Thousands of Gardening Answers.** (Garden Way Publishing, 1993)

Gardner, JoAnn. **The Heirloom Garden: Selecting & Growing Over 300 Old-Fashioned Ornamentals.** (Garden Way Publishing, 1992)

Hill, Lewis. **Secrets of Plant Propagation.** (Garden Way Publishing, 1985)

Kelly, John. **Growing Plants From Seed.** (Sterling Publishing, 1996)

Lloyd, Christopher, and Graham Rice. **Garden Flowers from Seed.** (Timber Press, 1994)

Loewer, Peter. Seeds: **The Definitive Guide to Growing, History and Lore.** (Macmillan, 1996)

Nau, Jim. Ball Culture Guide: **The Encyclopedia of Seed Germination.** (Ball Publishing, 1993)

Powell, Eileen. **From Seed to Bloom, How to Grow Over 500 Annuals, Perennials and Herbs.** (Garden Way Publishing, 1995)

Rogers, Marc. **Saving Seeds, The Gardener's Guide to Growing and Storing Vegetable and Flower Seeds.** (Storey Publishing, 1990)

Sears, Elayne, illustrator. **Step-by-Step Gardening Techniques Illustrated.** (Garden Way Publishing, 1996)

Thompson, Peter. **Creative Propagation: A Grower's Guide.** (Timber Press, 1992)

Watson, Benjamin. **Taylor's Guide to Heirloom Vegetables.** (Houghton Mifflin, 1996)

Glossary

Annual: A plant that grows, blooms, sets seed, and dies all in one year or one growing season.

Anther: Part of the male reproductive structure (stamen) of a flower that holds the pollen grains.

Asexual propagation: A form of propagation that produces offspring that are clones of the parent plant. Also known as vegetative propagation, methods of asexual propagation include division, cuttings, layering, and tissue culture.

Biennial: A plant that lives for two growing seasons, producing leaves the first season, then flowering and setting seed in the second growing season.

Binomial: Two-part botanical name for a plant. The first name refers to the genus and the second name to the species.

Bolt: To send up a seed stalk prematurely, usually in hot weather. Bolting often detracts from the quality of the edible part of the plant.

Calyx: All the sepals, the outer parts of a flower.

Cell: The smallest structural unit of an organism.

Cloche: A protective cover used to protect tender plants from cold weather.

Clone: A plant that is genetically identical to its parent.

Cold frame: A low frame or box set on the ground outdoors, with a transparent cover to admit light. Used to protect tender plants from cold weather and to harden off transplants.

Complete flower: A flower that contains both male and female reproductive parts. Also known as "perfect flower."

Cotyledon: The seed leaves, or first leaves, that emerge from a germinated seed.

Cross-pollination: The transfer of pollen from one plant variety to another.

Cultivar: A variation of a species, one that has been produced through breeding or deliberate selection.

Damping-off: A fungal disease that attacks seedlings, causing them to shrivel at the base. Damping-off is brought on by one of several fungi, including Pythium and Rhizoctonia, which thrive in stagnant air and high humidity.

Deadhead: To remove old flowers to prevent seed-pods from forming.

Dehisce: To disperse seeds when they are ripe.

Dicotyledon: A seed-bearing plant that stores food for the embryo in the seed leaves.

Dioecious: Bearing male flowers on one plant and female flowers on another plant, but not both on the same plant.

Diploid: Having two sets of chromosomes.

Division: A method of asexual (vegetative) propagation whereby parts of the parent plant are split off to produce new plants.

Dormant: Alive but in a state of suspended animation until all conditions are right for growth.

Drill: A shallow furrow for planting seeds.

Embryo: The undeveloped plant within a seed.

Endosperm: Stored food within a seed, used to nourish the embryo.

Fertilization: The union of a male pollen cell with the female egg cell, or ovule, to form a single cell, or zygote.

Filament: Part of the male reproductive structure (stamen) of a flower supporting the pollen-bearing anthers.

Fruit: An ovary that is ripe and contains seeds.

Germination: The moment when a plant's embryo breaks its dormancy and begins to grow.

Hardening off: The process of gradually toughening up a seedling for its transition to the outdoor environment.

Heirloom: Nonhybrid (open-pollinated) plant that was introduced over 50 years ago but is no longer commercially available (although heirlooms are now beginning to appear in seed catalogs).

Hill: A number of seeds planted in a cluster rather than a row.

Hilum: The scar on a seed at the point where it was attached to the pod.

Hotbed: A cold frame that is heated with electric cables or a layer of raw manure. Used for raising seedlings or cuttings.

Hybrid: A plant grown from seed obtained by cross-fertilizing two different plant varieties.

Imperfect flower: A flower that contains either male or female reproductive parts, but not both. Also known as an "incomplete flower."

Incomplete flower: A flower that contains either male or female reproductive parts, but not both. Also known as an "imperfect flower."

Monocotyledon: A seed-bearing plant that stores food for the embryo in the endosperm surrounding the seed leaves.

Monoecious: Bearing both male and female flowers on the same plant.

Open-pollinated: Pollinated by the wind, insects, birds or animals, not by human manipulation. Open-pollinated plants or seeds are also referred to as non-hybrid.

Ovary: Part of the female reproductive structure of a flower holding the ovules, which contain eggs that become seeds when fertilized with pollen.

Ovule: The female cell, or egg, within the ovary of a flower.

Perennial: A plant that lives for more than two growing seasons, bearing flowers and fruit every year.

Perfect flower: A flower that contains both male and female reproductive parts. Also known as a "complete flower."

Perlite: Ground, expanded volcanic glass used to lighten and separate soil mixes.

pH: A measure of the acidity or alkalinity of soil, on a scale of 1 (extremely acidic) to 14 (extremely alkaline), with 7.0 being neutral.

Pistil: The female reproductive structure of a flower, consisting of the stigma, style, and ovary.

Pollen: Tiny grains produced by the male reproductive organ of a flower and used to fertilize the ovule and make seeds.

Pollen tube: A tube (actually an extension of the pollen grain) that extends down through the style to the ovary, carrying pollen to the ovules.

Pollination: The transfer of pollen from an anther to a stigma, either on the same flower or from one flower to another. Pollination leads to fertilization and production of seeds.

Pricking out: Transplanting groups of seedlings from flats to individual pots.

Rogue: To weed out weak, diseased, and otherwise undesirable seedlings.

Scarification: Scratching, nicking, chipping, or notching a seed coat to allow water to penetrate more quickly and thus hasten germination.

Seed: The fertilized egg cell of a plant, consisting of an embryo, nourishment for the embryo, and protection in the form of the seed coat.

Seed leaves: The first leaves to appear on a seedling. In dicotyledons, the seed leaves provide nutrients to the dormant plant embryo. Also known as cotyledons.

Seedling: A young plant grown from seed.

Self-fertile: Refers to a plant's ability to produce fruit after accepting its own pollen.

Self-pollinated: Refers to a flower that is fertilized by its own pollen rather than the pollen of another flower.

Set: To develop fruit or seeds.

Set out: To plant a seedling in the garden.

Sexual propagation: A form of propagation whereby the offspring contain genetic material from two different parent plants. These offspring will not be clones of either parent plant. Also known as seed propagation.

Species: Closely related, similar-looking strains of a plant that occur naturally.

Stamen: The male reproductive part of a flower, consisting of a thin stalk topped by the pollen-producing anthers.

Sterile: Unable to bear fruit or viable seed.

Stigma: Part of the female reproductive structure of a flower, the stigma receives the pollen from the anthers.

Stratification: Chilling moistened seeds to hasten germination.

Style: Part of the female reproductive structure of a flower connecting the stigma and ovary.

Tetraploid: Having four sets of chromosomes.

Thinning: Pulling out excess seedlings that are crowded together, and leaving one or two in place to grow larger. Unthinned seedlings will compete for water and nutrients, and will have poor air circulation.

Threshing: Removing seeds from their pods by beating or flailing, or by striking the pods against a hard surface.

Transplant: To move a plant to another container or location. A plant moved in this way is also called a transplant.

Triploid: Having three sets of chromosomes.

True leaves: The leaves that appear after the seed leaves, or cotyledons.

Variety: A naturally occurring variation of a plant species.

Vegetative propagation: A form of propagation that produces offspring that are clones of the parent plant. Also known as asexual propagation, methods of vegetative propagation include division, cuttings, layering, and tissue culture.

Vermiculite: Heat-expanded mica (a shiny, scaly mineral) that is added to soil mixes to hold moisture and nutrients, and to lighten the mix.

Viable: Capable of germinating.

Winnow: Separate very light chaff from heavier seeds by pouring the seeds from one container to another while blowing on them or allowing a breeze to blow over them.

Zygote: A single cell formed when the male and female plant cells unite.

Illustration credits:

Illustrations on pages 32 (top), 35 (top left and top right), 53 (top left), 59 (bottom right), 75 (bottom), and 85 (top) by **Polly Alexander**; pages 10, 16 (bottom), 17 (middle), 21 (top), 22, 43, 79 (bottom), 87 (bottom), 131 (top right), 151, 153, 169 (top left), and 173 (middle) by **Judy Eliason**; pages 13, 14 (top), 15 (bottom), 17 (bottom), 20, 21 (bottom), 37, and 133 (bottom) by **Brigita Fuhrmann**; pages iv, 7, 8, 9, 10, 14 (bottom), 15 (top), 17 (top), 18, 19, 24, 25, 26, 34 (top), 36 (top), 37 (bottom and top left), 44, 45, 51 (right), 52 (top left, top right, and bottom right), 53 (top right, bottom left, and bottom right), 54, 55, 59 (top left, top right, and bottom left), 60 (top), 63 (top), 65, 66, 69, 71 (top and bottom), 73, 75 (top), 77, 79 (top and middle), 81, 83, 87 (upper middle and lower middle), 91, 93, 95, 97, 99, 101 (left), 103, 105, 107, 111, 117, 119 (top left and bottom), 121 (left), 123, 125, 127, 129, 131 (top left and bottom), 133 (top), 139, 141, 143, 145, 147, 153, 159 (bottom left), 161, 163 (bottom), 165, 171, 173 (top and bottom), 175, 177 (bottom), 179 (bottom), 183 (top), and 185 (top and bottom left) by **Alison Kolesar**; pages 137 (right), 159 (top), 177 (top), and 179 (top) by **Kathleen Kolb**; pages 33 (top), 52 (bottom left), and 85 (middle and bottom) by **Susan Berry Langsten**; page 11 by **Michael Lamb**; pages 3, 6, 8, 9, 12, 16 (top), 29 (middle), 35 (bottom left), 36 (bottom), 37 (top right), 50, 51 (left), 60 (bottom), 63 (bottom), 71 (middle), 87 (top), 101 (right), 119 (top right), 135, 137 (left), 145, 155 (top right), 157, 167 (left), 169 (top right), 183 (bottom), and 185 (bottom right) by **Elayne Sears**; pages 23, 28, and 29 (top and bottom) by **David Sylvester**; and pages 13 and 35 (bottom right) by **Mary Thompson**.

Index

Page references in **bold** indicate charts; those in *italics* indicate maps.

Other Storey Titles You Will Enjoy

From Seed to Bloom: How to Grow over 500 Annuals, Perennials & Herbs, by Eileen Powell. Easy-to-understand plant-by-plant format that includes information on hardiness zones, sowing seeds indoors and out, germination times, spacing, light and soil needs, care, and propagation techniques. 320 pages. Paperback. ISBN 0-88266-259-7.

Saving Seeds: The Gardener's Guide to Growing and Storing Vegetable and Flower Seeds, by Mark Rogers. Plant-by-plant, practical, and easy-to-use advice on how to raise, harvest, and store seeds for both vegetables and ornamental plants. 176 pages. Paperback. ISBN 0-88266-634-7.

The Herb Gardener: A Guide for All Seasons, by Susan McClure. Complete instructions on every conceivable aspect of herbs so the reader can grow and use 75 different herbs all year long. 240 pages with full-color photos. Paperback: ISBN 0-88266-873-0. Hardcover: ISBN 0-88266-910-9.

Just the Facts!: Dozens of Gardening Charts — Thousands of Gardening Answers, by the editors of Garden Way Publishing. An excellent reference tool for the home gardener with information about every aspect of gardening. 224 pages. Paperback. ISBN 0-88266-867-6.

Step-by-Step Gardening Techniques Illustrated, illustrated by Elayne Sears. Organized by season and appropriate for experts and beginners, this is a collection of 86 of the original two-page "Step-by-Step" articles published in *Horticulture* magazine, written by seven different horticultural experts and illustrated with detailed line drawings. 224 pages. Hardcover. ISBN 0-88266-912-5.

The Big Book of Gardening Skills, by the Editors of Garden Way Publishing. A comprehensive guide to growing flowers, fruits, herbs, vegetables, shrubs, and lawns. Organized by topic to help plan, plant, and maintain beautiful and productive gardens. Includes skills for garden basics, plant selection, safe organic growing, and a garden equipment guide. 352 pages. Paperback. ISBN 0-88266-795-5.

The Organic Gardener's Home Reference, by Tanya Denckla. Detailed information on how to grow, harvest, and store vegetables, herbs, fruits, and nuts. 288 pages. Paperback. ISBN 0-88266-839-0.

These books and other Storey books are available at your
bookstore, farm store, garden center, or directly from
Storey Publishing, Schoolhouse Road, Pownal, Vermont 05261,
or by calling 1-800-441-5700. www.storey.com